HEADPRESS 19: WORLD WITHOUT END • Published by Headpress, Summer's end 1999
ISBN 1 900486 08 3
ISSN 1353-9760
A catalogue record for this book is available from the British Library

HEADPRESS, 40 ROSSALL AVENUE, RADCLIFFE

Contents

Contributors

Gerard Alexander
Anton Black
Tom Brinkmann
Mikita Brottman
Michael Carlson
John Carter
Rick Caveney
Simon Collins
Maxon Crumb
Mark Deutrom
Dogger
Anthony Ferguson
Janet Gould
David Greenall
Mark Griffiths
Martin Jones

James Marriott
Pan Pantziarka
Anthony Petkovich
Progeas Didier
Rik Rawling
Jack Sargeant
H.E. Sawyer
Stephen Sennitt
Kerri Sharp
Marie Shrewsbury
Jack Stevenson
Johnny Strike
John Szpunar
Phil Tonge
Sarah Turner
Joe Scott Wilson
Will Youds

Editor DAVID KEREKES

Layout/cover David Kerekes & Walt Meaties
Inside front cover (doctored) magazine covers from
   the collection of H.E. Sawyer
Back cover (from top) Marlon Brando (in The
   Nightcomers); SMOKIN' STRIPPERS SPECIAL #1 (©
   Galaxy Publications Ltd); Traci Lords.

Acknowledgements
Laura Briscall (Taschen), Harvey Fenton (FAB Press), Mark Chapman (Titan), The Dark
Side, Mark Farrelly, Miranda Filbee (Creation Books), Barry Futterman, Antonio Ghura,
Marie-Luce Giordani, Dave Huxley, Jemma, Lesley Kerekes, Richard King (Screen Edge/
Visionary), KinoFilm, Stefan Jaworzyn, Craig Ledbetter (ETC), David LeFevre, Adrian Luther-
Smith, Mick Middles (Manchester Evening News), Tony Moore (Pluto Press Australia),
Steve Puchalski (Shock Cinema), Chris Reed (BBR), Lisa Richards (The Associates), Laurence
O'Toole, Roger Sabin, David Slater, Ralph Steadman, Jan Švankmajer, Claire Thompson/
Joe Prior (Turnaround), Pete Tombs (Pagan Films), Tomoko Sagara, Anna Vallois (Serpent's
Tail), Larry Wessel, Stephen Wilson, Stuart Wright.

EDITORIAL News of a public appearance by the elusive Robert Crumb and other luminaries of the art world stimulated your editor and companions into leaving one Saturday morning in April for the ICA in London. We were excited. First on stage was Ralph Steadman (curiously, under the guise of his FEAR AND LOATHING buddy Hunter S. Thompson) for an impromptu 'Live Painting Performance' with musical accompaniment by his son. Paint was flying in abandon and the genial Steadman was happy to sign numerous items thrust his way afterwards, including ticket

Photos © Kerekes

Steadman

stubs and one of my travelling companions' empty Anusol packet.

Crumb himself took to the stage with his new band Les Primitifs du future, playing a set of traditional French songs concerning the subway and unrequited love. Unlike Steadman earlier, Crumb was greeted with a packed room. He didn't disappoint with his reluctance to communicate (he refused the micro-

Crumb

phone at one point, prompting a fellow musician to remark in broken English, "Robert doesn't like electricity"), but genuinely seemed to enjoy playing his ukulele before an audience.

They almost had to push him onto the stage for the obligatory Q&A session that followed. When it was over, he ran off.

Lastly for us was Gilbert (FURRY FREAK BROTHERS) Shelton's boogie woogie piano. Having forgotten his sheet music, most of the numbers Shelton played stopped midway as he attempted to get to grips with what came next. Informal to say the least and very entertaining.

A good time was had by all.   **David Kerekes**

PORNO HAS A BRAIN

H. E. Sawyer in conversation with LAURENCE O'TOOLE

• • • • • • • • • • • • • • • • •

this is different. A pub in Shoreditch without the obligatory young women whipping their kit off for a handful of loose change? 'The Bricklayer's Arms' is an oasis of mental activity and bonhomie. The Chinese sit with the Asians and the Irish, and debate whether, if alive today, The Bard would be writing on the Net. I figure from the conversation that I'm in the right place; it looks interesting and intriguing, the kind of place a young cool author would hang out for a pint. My beer mat is the media section from THE GUARDIAN...

I should clarify, in case you aren't familiar with **pornocopia**, Laurence O'Toole's first book — it's about pornography for anyone who's even remotely interested in the subject, and solace for anyone who has ever had to listen in silence to the moral minority banging on about how wrong pornography is. I'm not going to con you, it's a book without pictures — no glossy tits or arses, just reams of fascinating text, where every point, every argument, for sanity and reason is backed up by the author.

The hubbub is seamless, and as I didn't die a death when I entered, I figure I blend in pretty well with the regulars. The appointed time draws near and I wonder if I will recognise Laurence from a brief soundbite on Channel 5's SEX & SHOPPING. The bar's crowded. How will he recognise me? I scan the faces. I'm the only one wearing specs. That's good. He'll figure I've got dodgy eyesight — being a porn connoisseur. Should I sit here with my hairy palms turned out? But we recognise each other immediately. We shake hands, and I like Laurence O'Toole.

He draws a fag from the pack and signs my copy of **pornocopia**. I'm unashamedly a fan. And now we're going to smoke, drink, and talk dirty.

HeadPress So basically... why did you decide to write PORNOCOPIA?

Laurence Otoole Because I felt that the arguments regarding pornography were stuck in a rut, and I didn't find them particularly persuasive. I wasn't persuaded that that was all there was to be said on pornography, and what had been said already I didn't find particularly interesting. I thought pornography had been treated as like a problem. But it could have been treated as an industry... a legal issue, a career, a film genre — and a viewing experience. They were all the kinds of things that I think had never been dealt with. If it had been treated as a film genre, it would be treated at a very high academic level. That book by Linda Williams, HARDCORE — it really gives you a nosebleed, and it doesn't get into the pleasure of pornography.

Do you think that was because she was too much of an academic, or because she was female?

I think it's because of being an academic, not because she's female. And subsequently she's continued to work in the field. She teaches courses on pornography — which is quite amazing — at a university in Southern California and I saw her give a lecture in Los Angeles last summer. I think she's now into the idea of the pleasure in pornography. But earlier on — and she acknowledges it was a flaw — she didn't. She thought it was important to be detached. And I think with cultural studies, you have to be involved, because you can't really comment unless you understand what makes it an interesting subject, i.e., it creates a physical as well as mental and intellectual response on the part of the consumer. So I felt that that hadn't been charted properly. I don't know... when I started out, I really did feel that things were stuck in a rut and the arguments were really circular — anti-porn, in defence of freedom of speech, but this stuff is disgusting, keep it at arm's length and hold your nose — and, I can't believe in the last couple of years how much the attitude has changed. And I was getting quite excited, because this was happening as I was writing the book, and I thought, "Jesus! I hope someone else doesn't do this!" because no one's written a book like this, and I can feel this ground swell of interest in the subject, which came to fruition last year.

Did you have a problem getting it published?

No — I never thought of taking it to anyone else [other than Serpent's Tail], because they're a leftfield popular culture publisher, and they are quite keen on civil liberties and freedom of speech. They've dealt with things by controversial writers — like Dennis Cooper — so they definitely had the balls to take it.

So what do you think was the defining moment in the last couple of years that has made pornography more acceptable?

I can't think of a defining moment. Obviously

the one that one would probably go after is the release of BOOGIE NIGHTS, because I kind of think it gave the mainstream media a chance to write about pornography again. But they couldn't handle it the same way they had in the past — some of them did, but a lot of them couldn't — and it was an opportunity, almost an excuse for them to write about it. And it became tied in with the fact that pornography had slowly gone mainstream in the States. I think another key issue is the internet. It really made people aware that they had access to pornography — stuff they'd been told they shouldn't look at. Virtually everyone when they come on-line, one of the first things they do is check out a porn site. Maybe it's not the best way to look at pornography — I don't think it is — but they've seen it and thought, 'Jesus, it's not so bad. What's all this fuss about?'

Do you think it's because the majority of people had problems going to get their porn?

I think a lot of people did — I think a lot of people didn't know they could tune into pornography as a leisure activity. I think pornography opened their eyes to that — on the internet I mean. But yes, I think particularly in this country, a lot of people have problems accessing it. But the fans know where to get it.

Well, we've always known where to get it, haven't we?

Yes, but not necessarily happy with the quality of the product. Not in the sense that it's not a very good film, but it's a ropy video — a third or fourth generation copy, or the magazines just aren't up to scratch. A lot of people might have

PERSONAL CALLERS WELCOME

checked it out, but not had the opportunity to get it. And that's how censorship works — not just absolute denial of access to material — just making it difficult to get hold of the stuff. And that's why I feel pessimistic about censoring the net — I think people can make it hard to get stuff.

But someone somewhere is working on a way to control the Net.

You hear stories about the police and MI6 and the government, talking about internet service providers giving them access on request, so they can access individual peoples internet counts and work out what they've looked at.

I was thinking more of big business

Yeah, that sort of thing is going on. Eventually there will be filters and blockers rigged up and ready to go, and people will have to learn how to dismantle them. But some people won't know from the start that it's actually there, do you know what I mean?

It's not hard to go down to the newsagent to buy a top shelf magazine, but I remember only too well in my early days how all the circumstances used to have to be right for doing that. So you were a fan of pornography from a fairly early age?

Yeah. I had issues about it. I came from quite a conservative sort of working class background, a working class area, and my parents were Catholic and so I think sex wasn't a subject for discussion really. And from out of that fairly insulated environment I went to college when I was 18, and arrived raring to go basically. But the shutters were just about to come down with the emergence of a very, very centred, orientated, feminist attitude — not the only feminist attitude, but one that started to take hold on campuses in the early Eighties in the UK and the US. And I think it made me feel for a number of years that there was definitely something wrong with looking — to look, to fantasise, to desire. So there one kind of system of thought that kind of made you feel bad — i.e., Catholicism — was replaced by another, and I think it

took me a long time to come out of that. I think the Eighties were a miserable time for many people because of that sort of 'thought police' thing going on. I'd read a bit about the theory regarding the male gazers, 'the gaze is male', all that kind of stuff — and objectifying women — I knew all that — never fully believed it but wondered if there was some truth to it. I knew some pornography, but knew I hadn't seen it all. I wanted to know if the horror stories were true, because I didn't know anyone who worked in the industry. A lot of people I've met have

Laurence O'Toole.

said about the American porn industry, that before they got into it they thought there was going to be everyone dealing cocaine on set, and then they find out it's a quite well-run business — it's got its problems, but it's not how they perceived it to be. So I needed to find out quite a few things I didn't know, and generally deal with the ideas around pornography and get them worked out in my mind. That's what motivated me to write the book, and that propelled me forward.

So you managed to reconcile your respect of feminism and your faith, with pornography?

Yeah — well it's not my faith — it's just the circumstances I found myself in really. I don't have a religious belief. My parents are very devout Catholics. I went to church for periods of times. In fact my parents weren't Catholics for a few years — they were hard-line Marxists, so we didn't go to church. And one weekend, they were no longer card carrying members of the Communist Party and we were going back to church again! I've always thought there was this interesting similarity between Stalinism and the Papacy. They're similar, centralised bodies, very top down, delivering the message of what you should think and how you should behave. I kind of struggled with coming out into a much more liberal environment at college, and in fact it wasn't liberal — it was another form of restriction, another form of conservatism, another form of overweening moralising. Just from a different angle. It's funny, because at the end of last year, I went to do a debate at Leeds University about the subject of porn, and the guy who invited me told me that there'd been loads of copies of GQ on campus, because it had been fresher's week, and someone had complained to the Student Union that she'd been sexually harassed by the image on the cover, a picture of Denise van Outen, and the Student Union pulped the lot. And I thought, "Jesus! That's how it was. It's still going on." And I followed up the story, and he wrote a letter to GQ saying, "I left home to go to college, expecting not to find hassle, not having to look over my shoulder with my parents no longer telling me what to think and what to do, and what not to look at, and now at college someone else is doing it for me."

How did you find people to talk about what is essentially a very private subject?

For a lot of people it is. How I got to talk to people? I put adverts in magazines and newspapers. GUARDIAN (funnily enough, on the woman's page), DESIRE, FETISH TIMES. Soft porn top shelf magazines wouldn't help me. I then had a few people who put me in touch with people they knew. That brought me in 40 to 50 people, and I posted to newsgroups on the internet, and that's where I got absolutely loads — from the States, the UK, Scandinavia, Australia. I drew up this enormous questionnaire, and some people just wrote in a pithy style, and some people wrote reams of text. And the reason it took so long to write the bloody book was getting that amount of data, selecting the right people. There were a lot of people I could have written case studies of, but I had to pick the right person. The character I write about under the pseudonym 'Nicholas White', he just seemed perfect. He gave me so much information, and he seemed symbolic and emblematic of what other people had said.

There was a whole book to be written on Nicholas White, because of the conflict he was undergoing. Personally I never had that kind of conflict. I was furtive. I kept it quiet from my male contemporaries, and when the subject was finally broached, it turned out that myself and my contemporaries we'd all been running after this stuff independently of each other, but we'd all been running pretty much parallel.

That is so true. When I was researching the book, I'd be at parties and people would sidle up to me and whisper in my ear, "Y'know, I like pornography". Men and women. Quite a few women would tell me about relationships that they'd been in where pornography was a key issue in their love making, stuff like that. It's much more common than people let on and understand.

Take America, it's a different generation that's watching porn now. They didn't find out about pornography by discovering dad's copy of PLAYBOY in the cellar — it's a cable society. They've had cable TV for a generation now. A lot of homes in America have been getting PLAYBOY channel piped in, and these people don't even know who Andrea Dworkin is, and it's kind of like intersected in a very complex way with youth popular culture. The young guns who are making porn in the States, like Johnny Toxic and Robert Black, Matt Zane, they reference not just porn — they reference Nine Inch Nails, FRIDAY THE 13TH, SOUTH PARK... This is where the action is.

Do you think MTV had anything to do with that? Because the videos there are highly produced and original, and slick and raunchy?

Yeah. The mainstream has got higher octane in its representation of sex, particularly in the area of youth culture, magazine and video culture. The porn industry has become closer to the mainstream. Now you've got surfing magazines, snowboarding magazines, that court their viewers by putting porn actresses on the cover. Or extreme-sportswear manufacturers using porn actresses to model their clothes for advertising campaigns, stuff like that. Do you see what I mean? And to be a porn fan now is not to be a social pariah.

Do you think it also has something to do with the fact that the Nuclear Family doesn't happen any more? In as much as I'm mid-thirties with absolutely no interest in marrying or settling down. More women are more independent, and therefore, maybe as a knock-on, men aren't getting married.

Mmm. Definitely. It's also a thing of the 'extended adolescence'. I think the ideal, for a large amount of people, is a long-term monogamous relationship, probably matrimony, although they'll test drive it first by living together. But a lot of people leave it a lot later and have this prolonged, slacker lifestyle.

It's bloody brilliant, isn't it?!

I think it's pretty good, yeah. It brings with it issues. I think for women it brings up issues with the human clock ticking away — whether to have babies or not. Maybe they're in a long-term relationship that started in their twenties, and then they get to their thirties — they're dead keen to start procreating because they haven't got much time left — men don't have to get their arse in gear. They haven't thought about a career, and still haven't given up on the idea of being semi-autonomous, struggling to commit themselves. And it's also about identity. How do you achieve your identity? With previous generations it was quite simple: you had your childhood, little bit of adolescence, then in your twen-

ties you got your job, the job was probably for life, you got married, started a family and you knew where you were. Nowadays we've got a pick'n'mix culture, a buffet culture where we choose our roles and lifestyles because there's so many more things available to us. I think it's great. But the increase in therapy culture, that's not a coincidence. It's consequential.

There was a piece in the book where you turned up on a film set, and you were talking to someone who said that everyone in the business was fucked up in one way or another. And he said, "Including you."

(*laughs*) Yeah, that's right. That's very funny. That's Paul Thomas. Yeah.

What's the matter with me? He's gone to sleep - now she's dropping off!

Photo cartoons taken from risqué humour magazine (circa 1970s) rescued from a skip. No publisher details listed.

"Roll on Christmas!"

He's a heavy weight in the industry. He's been around. Was that actually true?

What? That I was fucked up?

Yeah.

No. I didn't feel that way at all. I thought it was very funny. I thought it was worth putting in the book. I was thinking about this the other night — anyone who gets close to pornography, because of the social stigma attached, may have problems. Even someone as far removed as myself. I haven't been kind of like socially excluded — although I went to a quite high-powered launch party for a book the other day and I was talking to a woman who was from the Arts Council, and I was introduced, like, "Oh,

this is Laurence O'Toole, the author of the best-selling PORNOCOPIA, and he's Britain's biggest porn expert"! Which isn't true. And this woman literally stepped back, and said "Where do I go from here?"

Really?!

Yeah! She was some twin set. She should really be living in the Home Counties reading THE LADY. But the next day I was thinking about people, whether they'll look at me as a bit of an oddball to have done this — to have written a book like this. And if I were to write another book, would I struggle to get a deal because I was someone who had written about pornography.

Maybe it's a bit like the porn actresses who try to move into mainstream acting? But your neighbours are still talking to you, aren't they? The work hasn't dropped off because of the book, has it?

No. Not at all. The other great thing about being published by Serpent's Tail is that they've got cache. People see them as a...

A 'serious' publishing house.

Yeah. They're not sleazy. They're not like that. If they publish a book they probably think it's a pretty good book and think it's worth taking seriously. And give or take one bad review — I had one really bad review — the reviews have been excellent.

It was interesting about what you were saying, about the effects of porn, because I was fucked up, and then I got interested in porn. And I wondered that to be interested in porn — or work in it — you had to, at some time, have been fucked up.

(*sighs*) I think it's really hard if you work in the porn industry. I feel this even more now than when I wrote the book, and I'm thinking about it even more as I update the book. I think it's really hard to keep a relationship going. I think its really tough to live in the outside world and be taken seriously as a person. I used to say the only thing I noticed that changed in my behaviour — (*big smile*) which is really silly — is that I have trouble typing 'ph'. I got so used to writing 'pornography' — '-p-h-y' — that I can't write 'ph' without following it with a 'y'. So if I'm writing DAILY TELEGRAPH, it's DAILY TELEGRA*PHY*! (*laughs*) But I feel at this level, its the only thing I'm prepared to admit to!

That is interesting!

I think it opens your eyes to things which are really useful to have your eyes open to. The diversity of sexuality, the diversity of fantasy is a fantastic thing, and should be encouraged and nourished, rather than condemned and policed. I also think it opens your eyes to the issues that I think are going still, about the fact that we still have this dominant ideology and this culture, and we do have a mainstream. Everyone keeps talking about proliferating margins, and that's true to some extent. But it's fucking hard to kind of persuade people that porn can be treated differently, and this is why I bang on about it in my book, about taking it seriously as an art form — because we won't gain credibility unless it's seen as an art form. And unless it gains credibility, the laws won't change significantly. There is no adult conversation going on about pornography, and that is one of the things I really wanted to do. It's not talked about in an adult way. It's talked about as if it's a modern urban fantasy — a negative fairy tale. People constantly bang on about exploitation — it's like Steve Perry says, and I quote in my book, "People still think that porn actresses are apprehended outside dole offices in Tooting!"

Yeah, he said that to me.

It's so stupid.

There seems to be a trend from some directors in America where porn is dehumanising — stuff like a guy shoving a girl's head down a toilet bowl?

Yeah. That's Robert Black.

"OOOOH, PAUL, IT'S EVEN BIGGER THAN I REMEMBER..."

Maybe they've run out of road and are still trying to take things further?

I think what's going on there is a whole range of things. I think they're trying to announce their presence in the porn industry as the next generation. It's kind of like 'slaying the fathers', the ones who came before them. I think they desperately need to make their presence felt, in as much as if you're going to sell product in such an over saturated market, you've got to have some schlock going for you, otherwise you're not going to sell. It's like comedians coming on the scene and going, "fuck-fuck-fuck-fuck!" And someone says, "Who is this guy? he's swearing all the time!" Any mainstream article on porn in America — like the one in TIME magazine — the guy they go for is Robert Black, partly because they want to find someone to be disgusted by.

And it is a bit disgusting. But I also think there are other, deeper issues going on there, which I haven't fully worked out in my mind. I think it's something to do with consent in sexual relationships in real life. And I think in America, and to some extent in Britain, I think we're coming from a position where the idea of date rape and sex education is very fraught for young people, and they're being told, "Just say no. Whatever you do, say no. If you have sex outside of wedlock, and it's 'perverse sex', it can be bad for you."

Not only is it morally bad for you, but it can be physically bad for you. And they don't just mean AIDS. This is actual sex education in America. If you're going to run a sex education programme that's going to be funded by Congress, you are required to tell children, young adults, adolescents, that sex outside of wedlock is physically damaging.

Physically damaging?

Physically damaging. You've got that going on. Everyone's being told to say "no" to sex. No-one's being educated as to how you say "yes" to sex. And then they leave school, and a lot of

PSST! — SEEN ANY GOOD MOVIES?

video PORN

KEEPiNg iT UNDER WRAPS

An Argument for the
Brown Paper Bag
by
H.E. Sawyer

I have sympathy with those pioneers who strive to break down the barriers of suspicion and fear, and greater sympathy still with those victimised by zealous self styled censors. But the Obscene Publication Act as it stands doesn't affect me personally. Not with regards to my preferred medium of sampling porn: the video cassette.

And there is — surprise, surprise — an argument that advocates that hardcore pornography, certainly on video, should remain illegal and stay in the shadows.

Basically because it's in the punter's best interest. Correction. It's in the *wise* punter's interest. The chances are

them go onto college, experience a lot more freedom, 'Bang!' What do you have? What you have is a whole explosion of issues of 'date rape'. Now obviously some 'date rape' is clearly forced and non-consenting and is rape in the full sense of the word. Some of it — I know this is a controversial thing to say, but some of it's about women who've been taught to be demure and pure, not knowing how to just say "yes", they want sex. Do you see what I mean? And I think in that kind of environment, in that kind of very, very fraught troubled area, this is what gives rise to that kind of porn. This is where they're coming from. This is where sexual relationships aren't a battlefield, they're more like a minefield. You don't know where to start, things could go really, really wrong if you step in the wrong direction. Do you see what I mean? And I think these filmmakers are negotiating these issues in a very ham-fisted, unconsidered, obnoxious way, as well as all the other things — trying to make a name for themselves, trying to upset people. And porn has always been about upsetting people. If it stops upsetting people then it loses it's credibility with a lot of viewers. And for a lot of porn makers who feel they've got to wind you up, it's an anti-bourgeois statement. One of the great ironies I love is HUSTLER magazine — Larry Flynt. His mission in life — apart from making a fortune — apart from showing women exposed, naked — is he wants to piss off the elite. He <u>really</u> wants to piss them off. All the political correctness, any kind of taboo — he wants to have a go at it. HUSTLER distribute the NEW YORK REVIEW OF BOOKS! It's classic, because in many ways the NEW YORK REVIEW OF BOOKS embodies the beautiful Manhattan bourgeois lot that HUSTLER's gunning for. It's a white trash lower working class "up yours!" kind of thing!

You were talking about how hard it was to work in the industry, which I can appreciate — at the end of the day, the performers, men and women, they're all human beings.

But it's not hard for the people who are at the top and making the money, though, is it? It doesn't appear to me to be hard for Robert Black and Paul Thomas?

Paul Thomas — I think it was hard for a long while. He was an up-and-coming actor in mainstream stage and film, and he lost his friends, he's coming from that angle. He was seen as being a sad fuck for doing that. Robert Black — no I don't think it's hard, but I don't think he's making that much money. He's very heavily funded. He doesn't get the cable service because his stuff is too weird. Fifty percent of any profit you make in American porn is from cable and foreign sales. I don't think his foreign sales are too good and his cable is going to be zero.

There's the flip side. There's Vivid who seem to be making every dollar in the world.

Vivid, yeah they do. I think they would have been struggling if they hadn't had the Pamela Anderson/ Tommy Lee thing. There are always rumours going round about VCA... they've had to raunch up their product line. They've brought in various gonzo lines — they've brought back Marilyn Chambers. Did you know that?

No.

Yeah. She's making a porn movie with Jane Hamilton at the moment. STILL INSATIABLE I think it's called. She's got to be in her late-forties. I admire VCA for that, they're not ageist, not like a lot of companies.

But there's a trend for that, isn't there?

It's not like that though. It's a beautiful older lady in a romantic story. It's not going to be like pensioner porn. But, yeah, I think these guys struggle to make money.

Does it bother you — because it bothers me

you already have your own stash, know what you want, and know where to get it. Fools and the naïve will always be parted from their money in the quest for top quality porn on tape, and here I speak from personal experience. For in days gone by, I have entered into the dimly lit, musty atmosphere of one of those chain stores advertised in the salacious press and on the backs of various soft porn publications. I've hurried home with an over-priced copy of *Danish Dentist on the Job*, wrapped in the obligatory brown paper bag, zigzagging through the streets to avoid recognition... irrespective of the fact that I was 40 miles from my local turf at the time. With hindsight, I should have kept the bag — I might have had more entertainment with that — but I tore it to shreds in my haste to play with myself.

I had my flies down as the opening titles rolled, only for the tape to wow and disintegrate into a blizzard, followed by 90 minutes of amateur boxing from the York Hall Bethnal Green. No dodgy overdub ("Look at this little cutie! Her pussy is wet and wanting for your rock hard cock!"), just the dulcet tones of Reg Gutteridge eulogising the virtues of Southpaw and a good jab.

Laugh at my expense. Please. I wasn't surprised. An earlier adventure in Stockholm had culminated in an equally unsatisfactory purchase — a solitary copy of *Mayfair*. I cringe with embarrassment and humiliation now at the thought of what I passed over, but at the time I thought I was the dog's

VIDEOS

bollocks bringing this inoffensive publication back through Gatwick.

It's all very well buying your own 'dirty mag' — it is after all a long way from finding scraps of porn over the fields as a child — but to progress to the moving hardcore image, that was another matter. Help was evidently required. Isolated by embarrassment and uncertainty, who wants to broach the subject of porn with their contemporaries? Not at that age, not if you're middle class.

Luckily the media was at hand. A late night fly-on-the-wall cop show followed a vice raid into deepest Soho. Plainclothes coppers blazed a trail through the door, startled punters scurried from the emporium, trapped momentarily like moths in the lights of the camera crew before scattering into the night air. The roving eye depicted the layout of the shop. The counter here, a staircase there. Down we went to the basement, and the packed 'fridge of porno tapes. The vice crusade, filmed in glorious detail by the slavering media, gave me the layout of an establishment that had to contain something of note, I determined. Why else would they be there?

Illegality and frustration breed determination in the porno fan. All it takes is a rainy day when the streets are quieter than usual, when most people are engaged in their daily business — that and the nerve to pop your head round doors and through plastic curtains for a cursory glance at the floor plan — and the prize can be yours, young man.

The 'porn peddler' wasn't anything like the media would have you believe. Here in the same shop as featured in the late night cop show, it was all about customer service and satisfaction.

"Why should I rip you off, my friend?"

He was Dutch. That was a good sign. He waved a hand over the 500

How's your breast-stroke, Mr. Perrywinkle!

— that the legislation in this country forces porn underground, and that buying hardcore porn tapes means that we're funding organised crime?
Yeah it really pisses me off. Really pisses me off. I think the vast majority of vendors in Soho are scum. I really don't like them. I hate the way the sex industry is in this country. There's some reasonable people, but most of them are nasty.

You went to talk to them?
I spoke to some of them. I didn't like them. I've got no time for them. Yeah, I really resent that fact. It's so stupid, so gormless. The legislation, the way it criminalises.

Can you see it changing?
I find it hard to imagine the law being changed. Funnily enough, even although Jack Straw came down hard on Ferman for his restricted hardcore outburst, I hear the BBFC are going to go back to doing R18.

I remember BAT BABE and THE PYRAMID. As I understand it, even in R18 versions those

films have no anal sex—
No come shots.

And the penetration is very limited.
Likewise the blow jobs. But I think they're going to go to that, because some of the distributors decided that they've got public will on their side and they can take the Government and the censor on. Shepton Hurst have already done this. They presented a tape, the BBFC said "no", and they went to the complaints panel that the BBFC have — which is rarely used, and rarely disagrees with the BBFC, but for some strange reason they did this time. The BBFC were therefore required to release the tape but sat on it for ages, as is their habit. Shepton Hurst were expected to go away quietly, they didn't, and said "We'll take you to court". The day before they were due in the High Court to dispute it, the BBFC gave it a certificate. A few days later, Shepton Hurst sent them about six more tapes and said "We'd like certificates for these as well, please". So I think the Government are probably thinking we'll allow this. They won't make a policy decision about it — they won't announce it. But I can't see the laws changing, no.

Do you think it's inherent in our culture?
No. I really don't think it's anything. Well, it's to do with our limited culture — we won't broaden our horizons. But they will do eventually. That's why I go on about it so much in my book. I really think it

hardcore box covers on the shelves, opened the cupboards underneath, filled with something in the region of another 2000 titles. I nearly fainted.

"I'll pick a good one for you. I don't sell rubbish — ask anyone here."

Half a dozen punters shifted nervously. One left the shop. The portable TV flicked into life.

"Is that what you're looking for my friend?"

"Fucking Hell!!!"

He smiled.

"See? I told you I won't rip you off. I want you to come back."

Ten years later he's been proved right.

The tapes still cost the same now as they did then. It's £20 per tape with a £10 part-exchange deal. The cartel that operates in Soho means that any shop will take a returned tape if the original lender has nothing in stock that you fancy. Would such an arrangement exist, would the price remain constant, with legality? Not a chance. In Amsterdam's red light district a decent legal porn tape costs £70–£80.

Make hardcore porn legal in this country and not only will the price rocket (and the Government be embarrassed with what to do with the resulting revenue from a product they have assumed the public do not want), but the world and its grandmother will be churning out crap porn in an attempt to make a quick buck. As award winning porn director Steve Perry said:

"If they did legalise it here, everyone would be making it, and I'd go to being a very small fish in a big pond, instead of being a big fish in a small

pond."

Obviously Perry doesn't command a monopoly on porn, but he is one of the few directors — whether working for Private on 35mm features, where he honed his craft, or his latter-day acclaimed 'Gonzo' series — who genuinely cares about his product, and has got the essential ingredient to make good hardcore porn. And talent is becoming a rarity these days; more and more product is being released onto the market with inevitable cut-throat competition. Producers are selling porn to the distributors cheaper than the punter can buy a blank tape to copy it.

Whilst it remains underground, the Soho retailers can filter out the dross from the 9,500 tapes produced in America alone each year. The London boys take a risk to get hardcore onto their shelves, so there's little point in displaying sub-standard product. And they are already exercising self censorship. You won't find bestiality or child porn in Soho, and whilst I admit there's a greater variety of videotape in Amsterdam — including pseudo-rape and bestiality — who wants to pay that kind of money for it, especially when Customs and Excise are still forbidding material depicting masturbation into the country? Not only that, but who wants to spend hours trawling through 10,000 box covers in the hope of finding some cool Asian babe getting screwed in ripped tights?

OK, OK, I admit it. It took me three days, and in the end the only tapes featuring Asian babes (as opposed to Oriental babes) were those produced by Britain's Steve Perry, aka Ben Dover. These are easily purchased in Soho for a fraction of the price they are in Holland, and there's no way that an official box cover — the only difference — is worth that much money.

important that pornography is seen as valid <u>culturally</u>. It's only when it's valid culturally that it will be talked about. It's the old anti-censorship argument. If you can find some redeeming social quality to it, then it's no longer obscene.

I'm fascinated by fetish, and working out where it comes from. I remember going into a shop — very few people talk in porn outlets, but when you do hear conversation it's usually interesting — and there was a guy who wanted a tape featuring 'girls on phones in the backs of cars'... I overheard this, and for the life of me I couldn't work it out. I wasn't sure if he wanted girls to be talking on phones while riding in the back of the car, maybe just talking dirty to someone, or listening to someone else talking dirty to them; or if they were talking on the phone in the back of the car whilst being simultaneous screwed; or if they were 'on' the phone, in the sense of using the phone as a masturbatory device
It's quite creative in a way really, isn't it?

Oh yeah. I find girls wearing Alice bands and chokers a real turn on — and I thought that was weird, because I never got into SNOW WHITE **— I've never seen it! There's a lot of porn on TV these days, isn't there?**
I know. TV companies are <u>obsessed</u> with sex.

They've become so ratings orientated, and they realise there's a market for it. Take SEX & SHOPPING **— back in the Eighties if someone had told me there was going to be a 13-week series on the porn industry, I'd have said "In your dreams!"**
I know, It's incredible. One-and-a-half million viewers per episode they're getting, which is incredible for Channel 5. All that kind of soft porn stuff is getting good figures — HOTLINE and COMPROMISING SITUATIONS, they're big sellers.

Steve Perry [aka Ben Dover] has a theory that the main group of porn tape buyers are men who are young and inexperienced with

women, and men who have got married and had the family, and maybe are settled in a comfortable relationship.

I don't think that's true. I don't think you can pin it down. Apparently the biggest buyers in the States are the 20-30 bracket — mainly single. But the fastest growing demographic in that group is women. Single and married. It's like people say to me about 'Buttman' tapes, and 'Ben Dover' tapes, that they're male fantasies, but they're not. They're not just for men to get off on. Because a lot of women really like them, and I know that for a fact.

Do you think it's because of the actresses — they're not stereotypical porn women, not 'identikit' actresses?

Well I'm sick and tired of looking at silicone. I think it's because there's enthusiasm there.

But they're 'ordinary' women. They're like the women who are watching it. They're not supermodels, they actually look like women on the street.

I think that's true as well. I find it fascinating at how many women get aroused by seeing other women, and they don't identify themselves as lesbians, or bisexual. Straight women look at imagery that's supposed to be for men — they see close-up genital detail of a woman, and they find that really arousing. People get excited by seeing people who are excited. It's possibly a fascination thing... a projec-

Hold it, Mr. Willington! That's the tradesman's entrance!

The biggest advantage of Amsterdam is the database they have in the shops. If you're a connoisseur and after a specific tape, as opposed to someone merely looking for a wank tape, you can ask for a title and they'll tell you within seconds if they have it. This service isn't available in Soho, so it does mean that you have to visit a lot of stores and ask a lot of vendors who aren't interested if they have the original *Reves de Cuir*. Of course, while the porn fan lives with illegality and frustration, they also learn to live with disappointment. Although the shops in Britain do not have the plush fittings of their legal counterparts overseas, they do contain interesting people, and that vital ingredient — sleaze. We're British. We love it. Especially the nobbs and toffs.

In the recent BBC current affairs flagship, *Panorama*, the police admitted that the chance of a successful prosecution against porn on video was becoming less likely. Even a fire extinguisher being inserted into an orifice was deemed not likely to corrupt or deprave in the eyes of a jury. So why continue to fight a war they cannot win, especially when they have better things to do with their time? After all, the

MEN MADE ME INTO A LES

police service is all about results.

The police will still pursue the worst transgressions, which could be interpreted as kiddie porn and therefore applauded, but it seems that video porn is now frowned upon, rather than acted upon. Although the vice squad periodically turn up to deplete the shelves in Soho, the stock is back within hours and the business continues to thrive whilst the police wade through the resulting paperwork.

The recent relaxation on certain titles by the British Board of Film Classification has enabled the average punter to feast on snippets of hardcore. They flock to the Private stand at each Erotica exhibition to pay £15 for the 18R version of *Bat Babe* or *The Pyramid*, happy in the knowledge that they will be getting something of worth for their money. But porn should not be elitist. It should be there for everyone. Media scare-mongering has made Soho a forbidden zone, a rip-off waiting behind every narrow doorway.

Perhaps this is the price to pay for keeping video porn in the shadows. The climate is changing and whilst people are not proclaiming their love for blue movies from the rooftops, they are being relaxed about it.

Surprisingly, the British also benefit from content. In the US, fisting is not allowed — either anal or vaginal — so whilst fingers are OK, thumbs are not. The current crop of porn filtering into Soho from Stateside indicates the current vogue is to utilise European woodsmen shoving their fingers into the backsides of pretty girls of Eastern European extraction. In other words, they want to fist in the USA but their law prohibits it.

The updated version of *Pornocopia* by Laurence O'Toole will be out in paperback in October 1999. Pub: Five Star, an imprint of Serpent's Tail, at £8.99

FREE LOVE

INSTANT ACTION £1

tion thing.

Did you see ZAZEL? I personally thought that if you were going to show your girlfriend her first porno tape — that's the one you'd show her.
Sure. But I still believe that people who make these arguments about "this is what a man will go for and this is what a woman will go for" are missing the point. So many women like Max Hardcore tapes.

Do you think there's truth in the idea that men like the 'mechanics', and women like the romance and the set up.
See I don't think that's true either. I think it might be true to some extent that some women need the seduction in their apprentice years as porn viewers; I think they kind of need that transitory stage, where they go from reading fiction, or watching mainstream Hollywood movies, to watching hardcore pornography. There's this period of looking at this glossy movie, but it's also got hardcore sex. But you cannot pin things down like that. Some days you like this, and some days you like something else. It's not a very sophisticated theory, but I think it holds true!

How did your partner take it when you told her you were going to sit down and write the definite book about pornography?
She was good about it. She was interested in the subject, not necessarily as a fan. She was kind of like really curious about what I was going to come up with. She was really supportive and gave me a lot of feedback as I was writing it, and we were talking about it all the bloody time — it was really tedious. I still find it really difficult to have a conversation about anything and not bring it round to pornography. There's so many parallels in so many

things.

So will you continue to write about this subject, or will you move on to something else?

I think I want to sign off on it. I feel that it's such a fast-changing and broad area, that to keep on top of it, it has to be a full time occupation, and I don't want to spend the rest of my life being an expert on porn. To be an expert on porn you've got to watch it all the time — as an industry, as a legal event, as culture shifts and social changes occur. I don't think I want to do that. I'm doing the update of the book, which I'm really enjoying, because a lot has happened since it first came out. Once that comes out, I'll see how I feel, but I think I'll move on. I'll always be interested, I'll always follow it, and I'll subscribe to ADULT VIDEO NEWS and go round and look at what's on the top shelf and get videos to watch. I find it a burden really, to keep in touch with it, because every few days I've got to down-load stuff and sift through it and find any little nuances occurring in the law in America and the UK. I'd like to use the internet for other things occasionally!

Yeah! It does take up a load of time... Like having to get tapes copied, and if you're copying an American tape onto a four-hour blank, you need to find a 90 minute European tape to fill up the space...

Yeah, I know, I know!

I see people in the shops making notes in their little black books! A friend of mine recently started compiling a list of all the actresses that he'd seen in porn.

I think he should get out a bit more often! (*laughs*) ∎

Of course, Soho has tapes that carry not only fisting elements, but also watersports. In actual fact, in the UK — sitting pretty in a bootleg market with a distinct lack of legality, and laws telling us what we can and cannot see — we have the best of both US and Euro porn at a cheaper price. And this applies not only to Soho, but to the rash of free home delivery salesmen who ply 'adult videos for sale' in the small ads of the free papers.

If there's any immorality involved, it's the fact that producers of porn do not receive any revenue from the UK market, which, were it to be legalised, would be lucrative. There's no telling how much money is made by the bootleggers here. But look at the kingpins of legal Britporn: David Sullivan, the Gold Brothers and Paul Raymond, all having acquired personal fortunes. Imagine the turnover of the organised crime behind the illegal tide of hardcore in this country? Porn has proved to be fireproof no matter what the economic climate dictates. Porn either does well, or incredibly well.

But we will never know the true figure. It has to be offset with protection and extortion — elements that surely exist with any illegal trade. And there's the crux: the organised crime that is behind the video cartels that operate within the UK. And crime, organised or otherwise, is like the worse excesses in porn. By its very definition it does not require consent. ∎

17

Evangelical Mind Control and the Abuse of Altered States

Marie Shrewsbury

MOST PEOPLE HAVE SEEN ON television images of evangelical 'revival meetings' where people shake, babble incoherently, scream and collapse spectacularly in an experience termed the 'Toronto blessing'. What is really taking place here, how does it work, and what do these people actually experience?

To understand this, we must begin by looking at the potential of the human mind to be influenced and moulded. The term 'brainwashing', frequently used by the sensationalist media, can be unhelpful, but is a useful umbrella terminology for what is in fact a battery of tools for emotional and psychological manipulation. One of the more powerful tools is the use of altered states of consciousness, or trance states, the method being commonly known as hypnosis.

Trance states are in fact very mundane, we slip in and out of them many times a day. They exist to enable us to carry out more than one action at a time, so that a repetitive job does not prevent us from thinking or doing other things, however in doing so, some actions are performed with different cognitive functions enabled or disabled.

This is why it is possible to make ridiculous errors while performing a simple task.

Classical hypnosis differs from trance only in that the subject voluntarily surrenders the mind's

higher functions, rather than this occurring automatically, an action that by definition requires trust in the hypnotist, and thus a degree of compliance from the subject. Hypnosis is, quite simply, a state of relaxation in which the conscious mind is tuned out – there is nothing unexplained or supernatural about it.

Subjectively, it is very similar to the way one feels when waking up naturally — fuzzy and relaxed with absolutely nothing on the mind.

Induction – Into the Altered States

Many repetitive actions can induce a trance state. These are termed Trance Generating Loops — the state entered is termed a trance plane. An internal Trance Generating Loop (TGL), such as a thought pattern, spoken chant or meditation can induce a meditative trance. External TLGs, such as music, drumming or many people singing can create a hypnotic trance. Further external stimulation can cause a TGL to be established in an existing trance plane. This is an addictive trance, and is dangerous in that the ego is then moved into a dissociated plane, with some loss of contact with reality.

If the subject is consciously and purposely working towards this state, as in a hypnotherapy session, it can be sufficient to use a pleasant visualisation or simple repeated commands such as 'calm and relaxed' or 'sleep now' to induce a reasonable depth of trance.

A TGL which has a well established trance plane associated with it can become a trigger; one repetition may be sufficient to induce trance. This is similar to using a post hypnotic suggestion to establish a keyword, sound or other cue to access an altered state. As this avoids the need for a lengthy induction to achieve a good depth of trance, it is a very powerful tool.

Some common characteristics of trance states are fixed attention, a sense of dissociation and self-observation, an inhibited ability to make critical judgements, and the literal interpretation of words and events. Physically there are often involuntary movements, an increased rate of swallowing, rapid eye movement, pallor and a slight protrusion of the lower lip.

When a trance has been generated unconsciously by a TGL, this state will tend to terminate as soon as we become aware of it as our centre of attention has moved back to the designated task. In contrast, when we are consciously aware of being in a trance state it can be maintained for a time, even whilst carrying out other tasks. Prolonged use leads to habituation, in which the state will persist even though the individual can otherwise function normally, and may not be aware that they are still experiencing an altered state. To maintain this plane indefinitely requires that it is periodically refreshed, usually by repeated use of the original TGL or triggers.

Some young evangelists listen to 'worship' music on their personal stereos, enabling this refreshing to take place on the bus journey to and from work, or during their lunch hour.

The existence of an unacknowledged dissociated trance plane tends to give the subjective sensation of there being another presence, even when the individual is alone.

Trance Application in Evangelical Worship

All evangelical services begin with a period of worship, involving live musicians. The songs have a repetitive beat, and few lyrics which are repeated over and over. Many people dance and some clap. All of these actions are all potential TGL's, and are capable of inducing a hypnotic trance.

In this state, the suppression of critical faculties leaves an individual highly open to suggestion, particularly from seemingly affirmative statements. Simple words or phrases are most effective. If one of the TGL's is a repeated sentence, this will in itself be influential. The choruses sung contain lyrics to induce feelings of excitement, love, sanctification and submission. Some actual lyrics that I have encountered are:

In your arms of love, holding me near, holding me still

More love, more power, more of you in my life

In the presence of many TGL's, an addictive trance can readily be established, the association of the trance plane with pleasant feelings making it especially so. For some, especially those who may be experiencing symptoms of stress or nervous exhaustion, this may be the only way that they are able to relax. Dependence on a group who are capable of offering this experience will thus occur readily.

Critical thinking is further ameliorated when the speaker is a respected peer or perceived authority figure, when we are in a heightened emotional state, enjoying ourselves, or when a message is repeated many times. Any combination of these methods can be used for increased effect.

The effectiveness of any suggestion is proportional to the depth of trance already achieved, and the suggestion may in itself be designed to increase trance depth. Each suggestion acted upon creates less opposition to successive suggestions.

For most people it may take several songs to induce an altered state, those particularly sensitised or with triggers can enter in a matter of minutes, and in one case I witnessed, even seconds. Words spoken by some individuals during this period can hasten Induction for others, eg muttering 'Yes Lord' over and over, or glossola-

lia, which sounds like a string of gibberish syllables, 'Ai No Se Ca Ca Ca'. This is called 'speaking in tongues' by evangelists. It is reasonable to speculate that it may be a consequence of a trance state disabling the higher speech functions, further aided by the suggestion that they are able to do this and having had others set an example. I have also heard words used that sounded stunningly made up!

As glossalalic phrases are typically repetitions with minimal variation, they also have good potential to become established as TGL's or triggers, enabling some individuals to self-trigger by speaking their 'tongue'.

Falling for the 'Slain in the Spirit' experience.

At the end of the service is the ministry and prayer period, which also involves music. Those involved move to an open space at the front, where they are prayed for by a designated ministry team and perhaps their friends. Typically several people will lay their hands on the person being prayed for and may speak affirming comments, or 'in tongues'. The collapse, termed a Mesmeric crisis state, is rapidly induced and may be accompanied by expressions of extreme emotion, crying, laughing or moaning. Subjectively, one experiences powerful feelings of elation, surrender and detachment. There is also a sense that a higher power has taken over one's body.

Those with triggers will generally collapse to cue, in response to the touch of a hand, commonly on the forehead, or the phrase 'Come holy spirit'. An enthusiastic member of the ministry team may hasten this process by speaking loudly, using an excited tone of voice, and if all else fails, putting sufficient pressure on the person's forehead to virtually push them over!

The key to this experience is the achievement of an extreme trance state in which the conscious is so suppressed that a cathartic outpouring of otherwise unexpressed emotion can occur. For this reason the first occurrence, usually needing a considerable amount of stimulation, is by far the most powerful as it has a lifetime's anxiety to fuel it. Many cite this as their key conversion experience. Those who have not yet learnt how to achieve this are given tips such as 'Stop trying to think, you can't reason Jesus'.

Given that the degree of susceptibility to trance varies widely between individuals, how can be certain that those being prayed for will give a good performance? There are close parallels here with stage hypnosis. Prior to a show, the hypnotist will perform several tests on the audience to ascertain which individuals can and will submit most readily to hypnosis. A classic method is to induce a trance in the audience, instruct them to lock their fingers together, and then tell them that their fingers are stuck. Those least able to part their fingers are the ones who have achieved the best depth of trance, and thus will provide the best subjects. Some of the audience will have attended with a view to participation, and so will be more compliant.

In the evangelical service similar mechanisms are in place. The 'worship' has already induced a trance in the collective audience — a suggestion may then be used to draw out those who have already achieved a good depth. 'I can see that the holy spirit is resting on several people' or 'If you feel the palms of your hands prickling, come to the front' are absolute classics. Many of the audience will have attended specifically for this experience, so the sense of expectation is great.

Individuals with a very low susceptibility are less likely to be represented in this group to begin with, as these control methods will have had limited effectiveness in ensnaring them.

Further inductions become progressively easier as individuals gain awareness, consciously or subconsciously, of how to work towards the crisis, or as triggers become established. Strong emotion and hysteria aid this process, so the frenetic atmosphere at revival meetings (now called celebrations), with many people engaged in laughing, crying and screaming at once is highly conducive to the onset of a collapse state. (Some individuals also find hyperventilating helpful.) As this is alleged to be the work of the 'holy ghost' it is effectively done without the individual's educated consent.

Conclusion

In conclusion, we can look at how these events mirror the findings of Austrian physician Franz Anton Mesmer, ostensibly the pioneer of hypnosis, during the early eighteenth century. Consider this description of his activities:

> Mesmer marched about majestically in a pale lilac robe, passing his hands over the patients' bodies or touching them with a long iron wand. The results varied. Some patients felt nothing at all, some felt as if insects were crawling over them, others were seized with hysterical laughter, convulsions or fits of hiccups. Some went into raving delirium, which was called 'The Crisis' and was considered extremely healthful.

Once we have an understanding of trance theory, it is clear that there is nothing mysterious about these events (which had been debunked by science by the 1950s). However the lack of understanding about altered states means that such activities are not only widespread but also condoned by many in authority. In a disturbing article in RENEWAL magazine, a leading evangelist described how she induced an altered state of consciousness in a number of five-year-old children at a local primary school. There was no protest against this.

In a series of radio interviews that I gave on the subject, many people were keen to point out that these methods were not commonly used by charismatic Christian groups and were the domain only of a few extremist cults. Sadly this is not the case. The multinational organisation that I was involved with, perceived from outside as respectable, has churches in most cities in the US, UK and elsewhere.

REFERENCES
Dennis R Wier, *Trance*, Transmedia, 1996
William Sargent, *Battle For The Mind*, 1957
Roland Howard, *Charismania*, Mowbrey, 1997
Martyn Percy, *Words, Wonder and Power*, SPCK, 1996

Dr Anne Richards, *The Toronto Experience*, Church House Publishing, 1997
Alan Morrison, *We All Fall Down*, Diakrisis Publications, 1997
Eleanor Mumford, 'Spreading Like Wildfire', Renewal, July 1994

Marie Shrewsbury is an anti-cult campaigner with an interest in Fortean events, societal tension, and their expression in alternative music. In addition to giving radio interviews, she has recently contributed to a 'cult recruitment' feature in *Company* magazine.

21

GOD TOLD ME TO

REGRESSION, POSSESSION & CINEMATIC NEUROSIS

THE SYMPTOMOLOGY OF THE EXORCIST

DECEMBER 26TH, 1973. OUTSIDE CINEMA 1 IN NEW YORK CITY, A HUGE QUEUE OF MOVIEGOERS STRETCHES ALL THE WAY DOWN SECOND AVENUE, BETWEEN 59TH AND 60TH STREETS. THE LATE AFTERNOON IS GROWING DARK AND CHILLY, AND SMALL BONFIRES HAVE BEEN LIT IN BARRELS ON THE CORNERS OF THE PAVEMENTS TO WARD OFF THE COLD.

Mikita Brottman

It's the opening night of the controversial new movie THE EXORCIST. As word of the film spreads around, the cinema lines grow longer. Tickets are going for as much as fifty bucks a pair. On Friday night of the opening week, the crowd storms the cinema when it looks as though they're not going to make it inside after a four-hour wait. "It was like a riot", says Ralph Bailey, one of the security guards at Cinema 1. "We had to cancel the show". Four other Manhattan cinemas have lines extending for blocks from noon until midnight every day. In Beverly Hills, thousands of people gather early in the morning for an eight a.m. showing of THE EXORCIST at a cinema seating one and a half thousand. Every day in Boston, five thousand cinemagoers stand in the long queue wrapped around the Sack 57 cinema. In the Chicago suburb of Oakland, Illinois, police complain of vandalism, congested traffic and assaults around the cinema where THE EXORCIST is playing[1].

Within weeks of the first public screenings of the film come stories of audience members fainting and vomiting in the cinemas. Psyched into near-hysteria by their long wait outside, some of the film's viewers get genuinely sick. Many more report experiences of disturbing nightmares. Several cinema ushers, according to one source, have to be placed under doctors' care; several others choose to leave their jobs because of the harrowing aftermath of successive viewings of the film. In numerous cities where THE EXORCIST has run for several weeks, every major hospital receiving department has to deal with dozens of cases of fainting, nausea and hysteria. Hospital emergency room physicians report patients who, directly after viewing the film, appear to be both hallucinating and extremely distraught. Cinema ushers often have to clean up floors and rugs when vomiting patrons don't make it to the bathroom in time[2].

In LA, theatre manager Harry Francis estimates that each showing of the film produces four blackouts, half a dozen bouts of vomiting and multiple spontaneous exits. "I've been in this business 47 years, and I've never seen anything like it", he claims[3]. In New York, Ralph Bailey at Cinema 1 says that several people have had heart attacks during the film, and one woman even had a miscarriage[4]. In Berkeley, California, a man throws himself at the screen in a misguided attempt to "get the demon". Frank Kveton, manager of a movie theatre in Oakbrook, Illinois, complains that "my janitors are going crazy wiping up the vomit". He also complains

The cuckoo is a funny bird.
Linda Blair in happier times; THE EXORCIST.

that he's had to replace doors and curtains damaged by unruly crowds[5]. Film critic Harry Ringel, in his review of the film, mentions the "vomit-spattered bathroom... (you couldn't even get near the sink)"[6]. Another reviewer mentions being "especially menaced, because between the regurgitation on screen and the heady foetidness of the air around me, my own stomach complained of possession by some demonic force"[7]. Cinema ushers soon learn to be ready with their kitty litter for those who couldn't keep their dinners down.

Friedkin tells of people being carried out of movie houses on stretchers. H. Robert Honahen, division manager of the ABC/Plitt theatres in Berkeley, witnesses "two to five people" fainting "every day since the picture opened... More men than women pass out, and it usually happens in the evening performance, after the crucifix scene involving masturbation"[8]. "If THE EXORCIST had previewed, it would never have come out", claims William Friedkin, the film's director, "because people would have written 'This is terrible — you have a little girl masturbating with a crucifix, you dirty Jew bastard'. Those were the kind of notes we got anyway, afterward"[9].

There are also reports in the press of a broader, more emotional reaction to the film — of doctors, nurses, ambulances and priests being hired by cinemas to attend to distraught members of their audiences. Religious groups up and down the country give out warning leaflets to cinema queues; priests are persuaded by the press to reveal details of exorcisms they've recently performed. The Catholic Church is besieged with queries about possession, and a number of phoney cases are reported in the press. Lots of people are just freaked out by the film; it's held responsible for countless religious conversions and mental breakdowns. People are being driven to psychiatrists, faith healers, exorcists, necromancers, the Catholic Church, and sundry demonic cults. In the words of one critic, "the whole country has gone EXORCIST-crazy"[10].

Interestingly enough, the immediate hysteria begins to die down as soon as the popularity of the film widens — a phenomenon accounted for, by some, as a result of the picture moving from prestige movie houses with their sensitive patrons to ordinary cinemas in working class areas and urban ghettos. However, the emotional impact of the film seems to be long lasting. Audiences describe THE EXORCIST as variously "obscene", "fascinating", "reactionary", "deeply moving", "cheap sensationalism", "mindblowing", "blasphemous", "profoundly religious" and "propaganda for the Catholic Church"[11]. Priests of all denominations warn of the potential long-term spiritual dangers of exposure to the controversial movie. "This thing with the

Linda in the B-movie quagmire.

Devil has become an epidemic, and something has to be done about it", believes Dale Edwards, pastor of the Bethel Assembly of God Church in Rock Island, Illinois, who's organised a public book-burning of William Petter Blatty's novel, on which the film is based. "This stuff is as dangerous as pornography and drugs"[12]. In Boston, the Paulist Fathers at the downtown Catholic Center are receiving nearly one call a day for the services of an exorcist[13]. "If it were up to me now to decide whether to release the film to the general public, I don't think I would do it because of the danger of hysteria", warns Father John J. Nicola, one of the technical advisors on the film. "I think it could rival what we had in Europe in the Middle Ages with St. Vitus's dance"[14]. Canon John Pearce-Higgins, a leading Church of England exorcist from the diocese of Southwark, pronounces the film to be filthy, indecent and blasphemous, and warns that it will produce "a new crop of schizophrenics and a small number of cases of genuine possession"[15]. Rabbi Julius G. Neumann, the Chairman of the pressure group Morality in Media, claims that "the movie is adding to the frustration and confusion of our youth, claiming that whatever they do contrary to accepted religions and society's norm is not really of their own making, but that of the devil inside them"[16]. An official in the Church of Scotland writes that he'd "rather take a bath in pig manure than see the film"[17]. "It's a social and religious phenomenon", claims the Rev. Arthur Dekruyter, pastor of Christ Church in Oakbrook, Illinois. "We turned them away by the hundreds from my EXORCIST sermon"[18].

Religious authorities are joined in their condemnation of the film by doctors and psychiatrists, who warn of the potential psychological dangers of exposure to THE EXORCIST. "There's no way you can sit through that film without receiving some lasting negative or disturbing effects", warns Chicago psychiatrist Dr. Louis Schlan, Medical Director of Riveredge Hospital in Forest Park, Illinois, who has to place two young patients "under restraint" after they've watched THE EXORCIST. Schlan claims that four other moviegoers are now under treatment

— two because they reported finding demons in themselves, and two others because they have "a continuing fear of demons in their children". "We have many disturbed people in our society", claims Los Angeles psychiatrist Judd Marmor, "and a film like THE EXORCIST will spread like an infection"[19]. Manhattan child psychiatrist Dr. Hilde Mosse warns that the film provides a "deadly mixture of sex, violence and evil... The only thing THE EXORCIST can do... is pull young people down to a primitive level"[20]. People report nightmares and feel the terrifying, irrational presence of demons. Men and women walk out of cinemas and stand there, blinking in the sunlight, unable to shake off the effects of what they've just seen.

As the notoriety of the film increases, reports rapidly begin to circulate of cinemagoers who've suffered lasting psychological damage from exposure to THE EXORCIST. According to the TORONTO MEDICAL POST, four women are so traumatised by the movie that they have to be confined to psychiatric care. In Manhattan, sociologist and psychiatrist Dr. Vladimir Piskacek pronounces the film to be "dangerous for people with weak ego control"[21]. In Chicago, two young moviegoers are taken from the cinema straight to the psychiatric ward. "They're way out in left field", comments Louis Schlan. "They see themselves possessed by Satan"[22]. One publication, the SATURDAY REVIEW (WORLD), goes so far as to print a "Psychoanalyst's Indictment of THE EXORCIST" by the celebrated Hollywood shrink-to-the-stars, Dr. Ralph R. Greenson, Clinical Professor of Psychiatry at UCLA's School of Medicine.

During one experiment intended to gauge levels of neurotic and psychotic reaction to the film, a test group is shown photographic stills from THE EXORCIST several weeks after they've first seen it, including slides of the actors' faces, staircases inside and outside the house, and the exorcism itself. The slide show lasts an hour, during which several people leave the room, reporting that they've become nauseous. Almost the entire group reports severe depression after the slide show is over, and many are openly annoyed at having to undergo the experience. Comments reported include feelings of "agita-

tion", "anger", "rage", "persecution", "fear", "extreme annoyance" and "upset stomach". During the following week, well over half the test group report unusual and vivid nightmares related to the movie, including dreams in which they're tortured and persecuted by the devil, and dreams involving sexual experiences with the devil[23].

Significantly, Friedkin's powerful film is also held to be connected with a number of serious crimes. In West Germany, 19-year-old Rainer Hertrampf shoots himself in the head with an automatic rifle some time after seeing THE EXORCIST. In England, 16-year-old Jonathan Power is found dead one day after watching the film, although an inquest into the death reveals he's suffered an unrelated epileptic attack. The destructive power of THE EXORCIST is used as a defence by murderer Nicholas Bell, who claims he's been possessed by the film. In October 1974, THE EXORCIST is cited as the cause behind the murder of a 9-year-old girl by a teenager, who tells York Crown Court: "it was not really me that did it. There was something inside me. It is ever since I saw that film THE EXORCIST. I felt something take possession of me. It has been in me ever since". And in the same month, October 1974, in the village of Ossett in Yorkshire, 31-year-old Michael Taylor undergoes an all-night exorcism to drive the devils out of him. The next morning, Taylor attacks his wife with his bare hands, tears out her eyes and tongue, and rips her face almost from the bones until she dies, choking in her own blood.

So similar and recurrent are these traumatic reactions to the film that they lead to the establishment of a new clinical condition known as "cinematic neurosis" — a condition that can be precipitated by the viewing of a particularly disturbing film by previously unidentified psychiatric patients. In a paper published in THE JOURNAL OF NERVOUS AND MENTAL DISEASE entitled "Cinematic Neurosis following THE EXORCIST", James C. Bozzuto considers that Friedkin's film "seems to be directly related to traumatic neurosis in susceptible people". He points out that "classical symptoms and disability were observed following viewing the movie", concluding that "there are elements in the movie, such as possession with resultant loss of impulse control, that are likely to threaten people with similar problems, and to exceed their 'stimulus barrier'"[24]. One of the most significant aspects of Bozzuto's article is his claim that THE EXORCIST is the first film that has been reported to produce a widespread neurotic reaction in its audiences, and that other examples of trauma following cinema are virtually unknown, although one therapist reports a single case precipitated by a viewing of Hitchcock's PSYCHO[25].

Bozzuto's seminal article leads to the identification in various other clinical publications of further cases of cinematic neurosis after viewing THE EXORCIST. Since each case produces such a variety of somatic responses — ranging from fainting, anorexia and vomiting to acute panic and severe regression — it is worth looking at a selection of these fascinating cases in more detail.

CASE 1 Norman N., an 18-year-old white male, arrives at the emergency room of the Cincinnati General Hospital three weeks after first seeing THE EXORCIST with the complaint that he's unable to take his mind off the film. Symptoms include decreased appetite, irritability, and the inability to remove certain scenes from his mind. He leaves home and begins drinking and abusing multiple drugs in an attempt to obliterate all memory of the film[26].

CASE 2 James V., a 23-year-old white male, is referred by a priest to the psychiatric outpatient clinic in Cincinnati approximately one month after seeing THE EXORCIST. During this time, he reports such symptoms as insomnia, paranoia, irritability, and decreased sexual functioning. He's unable to stay alone for any length of time, has persistent magical dreams about the devil, and tends to "misinterpret" sounds.[27]

CASE 3 Martha B., a 22-year-old white female, calls the Psychiatric Clinic in Cincinnati claiming that she's been unable to sleep for approximately one week after seeing THE EXORCIST. Symptoms reported include anxiety reactions such as abdominal cramps, hyperventilation, and the feeling that someone is after her, or that she's going to die[28].

CASE 4 Lyle H., a 24-year-old black male, arrives at the emergency room approximately one month after first seeing THE EXORCIST. Symptoms include flashbacks to the film, feelings of nervousness around his two children and his wife, insomnia, the sensation that certain people "look strange", and the suspicion that his five-year-old daughter is possessed[29].

CASE 5 Ruth A., an intelligent young woman, becomes symptomatic immediately after seeing THE EXORCIST and seeks urgent psychiatric help. Almost from the moment she leaves the theatre, she experiences a return of intense fears and phobias she can dimly recall from her early childhood. Other symptoms include a pervasive fear of being alone, especially at night, the insistence that her husband be with her at all times, and a refusal to go to work[30].

CASE 6 John M., a young university professor, is referred for emergency psychiatric treatment because of his urgent need to let the "devils" inside him "come out", and he feels that a psychiatrist would not be killed by his devils. Three times in a single day he regresses into fits of raving, ranting, crying, stamping his feet and banging his fists until he becomes exhausted. He admits that he has long felt possessed of an evil, psychotic core, and that THE EXORCIST has convinced him that this core is the devil himself[31].

Related cases are reported by psychiatric institutions all across the country, generally involving patients who overidentify with events and characters in THE EXORCIST, especially because of fears related to loss of control and issues of separation, to the extent that symptoms of traumatic neurosis are superimposed on a pre-existing borderline personality disorder.

When asked to recall their own experience of watching THE EXORCIST, most people think of the demonic figure of the possessed Regan, tied down to her bed, her face and body distorted into a hideous, discoloured travesty of the 12-year-old child we've met earlier on in the film. Surprisingly, though, out of the entire 113 minutes of film, the scenes in Regan's bedroom take up only 16 minutes and 20 seconds, and some of this is devoted to the reactions of onlookers — Chris, Sharon, the doctors and priests. The relative brevity of the scenes of demon possession suggest that the film's power to shock is based on more than the forceful and striking visual displays for which THE EXORCIST is so wholly condemned by its detractors.

In fact, much of the force of THE EXORCIST lies in the way it gradually and inexorably undermines the confidence of its viewers by inducing a sense of anxiety which cannot be satisfactorily allayed, even when the film is over. The effects of this anxiety state are the result of what CAHIERS DU CINÉMA aptly describes as the "cinema of crisis" — the cathexis of trauma, at all costs, until, "at the end of the film, the two exorcists are killed by the devil", and "the spectator is left all alone — it's now up to him to know how to deal with the consequences of his own fear"[32].

Perhaps most important in evoking this state of crisis in the audience is the film's soundtrack, for which it won an Academy Award. The music is basically a collage of largely contemporary serious pieces from existing phonographic recordings of the works of Krzystof Penderecki, Hans Werner Henze, George Crumb, Anton Webern, Mike Oldfield and David Borden, with additional music by Jack Nitzsche. But it's the unaccredited sound effects that play perhaps the foremost part in evoking a sense of menacing peril.

Friedkin, acting the part of the tricksy publicist, makes so many claims and counterclaims about the sound effects used in THE EXORCIST that at times it's hard to separate truth from fiction[33]. Two sounds in particular that are almost certainly mixed into the soundtrack include the buzzing of agitated bees (recorded then re-recorded at a number of different frequencies), and the terrified squealing of pigs about to be slaughtered[34]. Both sounds are mixed into the background noise of the movie with the intention of evoking discomfort, threat, anxiety and

fear at an unconscious level. A third sound rumoured to have been used for "demon voices" is the roaring of lions or big cats.

Most controversial of all, however, is the rumour that mixed into the film's soundtrack are the actual demon voices recorded during a genuine exorcism. Friedkin knowingly encourages the rumour by claiming to be in possession of "a cassette recording of an actual exorcism performed in Rome. It's in Italian. It involves the exorcism of a 14-year old boy. I got the tape

William Friedkin and Linda Blair at the reception thrown to prove Linda "couldn't be in better frame of mind or better health".

through the Jesuit Provincial of New York and on the tape are the sounds produced by this young man supposedly possessed"[35]. Whilst Friedkin never claims to have used the recording in the film's soundtrack, he does claim that "it's those sounds on the tape that I emulated for the demon"[36].

It's this rumour that provokes angry claims that THE EXORCIST is somehow dangerous, evil and incendiary. Evangelist Billy Graham declares there's an evil embodied in the very celluloid of the film itself. Fundamentalist author Hal Lindsay believes "there's a lot more going on in that film

Friedkin and Linda on set.

deliberate and careful use of rapid cutting, unexpected camera-movement, slow-motion sequences, sudden close-ups, and abrupt shocks created by visual and verbal intrusions. One reviewer, for example, is especially disturbed by a "hair-raising moment when, almost at the edge of one's perception, one realises that the child's head has turned round far too much for human possibility"[39].

Rumours circulate about the use of a number of "subliminal induction techniques" in THE EXORCIST intended to induce levels of panic and hysteria among some individuals[40]. In fact, there are two subliminal cuts used in THE EXORCIST. One occurs in Karras' dream sequence, when Karras' mother comes out of the subway entrance and Karras watches from across the street, and the other can be found when Regan is strapped down in bed, tossing from side to side, towards the end of the final exorcism sequence. Both consist of two frames spliced into the film, lasting approximately one forty-eighth of a second each, and both depict a leering, skull-like face surrounded by a dark background — in fact, frames from a make-up test which didn't work that Friedkin did with Linda Blair's double, Eileen Dietz[41].

THE EXORCIST also juggles a number of disquieting visual motifs, such as the discoloration of eyes witnessed first in the face of a blacksmith in Iraq, then, moments later, also in the prologue, in the eyes of the black figure in the carriage, then in the old tramp Karras bumps into in the Georgetown subway, then in the eyes of the demon, and finally in the eyes of Karras himself[42]. Other notable visual motifs include the recurrent image of the narrow, concrete flight of stairs that connects the MacNeil house with the street below — down which Burke Dennings falls to his death, where Karras takes his final

than just shock value. There are spiritual powers at work during the showing of that film. It is setting the stage for the future attack of Satan"[37].

Most effective in creating tension is the way the soundtrack builds slowly from plateau to plateau, always intensifying the audience's perceptual response[38]. The slow-moving scenes in Iraq at the opening of the film, for example, are contrasted with noisy scenes of unrest on the Georgetown University campus film set. The complete silence of Father Karras's eerie dream is broken by Regan's screams as she attacks the neurologists in the hospital, and the tense, low-pitched conversation between Chris and Kinderman contrasts with sudden bangs, growls and loud screams coming from upstairs. In general, the sonic pattern of the film contrasts long, tense scenes of silence or virtual silence with loud, discordant noises, devilish laughter, and the deep, guttural voice of Mercedes McCambridge speaking the words of the demon. The tense, silent scenes are relieved only by uncomfortable levels of noise, establishing a pattern of emotional anxiety and stress.

28 The visual effects of THE EXORCIST share a similarly hypnotic rhythm to that of the soundtrack. Anxiety levels are heightened by the

sacrificial plunge, and where Kinderman spends a good deal of time in contemplation[43]. These shots are paralleled by similar shots of the stair-case inside the MacNeil house leading up to Regan's bedroom. Symbolic resonance accumu-lates from repeated images of flowers, dark sil-houettes, skulls, or skull-like outlines (as in the X-ray of Regan's brain), mirrors and crucifixes.

The combined result of this onslaught of aural and visual techniques is to carefully train the film's viewers into heightened levels of anxiety and anticipation every time the camera goes up-stairs and moves towards Regan's doorway. We learn to anticipate worse and worse horrors every time somebody climbs the stairs. This gradual and methodical building of anticipation is often followed by a distinct anti-climax and then, just as the audience begins to get restless from the letdown, the real surprise climax strikes[44]. As a result, the film's shocks are alter-nated with our expectation of them, ensuring that the by-play of images continues long after the audience has left the cinema. Friedkin, who's deliberately secretive about the use of special effects in THE EXORCIST[45], claims that the film's "expectancy set", as he terms it, is constructed with a great deal of care:

> People are afraid while they're standing in line. And for the first hour of the film, while there's little more than exposition, and some of that very hard to follow unless you've read the book, people are working themselves into an emotional state that is inducive to becoming terrified... Fear is generally something behind a door that's about to be opened. Most of the nightmares that you read about someone having involve someone coming up to a closed door behind which there is the unknown[46].

As the notoriety of THE EXORCIST increases, a number of additional rumours begin to circu-late about the psychological health of Linda Blair, who is 12 when the film begins pre-production, and 14 by the time it hits the cinema screens. Friedkin unintentionally fans the flames of these rumours by asserting that Blair has "no stand-in, no substitute", and performs every scene in the movie herself, including the notorious "cru-cifix masturbation" sequence. Rumours spread

that Linda Blair has herself somehow become "possessed" during the shooting of the movie, and that she bears psychological scars. The ru-mours fuel widespread curiosity. Eventually Warner Brothers are forced to bring Blair out in public to dispel gossip about her purported psy-chological breakdown. A reception is planned, according to Friedkin, to prove that Linda's been unaffected by the production of THE EXORCIST.

Blair's healthy frame of mind at such a young age is called into question by Biskind's recent description of the film in his book EASY RIDERS, RAGING BULLS. Here, Biskind reports the follow-ing conversation, reputed to have taken place between Friedkin and Linda Blair when Friedkin was looking for an actress capable of dealing with the role of Regan.

> "Did you read THE EXORCIST", Friedkin asks her.
> "Yes."
> "What's it about?"
> "It's about a little girl who gets possessed by the Devil and does a lot of bad things."
> "What sort of bad things?"
> "She pushes a guy out of a window and masturbates with a crucifix and— "
> "What does that mean?"
> "It's like jerking off, isn't it?"
> "Yeah. Do you know about jerking off?"
> "Oh, sure."
> "Do you do that?"
> "Yeah, don't you?"
> She got the role.[47]

Claims Linda Blair:

> They wrote all these articles about how deranged I was and the psychiatric problems I was supposed to be having... maybe they wanted to believe all these rumours because it helped the whole process. Maybe people wanted to believe weird things happened because it helped them to be scared[48].

However, whilst Blair's psychological health is never in question during the making of THE EXORCIST, she quickly finds herself a victim of the film's notoriety during the years following its initial release — a condition that eventually takes its toll. "I'd be in a supermarket or a cloth-ing store or somewhere public, and... people would literally look at me and just about come out of their skin", she recalls. People questioned if I was the Devil... it really scared people. It got to the point where I just didn't go out publicly". The studio could do very little, in the end, to protect her from becoming the focus of the attention of an assortment of fanatics, zealots, and people's various projections. "The press literally scared me to death", claims Blair now. "They had my eyes on billboards that would change colour. Who wanted to go out in public with all that going on? It was crazy. I just kept away from the public".

Eventually, the combinations of her fears of kidnapping and her receipt of a number of serious death threats convince Blair to go into hiding for a time. Her disturbing confrontation with the dark side of mankind has made her decide, she claims, never to have a child of her own. Despite her temporary retreat from public life, however, stories persist that Linda's parents have struck a pact with the Devil, that her mother has been struck blind and her father dumb, that she'd given birth to a child born without eyes, that she keeps a room in her basement where she says Black Mass, and — most consistently — that she's committed suicide. Some of these

Linda Blair returned for further treatment in John Boorman's EXORCIST II: THE HERETIC. Father Richard Burton looks on.

rumours may have been fanned into flame by Blair's widely publicised arrest in 1977, at the age of 18, when she was charged with conspiracy to supply cocaine, and sentenced to three years community service.

NOTES

1   *Time*, February 11th 1974, p53; Klemesrud, Judy, "They Wait Hours — to Be Shocked", *New York Times,* January 27th 1974: 12; Woodward, 28.

2   Key, W.B., *Media Sexploitation*, New Jersey: Prentice Hall, p99.

3   *Time*, February 11th 1974, p53.

4   Klemesrud, p12.

5   Bartholomew, p10 and woodward, Kenneth L., "The Exorcism Frenzy", *Newsweek*, February 11th 1974: p28–33.

6   Ibid. p26.

7   Willson, Robert F. Jr., "*The Exorcist* and Multicinema Aesthetics", *Journal of Popular Film* no. 2, 1974: 183-187.

8   Although Friedkin has

always claimed that it's the scene where Regan undergoes an arteriogram that leads audiences to respond so viscerally.

9   Biskind, Peter, *Easy Riders, Raging Bulls*, NY: Simon & Schuster, 1998:92.

10   Farber, Stephen, "*The Exorcist*, A Unique Freak Show", *Film Comment* May/June 1974, p34-5

11   McCormick, Ruth, "The Devil Made Me Do It! A Critique of *The Exorcist*", *Cineaste* 3: 1974: p19.

12   Woodward, p31.

13   Ibid.

14   Ibid. p33.

15   McConnell, p172.

16   Bartholomew, p10.

17   see Biskind, 1998: 92.

18   Woodward, p28.

19   Ibid, p29-31.

20   *Time*, February 11th 1974, p53.

21   Ibid.

22   Ibid.

23   Key, W.B., p101.

24   Bozzuto, James C, M.D., "Cinematic Neurosis Following *The Exorcist*: Report of Four Cases", *The Journal of Nervous and Mental Disease*, 161:1, 1975: 43.

25   Bozzuto personally suspects that such cases may arise, "but usually with mild symptomology, and the patients do not seek treatment". Ibid, p47.

26   Reported by Bozzuto, p44.

27   Ibid. p44.

28   Ibid. p45.

29   Ibid. p45.

30   reported by Hamilton, James W., "Cinematic Neurosis: A Brief Case

Ironically, however, despite the enormous notoriety of Blair's role in THE EXORCIST, the film virtually ruins her subsequent acting career, making it all but impossible for her to get work in any picture other than B-movies and low-budget horror films, of which she's made more than 20.

T HE EXORCIST is not about Satanism and the occult"[49], says Friedkin. Nor is it, really, a film about demonic possession, or the supernatural, or the possible existence of evil. What Friedkin has made is a film about what's really going on when we buy tickets to a horror movie. THE EXORCIST is a film about humanity confronting its own horror, its own ugliness, the vileness and indignity of the human body. It's a film directed entirely against its observers, a film to assail the bodies and minds of those anxious and excited audiences queuing for hours round the blocks all the way down Second Avenue, a film to make us despair at our own bodily nature. And , as Friedkin neatly puts it, "if you go looking for the devil, chances are you're going to find him"[50].

A different version of this article appears in Mikita's book HOLLYWOOD HEX, pub: Creation, 1999.

COMPETiTiON TiME

Is the above a still from THE EXORCIST? A publicity shot, perhaps? So many 'possession' films followed in the wake of THE EXORCIST we at HEADPRESS are inclined to think the devil-girl here isn't Linda Blair. If you think you know for sure or have any suggestions, get in touch.

Report", *Journal of the American Academy of Psychoanalysis* vol. 6, no.4 (1978): 569.

31 Reported by Greenson, p41.

32 Kane, Pascal (review), *Cahiers du Cinéma,* October/November 1974.

33 His claim that no special effects have been used in the film is made possible by the fact that he repeats the scenes involving these effects again and again until they're perfect. John Calley of Warner Brothers claims that Friedkin would come up to him every day on the set and say '"You've seen the dailies – are they ok?'. I'd say, 'Billy, I can see the wires when she does the head thing. It's a bad joke'. He said, 'Look, I don't want to

bury you. Maybe I can cut it'. I said 'No, we gotta do it again. The point of this is, it has to be perfect'". And Friedkin would comply every time, and re-shoot the scene until the special effects were no longer visible (see Biskind 1998:91).

34 Key, p111.

35 Friedkin, cit. in Bartholomew, p9.

36 Ibid.

37 cit. in Woodward, p28.

38 Key, p113-115.

39 Milne, Tom, (review), *Monthly Film Bulletin* 41, April 1974: 332.

40 see, for example, Key p101.

41 Kermode, Mark, *The Exorcist*, BFI Cinema Classics, London: BFI 1997, p45.

42 Bowles, p202.

43 Key claims that the "consciously unnoticed" word "PIG" is written as graffiti on a ledge at the left side of the stairs. See Key, p112.

44 Bowles, 203.

45 He claims, for example, that "there are no optical effects... they were all done live, including the vomit", and "the levitation was done without wires and involved the use of a magnetic field" – see Friedkin interviewed in Bartholomew, p9.

46 Ibid. p13.

47 cit in Biskind, Peter 1998: 86.

48 Blair, cit. in Kermode, p73.

49 Friedkin, interviewed by Bartholomew, p43.

50 Ibid. p43.

Meeting Jan Švankmajer

THE EXCITEMENT BECAME almost unbearable as myself and holiday companion Rick made our way into the still-hot day after an almost impossible trip on a Prague tram stuffed with tourists. I was unfortunate enough to have been seated next to an elderly Czech woman who was wrapped in at least 16 layers of clothing and who insisted on slamming shut all nearby windows. The only consolation I got was from scanning the faces of shocked tourists who dared to try and open them. Cold eyes burned at them as if wishing them dead, and the old woman jumped at reaching hands and snatched the windows shut again.

We had successfully negotiated the Republican streets and, in a peaceful area of the city far from the low murmur of bustling tourists, found our goal: the Gambra Surrealist Gallery, part owned by Czech filmmaker and surrealist Jan Švankmajer. I quickly pulled out a trusty Agfa — *'Let's go!'* — camera and snapped a shot of the gallery where Švankmajer exhibits his own artwork together with that of many other Surrealists.

"I hope we meet him," I confided to Rick as we entered the building.

The tiny gallery, stuffed with art, was more than everything we expected. To the left at a desk sat Eva, a kindly lady who it transpired had worked in the gallery since it opened in 1992. To the right was a door with a curtain pulled across it, and everywhere paintings, sculptures, sketches, and ceramic jugs depicting open female genitals. I scanned the room and met Rick's eyes, both of us sharing the same expression of joy, like we were kids in a toyshop.

"Do you speak English?" I ask Eva.

"Yes, yes I do," she replies with a big grin.

I handed her the package I had prepared before I set off. Inside was a copy of HEADPRESS 13: PLAGUE — a present for Mr Švankmajer.

"I would love to do an interview," I pushed.

"Ask him, he will be back soon. He's just taking his dogs for a walk."

Trying to contain our anticipation we busied ourselves round the shop, both of us with our eyes on the door. Our patience paid off. In strolled a dog with what seemed a beaming smile across its face, soon followed by Mr Švankmajer himself and a second dog.

Švankmajer stood in the middle of the room and eyed us with curiosity. Eva kindly explained who we were and together they spent a few moments casually leafing through HEADPRESS and the letter I put inside. We stood quietly waiting for a reaction. Finally, Švankmajer took his eyes away from the book and gave us a large sincere smile and offered his hand.

"I'm so pleased to meet you, Sir," I spat as we furiously shook hands. Eva translated my gushing accolades.

"I would love to ask you about your new projects," I said, Eva again translating.

"I'm very busy working on the screenplay for my next film, as well as many other artistic projects," he offered.

We spend the next 10 to 15 minutes quietly looking at the work on the walls together, the language barrier more of an inconvenience than a problem — but how I would have sold my soul to speak fluent Czech for just those minutes! We came to the few bookshelves in the gallery that offered a wide selection of books on Surrealism as well as many publications about Švankmajer's work. Here he thrust a copy of INVENTION, IMAGINATION, INTERPRETATION into my hand, a retrospective collection of artwork by the Surrealist Group of Czech Artists, of which Švankmajer is a key member. He pointed and fingered the book, making clear it wasn't about his

A sugar sachet from the Franz Kafka café, Prague.

ALICE

dir: Jan Švankmajer

Switzerland, 1988; reVision, Cert PG

Contact: Visionary, 28/30 The Square, St Anne's, Lytham St Annes, Lancs., FY8 1RF

"Alice thought to herself... now you will see a film... for children... perhaps."

So says Alice at the beginning of Švankmajer's interpretation of Lewis Carroll's ALICE IN WONDERLAND. It's a sentiment that rings true of the director's most disturbing films: they may well delight children, but to grown-ups — who are burdened with reason and require some semblance of formality to cling to — they are dark and scary. And the strange thing is, they are dark and scary in a completely child-like way.

In ALICE we, as adults, will question the significance of the draftsman's worktable that provides the gateway to Wonderland. Until, that is, we reflect on why it is we so readily accept the rabbit hole of Carroll's original story as a gateway? They are both absurd concepts — but one is less absurd because it is founded in tradition.

Referring to herself in the third person (narrating the story in a series of clipped phrases), Švankmajer's Alice is subjected to more shocks, knocks, bruisings and scrapes than Bruce Willis in any number of his Action Hero roles. She bashes her head constantly, ingesting the 'grow potion' that sends her spiralling into the ceiling. It really seems that the other characters — which include a rat who builds a campfire in her hair, and an army made of ill-matched animal bones — are out to do Alice real harm, even kill her given the opportunity.

Lewis Carroll is a 'pre-surrealist' whose work Švankmajer has adapted on more than one occasion. (Another is Edgar Allan Poe, whose THE PIT AND THE PENDULUM was subject to a great interpretation by Švankmajer in 1983, almost a dry-run for his own FAUST several years later.) ALICE marked the Czech director's feature film debut, and continued a shift away from overt — some might say 'serious' — symbolism toward phantasmagorical dreamscapes routed in the real world.

A nightmare for grown-ups everywhere.

David Kerekes

PEOPLE WHO READ HEADPRESS Jan and Rick outside the Gambra gallery.

own work and projects, but — as stated in his rare interviews — concerns a collective of artists all working for the same goal. The refreshing lack of any ego swamped me with emotion.

"Photograph time!" I announce and in the next moment we are outside with my *'Let's go!'* camera.

After several shots, Rick shuffles into frame with a "May I?" He's met with another large grin and beckoning hand gestures.

After the shoot we congregate back inside the gallery and Eva explains, "Jan has to leave now. He's very keen to continue his screenplay."

Big handshakes and thank you's are exchanged as Švankmajer heads towards the curtain at the far side of the gallery. He opens the door and, with HEADPRESS under arm and dogs trundling behind, he disappears into the darkened room, closing the door behind him.

"I'm so glad we have seen him," I tell Eva.

"You should be. Nobody usually sees him," she replies.

A further 15 minutes are spent chatting idly to Eva and choosing mementoes to mark the occasion, then we say our farewells and leave with books and prints... straight to the nearest bar for a celebratory Staropramen. 🐆

Will Youds, Prague 1999

RUBBER DOLLS!

· ·

eptember 1988 and I arrive at University in Manchester. Due to a cock-up on the accommodation front, I was forced to share a room with a Physics student from Barnsley, called — for anonymity's sake — 'John'.

It was an uneasy co-existence: beds and desks at either end of a very high square room and one wash basin to share. He developed a passion for Jethro Tull, whose music has haunted me ever since. I am loathe to use the term 'Geek' or 'Nerd', but that's what John was. He wore a SOUTH PACIFIC sweatshirt and glasses, had kitten posters, an abiding love of Warhammer figures and kept a box under his desk which held 'bedclothes and stuff'. Needless to say, my sex-life was effectively

annihilated by this grinning Yorkshire idiot. The one time that I did get a girl back just for a cuddle, he insisted upon getting ready for his evening bath by stripping down to yellow men's briefs in front of my companion. (I fear he was trying to initiate some sort of threesome.)

We 'got-on'. Just. When I went home for the weekend, fellow inhabitants of our building would talk about his strange behaviour. Locking himself away and so on. I just believed it was part of his general prattishness. I was quite wrong.

One weekend, a group of friends crashed over and we needed some extra bed linen, so I went to the (TV-sized!) box under John's desk to 'borrow' some bedding… Stunned. Shocked. Perplexed. That was our collective response to what we found in that box. Not only was there a Rubber Doll (called 'Kitty' if my memory serves me

correctly) but stockings, two syringes, a vibrating egg connected to a vari-speed controller and the biggest stash of hardcore porn that we had ever seen! Not only 'straight' porn but dwarf stuff,

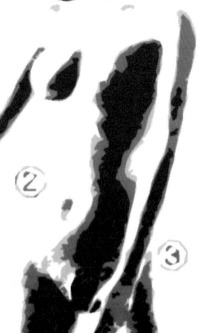

① ② ③

lesbian stuff, she-males and a couple of books on sex-change operations. We counted some 40-ish titles. An absolute fortune!

It was Kitty that drew our attention. I have a photo of the four of us holding her in her uninflated state. She felt moist. Inevitably we blew her up and ran around the corridors giving her a 'piggy-back'. None of us were interested in sticking our dicks anywhere near where John's had been so we put her back as we didn't wish to let on that we had found his stash. We now had our own supply of stroke-mags that would be the envy of the rest of the all-male hall!

Inevitably the word got round, it was too good a secret to keep. Soon people were coming round to the room demanding to meet Kitty when John was out. My notoriety was secure. I was "The Pervert's Roommate". At the end of the academic year, a group of drunken students stood under our window calling out for Kitty to make an appearance. John threw water at them.

I would like to be able to say that I caught John balling Kitty one day, but that would be untrue — he was too sly to get caught. When I did confront him, he claimed he was holding the stash for someone from his old school who had threatened him. We did try to sabotage the box so that his parents would find

out about him. No chance.

We didn't try to keep in touch. I don't know if he got a girlfriend or even got laid at Uni. People I knew kept running into him [after he left University]. He hadn't changed at all. I just assume that the stash got bigger and his interests became more varied... **Grant Hobson**

n the subject of rubber dolls, the first ad I ever saw for one was in a 1968 issue of THE MAGAZINE OF HORROR, a great little pulp reprint title featuring R.E. Howard's 'Kings of the Night' and an Algernon Blackwood story. Anyway, there at the back was an ad for the 'perfect bedmate' (!) for only $9.98, or some such, leading one to wonder whether the product in question *really* resembled the knockout dolly bird (with blonde hair piled on top of her head) who was doing the modelling with black tape over her offending nipples (ouch!).

The first 'real' rubber doll I ever saw confirmed my scepticism over this matter. After I'd just left school a friend of mine took me to the hideously scruffy house of one Roddy (his nick-name) with whom I had only a previously passing acquaint-ance. Up in Roddy's bedroom was the most gigantic pile of 'niff' mags I'd ever seen, including some hardcore porn titles — a real novelty for me

in those days. In the midst of his seedy lair, Roddy also showed us a hideously wide-mouthed rubber doll he's sent off for and proceeded to inform us, unnecessarily, how many times he's "shot off into it", to repeat his delightful phrase. He also showed us a milk bottle he'd "zonked into", so at this point I made my

●　●　●　●　●　●　●　●　●　●　●　●

Readers respond to Anthony Ferguson's SHE AIN'T HEAVY, SHE'S JUST RUBBER article in HEADPRESS 18. Why don't you? Write to the editorial address with your own inflatable-partner stories.

●　●　●　●　●　●　●　●　●　●　●　●

apologies and left.

Some months later, I heard that Roddy's doll had burst and that he'd tried to mend it with black electri-cian's tape (synchronicity, or something more sinister?) but gave it up as a bad job and "just saved the tits", which, I was informed, were under his bed. I spent many restless nights subsequently trying to banish the image of the acne-scarred Roddy banging away at these dismembered rubber mammaries to no avail. I often wondered if he wiped them before he returned them into the filthy dust balls under his bed ...

'Those were the days.'
Stephen Sennitt

Kerri Sharp

RECENTLY, A RARE SCREENING of Walerian Borowczyk's **La Bête** was organised at the NFT on London's South Bank. I'd seen his five-section film, **Immoral Tales**, in 1997 and at the time had been impressed by the inclusion of an uncompromising scene of female masturbation in**Therèse the Philosopher**. Given the director's fascination with the accretions of the *mise en scène*, it's still not a bad effort in getting right in there and portraying on screen something which is absent from most films which attempt to explore female sexuality.

It would be a joy to write a piece about the obsessions of Walerian Borowczyk and his influence on directors who deal with the picaresque fantastic, but this article isn't it. Those matters are eloquently covered by Colin Davis's piece in **Shock Xpress**. In this article I want to concentrate on the specifics of his film of 1975 — **La Bête** (The Beast) and why

I think it is a fine execution of the difficult-to-represent machinations of female desire.

HOW MANY TIMES HAVE YOU SEEN FEMALE masturbation in a movie that isn't straight porno? It's rare by anyone's estimation. Aside from another Borowczyk creation, **Immoral Tales**, it's in **Being There** (Shirley McClaine's spiritual scratchings) and, er... that's about it. When female orgasm is portrayed on screen it's nearly always the obviously phoney result of being penetrated by some lantern-jawed stud in a soft-focus darkened room. You get the picture? The mainstream cinema has a problem with masturbation generally, but female onanism is a big number. Not only does it wipe out the need for the hero and his dick, any realistic portrayal is going to acknowledge female desire is capable of functioning on its own terms and that female onanism is an ordinary practice.

37

By 'ordinary' I mean as not part of a cathartic steamy lovemaking scene with the hero. (Why are sex scenes always so tumultuous in mainstream and art house cinema?) There's a lot of fucking in the movies but how much of it is realistic? The expressions of sexual rapture we see in most films wouldn't be out of place in an ad for chocolate or moisturising cream. The metaphorical usage of states of female sexual ecstasy by the advertising industry has become primary while representations of the thing itself are absent. What you get in **La Bête** *are* glimpses of the real thing: hands going into pants and objects rubbed between legs in the broad daylight, in the afternoon.

For those of you who haven't seen **La Bête**, here's a rundown of the narrative. The film begins with graphic footage of rutting horses in the stable courtyard of a chateau. The stallion snorts and bites his mate; the filly's calm complicity is touching in its acceptance of her priapic aggressor. But she wants it as much as he does, given the shot of her oozing horsy hole. She does very little except flaunt it for him; he's hard and gagging for it and making a right tool of himself. This allegory will be repeated throughout the film.

Watching the beasts mate is Mathurin, educationally challenged son of the Marquis de l'Esperance. The Marquis's estate will crumble unless he can marry off his backward progeny to foxy and wealthy American girl,

Lucy Broadhurst. Lucy arrives, accompanied by her aunt, in a state of youthful enthusiasm for the beauty of her surroundings. She's photographing everything on her journey to the chateau, including the mating horses.

There are complications to the Marquis's plan to marry off Mathurin to Lucy. Family law dictates that only the Marquis's uncle, a cardinal, can marry Mathurin and his betrothed but the uncle won't comply as Mathurin is a pagan (idiot other) and has to be baptised. And who does the Marquis bring in to the house to perform the baptism? None other than the ageing roué that is the local pederast priest — who is always accompanied by his achingly beautiful choirboy helpers, desperately gorgeous in their androgyny. This is better than Buñuel. Not only does the director poke fun at the clergy; he effortlessly

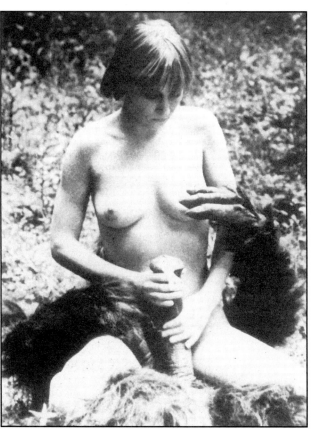

La Bête.

disempowers the sanctity of the church, making them out to be nothing more than confidantes of the French aristocracy. The irrational and 'ungodly' has encroached onto the proceedings at the same time as the 'destructive' distraction of desirable female flesh. Everyone is thrown into a spin by this collision of elements of disorder.

Borowczyk is in tune with the narcissistic female fantasy: the one that lets you be gorgeous to the point of causing chaos, and allows your sexual attraction to exact a power of such magnitude that male subjects will be confused by its efficiency while you reap whatever benefits are on offer. Lucy — having just arrived at the estate — finds dusty reminders of her forebears. A corset — preserved under a belljar — attracts her gaze. Rather than passing it by, this loaded exhibit exacts a powerful influence on our voluptuous subject. She then discovers an old family album belonging to the eighteenth-century Marquise Romilda de l'Esperance. In the album is a drawing of a hairy creature — The Beast — and the inscription 'I fought and defeated him'. This beast is due to reappear every 200 years. Lucy's unconscious mind seizes upon the bestial theme, which permeates the house, and it isn't too long before she's in her room using the Polaroid snaps of the rutting horses as wank material. She's interrupted once when a servant arrives, bearing a rose — supposedly a gift from Mathurin but actually sent by the Marquis. The servant has been called away at an inopportune moment: the Marquis's daughter has been seducing him in her room but now, left alone, pursues completion through the vigorous use of the bedpost. (All the women are at it in **La Bête**.) The rose fails to impress Lucy — for the time being at least. She is far too immersed in her imagination, fuelled by the longer-lasting erotic souvenirs which she inexorably stumbles upon.

Lucy, back in her room, lying on her sumptuous bed clad in a soaking wet diaphanous gown, begins to dream about the eighteenth-century Marquise and her coupling with the beast in the forest which caused the famous, now-preserved corset to be ripped from her body. This fairytale-like dream sequence is accompanied by harpsichord music by Scarlatti and manages to be uplifting, sexy, liberating, scatty and beautiful. It is this scene which is the most memorable in the film. This sequence was filmed originally as an 18-minute short, **La véritable histoire de la bête du Gévaudan**, which was devoid of any framing story featuring other characters. Borowczyk makes no concession to subtlety in this short film/sequence: a man in an ungainly but unclassifiable 'beast' costume cavorts, captures and ravishes the Marquise in the seclusion of the woods. During the pursuit the Marquise loses her powdered wig and by this seems to transform into a contemporary woman, sporting cropped hair and a very slender, almost boyish, frame. After her initial reluctance, she gives in to the power of the beast — his complete necessity to possess her — and applies enthusiastic oral and manual stimulation.

The beast oozes copious amounts of ejaculate (it's rumoured the film crew used potato soup for these shots) lovingly captured in close-up, before he dies, spent. We get to see a prolonged display of the huge spurting beast-cock — a treat for any female filth-hound despite (and maybe because of) its ridiculous size.

Lucy wakes up and begins once more to masturbate, this time using the rose to good effect. By this, Borowczyk cleverly ameliorates any need for subtle metaphor as cunt and rosebud collides in glorious close-up. The camera stays focused on Lucy's holiest of holies long enough to earn the film the 'slur' of pornography. This scene caused outrage

39

when the film was originally shown and was still powerful enough to make a significant number of the audience walk out of the 1998 screening. Could this be the shock of seeing female masturbation stripped of its soft-focus veneer?

In this sequence the character of Lucy is Everywoman in an hotel room with time on her hands and lust on her mind. But she does not need to find anything so tangible as a lover. She's happily self-contained in her onanism and is quite content using the *idea* of untamed or bestial lust as her trigger.

Lucy dreams again and wakes with the sound of the expiring beast ringing in her ears. She gets out of bed and goes to the idiot Mathurin's room where she finds he is dead. His corpse is laid out later on, and he is found to possess a hairy paw and tail. (He had kept his hand bandaged while alive.) Lucy and her aunt flee the house and the closure of the film shows the Marquise Romilda covering the poor dead beast with leaves and walking away slowly from the place of her carnal coupling.

IT WOULD BE FAR TOO GLIB TO SAY THE film was a metaphor for the power of female sexuality; it shows the power of female sexuality. The entire focus is on Lucy's newly discovered carnality, prompted by the beast of her imagination. Like Angela Carter's **The Company of Wolves**, **La Bête** rejoices in the profane and the pagan and returns nature to sexual culture. Puritans and anti-sex feminists would have a problem with the bestial scene. The Marquise is, effectively, raped by the beast and enjoys it. And so what? He's not everyman; he's a mythical creature thrown up by the female carnal imagination. He's going to know what you want without you having to ask. You're going to get the fuck of your life without having to listen to chat about football. What's the problem?

As Colin Davis notes in his article,

'True To His Own Obsessions: The films of Walerian Borowczyk',

> Makers of such movies are customarily accused of having a profound fear of the sexual woman but Borowczyk, though he often deals with the power of aroused femininity, doesn't seem to be afraid of it.

I'd agree with this and add that he doesn't see a need to punish his female characters, either. None of them wind up dead — punished for their carnality in some paternalistic Judeo-Christian 'told-you-so' nasty ending. One could say the underlying message of the film is that the sexual imagination is chaotic and bestial, and the sexual female is devouring and dangerous; the women go on to revel anew, unscathed, while Mathurin and the beast die and the Marquis is left to his financial problems. As someone who is sick of seeing female sexuality represented on screen as something tepid, cosy and not as enjoyable as shopping, it's refreshing to see the subject handled in a way which is liberating, creative, aesthetically original and arousing — and this film is 25 years old. In 1998, when we're still not allowed to see an erection in mainstream cinema and the county is becoming even more censorious, we have a duty to corrupt ourselves with such delightful transgressive material!

Of course, **La Bête** is not available in the UK but can be found in specialist video outlets elsewhere in Europe. 💀

BIBLIOGRAPHY

Colin Davis 'True To His Own Obsessions: The Films of Walerian Borowczyk.' *Shock Xpress 2*, London: Titan Books, 1994.

Pete Tombs & Cathill Tohill 'A Private Collection: The Films of Walerian Borowczyk.' *Immoral Tales*, London: Titan Books.

enjoyed everything in HEADPRESS 18, but especially the interview with Antonio Ghura. At the age of 13 or 14, I bought a copy of AMAZING LOVE STORIES. I vividly recall how shocked I was when I opened it! Not because of the graphic sex, though. As a young punk, I was utterly horrified by the drawings of the long-haired, flare-wearing characters in the first story! Oh no, hippies! I liked the art though, and the lesbian scene in the soft-top Beetle remained a favourite. I don't remember what happened to my copy, but I no longer have it. Hadn't thought about it for years actually, as it was eclipsed in my mind by Crumb, and to a lesser extent CHERRY POPTART (until HM Customs stepped in

anyway). Seeing the interview with Ghura bought it all back. The interview was pretty depressing stuff, I thought, although it had a kind of universal resonance. It remains true that talent doesn't always out, I suppose.

Adrian Horrocks,
Dorset

beautiful lettuce pages

Write **Headpress, 40 Rossall Avenue, Radcliffe, Manchester, M26 1JD, Great Britain**
Email **david.headpress@zen.co.uk**

hanks for the copy of the latest HEADPRESS. I've read it cover to cover and it's just as sparky as usual. I guess I should make some comments about the Antonio Ghura piece and my memory of how the sales of his comics went.

Knockabout probably sold more of his comics than anybody else. We supplied Robbie Robertson at Planet Wheels in Scotland and worked with John Muir.

Here's the pedantic bit. Antonio printed a cover price of 95 pence on AMAZING LOVE STORIES No 1 but could only give us 40% discount which is the same discount we were giving our customers. So we, that is Knockabout and Planet Wheels, had a meeting with Antonio at which we agreed that we would sticker the books at £1.50 so we could give a 40% or sometimes higher discount to our customers. Sometime later Antonio got it into his head that we were ripping him off over this despite several

© Antonio Ghura

> HOW CAN I POSSIBLY MAKE LOVE TO YOU? I...I'M NOT A LESBIAN!

**Prelude to "the lesbian scene in the soft-top Beetle".
Panel from Antonio Ghura's 'The Inevitable Truth!'
TRULY AMAZING LOVE STORIES No 1.**

41

HEADPRESS 19 cover inspiration courtesy of FREAK OUT, USA (circa 1967).

Photo © Anthony Petkovich

PEOPLE WHO READ HEADPRESS Brooke Ashley, circa 1997, on the set of Rob Black's GANGBANG ANGELS 2. Brooke was diagnosed HIV in early 98. She is suing the company for which she made THE WORLD'S BIGGEST ANAL GANGBANG and on which porn star Marc Wallice starred, claiming he faked the validity of his AIDS test.

meetings and him being paid the price he asked for.

In 1982 Knockabout got busted under the Obscene Publications Act and included in the seizures were AMAZING LOVE STORIES, SUZIE AND JONNIE, RAW PURPLE and HOT NADS all by Antonio Ghura. I was prepared to defend all these titles in court of which Antonio was aware because I thought some of them were great stuff as I still do.

We didn't go to trial until 1985 at the Central Criminal Court in London (the Old Bailey). In the meantime Antonio decided to bring a prosecution in the civil courts about us ripping him off. The Judge thought Antonio was a bit weird (as at the time he certainly was and he nearly got arrested in court for contempt) and having seen all our invoices from Antonio and our sales invoices and heard the explanation about the increased cover price, found in Knockabout's favour. So we stopped selling his books even though I still had the Old Bailey trial to come at which I was going to defend them. (We won the case: R. v. Toskanex Ltd. and R. v. A.R. Bennett). It was after this that Antonio started making a series of phone calls to myself and Carol threatening to cut our throats. He also attacked me physically at a comic mart in Westminster Central Hall in London during 1983 or 84.

There never was a cartel or an exclusive deal with Last Gasp. Haw it worked then

and how it still works now is that neither Ron Turner at Last Gasp or us at Knockabout like parting with money. So whenever possible we have always traded books with each other. Knockabout sold/sells to Last Gasp lots of UK produced books and comics that we distribute here and bought/buys from them titles to sell here. It is also easier for both of us to have one main supplier and shipper. AMAZING LOVE STORIES No 1 we invoiced to Last Gasp at a penny more than we paid Antonio for it because we thought it was a great comic.

I don't know if Antonio ever sold any books directly to Last Gasp — I don't think so but maybe he could have done. We sold lots to Last Gasp and if you ask you may find that they still have copies of SUZIE AND JONNIE. There was never any 'move between Knockabout and Home Grown to sell the rights to Last Gasp'. We much preferred selling UK copies to Last Gasp as we could use them as collateral for importing comics and books we could sell here and we have never done any joint deals with Home Grown. The comics distributed by Real Free Press in Holland I think were the ones that Knocka-bout supplied to Bill Daley who was a distributor in Amsterdam.

Best wishes. Crusty Old Curmudgeon,

**Tony Bennett
Knockabout, London**

...ere's a few corrections, additional pieces of information and assorted rambling anecdotes inspired by reading HEADPRESS 18.

Further to Anton Black's letter about Wayne/Jayne County and the Electric Chairs — like the old Maurice Chevalier song says, "Ah yes, I ree-mem-burr eet well!" For as a teenage punk rocker, I was the (fairly) proud owner of not one, but *two* Electric Chairs albums. The first of these was their self-titled debut, which opens with the track 'Eddie & Sheena'. Other stand-out tracks on this record included '28 Model T', a Beach Boys pastiche, and 'Worry Wart'. The other Electric Chairs album I had was STORM THE GATES OF HEAVEN, and I can't remember too much about this one, because frankly it was crap. The best thing about it was the cover, which depicted a (still pre-operative) Wayne County dressed as a transves-tite Pope being carried in a sedan chair. On the back cover, he/she was strapped into a sort of medaeval-looking electric chair, pretending to be electrocuted. The record itself was pressed on the nastiest coloured vinyl I've ever seen — a kind of spunk-mucky white with snot-green and blood-red streaks running through it. The only track I can remember from it, apart from the title track, is 'Man Enough To Be A Woman', which of course later lent its name to County's memoirs (reviewed in HEADPRESS 17). I never owned a copy of the Electric Chairs' finest hour (well, three minutes), the glorious full title of which was '(If You Don't Want To Fuck Me) Fuck Off', and my copies of the albums have long since gone the way of all vinyl, i.e. to the secondhand shop. Can't say I miss 'em much. Apart from that, I can only concur with David Kerekes' judgment that, even for a punk singer, Wayne/Jayne was way too ugly to make it big!

Darren Arnold, in his review of I JUST WASN'T MADE FOR THESE TIMES, wonders whether Charles Manson wrote the song 'Never Learn Not To Love', which was recorded by the Beach Boys and released both as the B-side to a single (sorry, can't remember which one) and on the album 20/20. The answer is yes, he certainly did. It was originally entitled 'Cease To Exist' (no, really! — this is apparently a phrase borrowed from Scientology, rather than a blatant death threat), and Dennis Wilson, finding this too heavy a trip, changed the title to 'Cease To Resist' before settling on 'Never Learn Not To Love'. Manson was — and apparently still is — very put out by this meddling with his lyrics, and this precipitated the deterio-ration of the relationship between him and Wilson, culminating in the half-hearted kidnapping of Wilson's son and the "Tell Dennis this is for him" incident. Manson's own version of 'Cease To Exist' can be found on his LIE album, recorded in 1968 and available in a number of more or less dodgy pirated editions. Further details about the Manson/Wilson connection and specifically about this song can be found in THE FAMILY by Ed Sanders, Chapter Six.

Finally, a somewhat embarrassing correction. In my review of LORDS OF CHAOS by Michael Moynihan and Didrik Søderlind in the last HEADPRESS, I opined that the authors are "clearly not apologists for Satanism". It has since become apparent to me that Michael Moynihan is, in fact, a fairly *major* apologist for Satanism — a pal of Boyd Rice, a priest in Anton LaVey's Church of Satan, founder of the occult fascist band Blood Axis etc, etc. I feel this is the sort of thing I should already have known. However, my feelings of admiration for the book LORDS OF CHAOS are undimin-ished: it's a fine piece of work, though perhaps not as impartial as I believed. The Norwegian Black Metal crowd still come across as a pretty laughable bunch. It would be interesting to know whether Mr Moynihan regards their actions as glorious, defensi-ble, Satanically correct, misguided, pathetic — or what?

**Simon Collins,
Leicester**

The world of

EL MONJE LOCO

Gerard Alexander

N 1968 I WAS SIX-YEARS-OLD and lived with my parents in Montevideo, in my native Uruguay. I had learned to read when I was four, and had read many books before I picked up my first comic. On one of my trips to the Magazine Swap Shop that year, I first spotted *El Monje Loco* (The Mad Monk). That issue featured the story 'Beyond Science'. Across the top of the cover was an old monk with rotted teeth and long claw-like fingers. Beneath the comic's title, a fanged monster drooled before a frightened man. The story involved a doctor trying to invent a regenerative

formula. His wife, also a doctor, was constantly pushing him to try dangerous experiments so that he would become famous and wealthy. Eventually, he tests a chemical on a rabbit and a gas is emitted. He wakes up in another dimension and is faced with a horrific creature. Using his scalpel, he kills it and passes out. When he comes

"... Y PERDIÓ EL SENTIDO. AL RECOBRAR LA RAZÓN, ADVIRTIÓ QUE HABÍA ASESINADO A NAT, SU CAPATAZ.

to, he finds the dead body of his wife next to him. The gas had merely caused him to hallucinate and he had thought his wife was the creature!

My young mind was very impressed by that little tale. So from that day on, whatever money I could get from my parents would go to funding my obsession with *El Monje Loco*.

Let me explain the format of the comic to give you an idea of how much it differed from the norm. It was published in Mexico by Revistas Populares, starting in 1968, coming out *weekly* (!!), 32 pages with no ads. There was a claim on the inside cover of every issue that it had the approval of the Secretary of Public Education.

It wasn't a colour comic, but instead of standard black, the printers would use another colour for the base. So one issue would be brown and white, the next blue and white and the following green and white. The artwork was variable, sometimes approaching the standards of US comics of the time, but usually looking somewhat rushed. The Mad Monk, the narrator of each issue, would either be walking around his chapel or playing the organ, cackling maniacally.

What really came across though was an aura of putrefaction. The Mad Monk was constantly drooling, saliva cob-webbing his gaping mouth. There was always at least one scene where somebody had an eye gouged out. One story had a character whose eye dangled from its socket for the whole tale!

In 1969, the comic started four-part serials. One in particular, called 'Delirium tremens', involved a guy who had hallucinations because of his alcoholism and believed he was wearing gloves made out of human skin. The skin of a murderer, to be precise... and it was turning him into one as well.

'The Telephone of Death' told of an African adventurer whose wife was tortured by the natives who wanted revenge for their exploitation. Our 'hero' finally catches up with the natives, ties

El Monje Loco **cuenta sus historias de auténtico terror...**

45

them to burning pyres and pours salt in their wounds. Very educational indeed.

Such purity of expression couldn't last forever, of course. As the new decade began, the stories lost all their touches of grue. No more serials such as 'Satan's Slave'. By early 1971, I was heading for my new home in Australia. Due to baggage restrictions, I was only able to bring a couple of comics with me on the plane. I felt as if an era had ended.

In 1991, my father returned from a visit to Uruguay with a dozen issues of *El Monje Loco*. My inquisitive mind needed to know more, so I began to research the character.

In the late 1930s, Mexican radio actor Salvador Carrasco created *El Monje Loco* as a weekly anthology programme. His catchphrase became "Nobody knows, nobody knew".

The show, on station XEYZ, was very popular and was syndicated widely across Mexico. His organist, Nacho Irigoyen, supplied suitably eerie themes for his macabre tales.

In 1940, director Alejandro Galindo shot *El Monje Loco*, the first feature involving the character that had become

an icon in Mexican culture. By 1951, he had become an object of ridicule, appearing in the popular Tin Tan's comedy *Kill me because I'm dying*. It wasn't until the late Sixties that the character was revived in his true sadistic incarnation.

The comic lasted until 1975, but in name only, as the stories had by that stage been filtered of any passion. But for a youngster in 1968, *El Monje Loco* was a revelation, and one which I am most grateful for. Thanks Salvador. Adios.

© EC Comics

Top **El Monje Loco knocks out a tune.**
Above **The Crypt-Keeper from EC's** TALES FROM THE CRYPT **comics in the Fifties. Note the similarities.**

"it's not that popular of a picture..."

on the town with joel m. reed

John Szpunar

It seems as though the world will never forgive JOEL M. REED for his 1978 sleaze-fest, **BLOODSUCKING FREAKS**. The film's off-centred mixture of utter nastiness and low-brow humour has shocked and sickened almost everyone who's seen it. **BLOODSUCKING FREAKS** is the last word on cinematic debauchery, a film that goes so far over the edge, you have to question the sanity of the mind behind it.

Joel M. Reed is a filmmaker from another time. Born in the Thirties in New York City, Joel began his career in the Joe Sarno school of sexploitation, working in that magical period of film his-

Joel in BLOODSUCKING FREAKS
publicity shot.

tory when the film-flotsam flew fast and furious through the run-down theatres of 42nd Street.

Age hasn't mellowed Joel a bit. Sitting at his stool in the upstairs bar at Sardi's, he talked freely about his mind-boggling adventures, both behind and away from the camera. What follows only adds to the legend that surrounds the man. Sit back and get ready. The first round is on Joel and you're in for one hell of a ride.

47

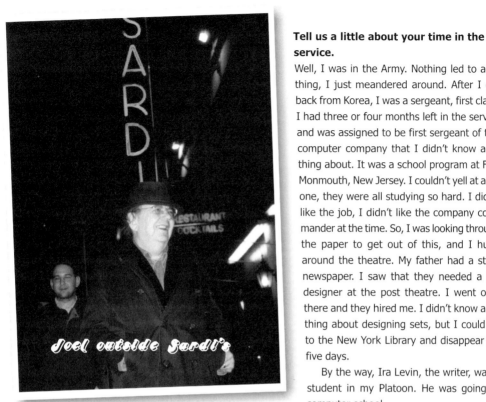

Photo © Brian Krueger

Joel outside Sardi's

headpress **Have you always lived in New York?**

joel m reed Yes, I've lived here my whole life. I was born in Brooklyn. Many people in the neighbourhood went on to fame and fortune, including Marty Engles.

Where did you go to school?

I went to public school in Brooklyn and I went to Erasmus Hall High School but I dropped out. I joined the army and was in the Korean war. I was in the army for about four years.

Was anyone in your family involved in show business?

More or less. My father was a singer and I had some other aspiring relatives. I think Joe Layton, the choreographer, was my cousin. Joe Papp was my baby-sitter and Kirk Douglas rented a room in our apartment. We were poor, we had to rent out rooms. He went to school upstate with my uncle.

Tell us a little about your time in the service.

Well, I was in the Army. Nothing led to anything, I just meandered around. After I got back from Korea, I was a sergeant, first class. I had three or four months left in the service and was assigned to be first sergeant of this computer company that I didn't know anything about. It was a school program at Fort Monmouth, New Jersey. I couldn't yell at anyone, they were all studying so hard. I didn't like the job, I didn't like the company commander at the time. So, I was looking through the paper to get out of this, and I hung around the theatre. My father had a story newspaper. I saw that they needed a set designer at the post theatre. I went over there and they hired me. I didn't know anything about designing sets, but I could go to the New York Library and disappear for five days.

By the way, Ira Levin, the writer, was a student in my Platoon. He was going to computer school.

Have you talked to him lately?

I've seen him over the years. He had just finished a book called A KISS BEFORE DYING. He was sort of a celebrity there, getting a lot of time off. I have a funny story about Ira. I went to New York on leave once and this guy that I knew from high school was with me. He was in the air force. He said, "Where are you going?" I said, "I'm going to the movies." He said, "I'm going to take out two actresses. Maybe you should come along." I was a horny young guy, so I went with him. We went to this apartment on the west side. At the time around seven girls lived there. Two of the girls were the Seitz twins. They were in a play called ONDINE with Audrey Hepburn and Mel Ferrer. I went over and we had lunch. One of the twins said, "Come over some day and meet us back stage." Well, I was in my uniform when I went back to see them. Audrey Hepburn came over to me and said, "Oh, you're a soldier." I told Audrey and Mel war stories and they took me out to dinner.

So one day at Fort Monmouth, Ira Levin said, "I'm going in for a press conference for my book.

What are you doing?" I told him that Audrey Hepburn invited me to dinner.

That inspired me, to some degree, to get into the theatre. I knew that I had to get out of the army before anybody caught up to me. They said, "If you sign up for college, you'll get out." So, I signed up for a number of colleges. I think I got into Yale, but I couldn't afford it. Anyway, I attended the American Academy of Dramatic Arts, for lack of anything else to do. I started acting and was in a number of plays and things. I got into advertising, into promotion.

Where were you working?
I was very active on and off Broadway as an actor. I got involved with public relations and publicity. I worked at MGM for Cy Siedler and Howard Dietz. I wrote captions on the back of pictures. One day Cy Siedler said, "Go over to the Warwick hotel and take Elizabeth Taylor to lunch." The columnist Earl Wilson was going to interview her. I almost fainted. Cy gave me $50 and I went to the hotel. Liz said, "Come up-stairs," and I was shaking. I thought, "No, I'd better not." After she finished the interview, she wanted to do something. I said, "I've got to take you back to the hotel." I went back to the office, gave Cy the change, and asked him if I

could eat lunch. He told me I was supposed to eat with the money he gave me. Then he asked me how things went. I said, "She gave me a lot of trouble, but I got her back to her room." I told him that she wanted to go out for a night on the town, but I put my foot down and got her back. He said, "You were supposed to do *whatever* Elizabeth Taylor wanted you to do!" I got a reputation as the guy who told Elizabeth Taylor to go home. I was young and stupid.

After that, when any starlet came up, they called me to pick them up at the Warwick Hotel. The girls would all say, "Get your ass up here!" You weren't going to reject them.

Let's hear a little more about the people you used to run around with.
Well, I was here at Sardi's with Lauren Bacall, Jason Roberts, people like that. I first came here on New Years Eve, 1953. They didn't have this upstairs bar then. There was this guy named Rhett that used to hang around down there. You had to buy him a drink. I used to hesitate, because he'd make such an asshole of himself. He'd start foaming at the mouth, like it was his God given right for a free drink. I used to hang around at a place called Downey's where I met Marilyn Monroe and Kim Novak. I sat with Marilyn for about two hours. I didn't know it was her. Eddie Bracken and I went over to sit down with Eli Wallach. He was with this girl with this babushka-thing wrapped around her head. She was reminding Eddie about the time her car was stuck at the bottom of a hill. Eddie whis-pered to me, "I'm leaving, this girl's nuts!" Just then, a waiter came over and said, "I'd like your autograph, Miss Monroe." Eddie hadn't recog-nised her. She was talking about when they made WE'RE NOT MARRIED. Marilyn was very plain, you would never recognise her in person. I used to see her all the time, we used to go to the same places. She lived on 57th Street.

What was it like in New York after you left Korea?
There used to be a whole night-club thing that doesn't exist anymore. When I was a kid, we'd have five or six places to go a night. We'd go to the Copa Cabaña and then to the Storch Club,

49

the Harwin, the Morocco. We'd wind down at about four in the morning. We couldn't afford to eat at any of those places; we'd stay for one or two drinks and then move on. We'd get hamburgers at PJ Clark's.

I know that you were once friends with Oliver Stone.

Oliver came over as one of my fans. He was doing work on Ted Gershuny's SUGAR COOKIES. He went to Yale with Lloyd Kaufman, Michael Herz, and John Avildsen. He saw one of my awful pictures and we started hanging around. Oliver went up to Canada to make his first picture, THE QUEEN OF SPADES [aka SEIZURE]. He was married to a Moroccan girl at the time. Oliver was younger than me, he had hair down to his ass, and he spoke French, you know. This was sort of in the hippie era. He said, "I'm going to have a birthday party and I want you to come over for lunch." He gave me some address on 53rd street. I figured the house was west, considering the way he always dressed. I started off and I got to 11th or 12th Ave and I couldn't find the place. I called him up, trying to figure out where he was and he said, "Go east." He was at

Joel and Barbara Streisand in New York in the late-Fifties.

some ritzy building that his father had. I was at this elegant apartment in my ripped dungarees and everybody else was all dressed up.

How soon after you got out of the army did you meet Joe Sarno?

That was years later. In 1966, I got the idea to make a softcore porn picture. That turned out to be CAREER BED. Someone introduced me to Joe and I wrote a script. I started to work on production. When I got things together, I called Joe and he said, "I'm going to Sweden. You direct it." So there I was. I got out two books: THE FIVE C'S OF CINEMATOGRAPHY, and Carl Reese's THE ART OF EDITING. I hired a NYU student, Ron Dorfman who went on in the business. We rented a camera from this place, and we didn't know that their cameras never worked. We were ripped off.

Was this the first film that Ron Dorfman worked on?

Yes. He shot and edited it. He went on to do GROUPIES — he won a lot of awards for that. He did some real classy stuff. At this time he was still in film school, he didn't know anything. Ron was the king of porn for a while. He was partners with Joe Sarno.

Who put up the money for your films?

Different people. For CAREER BED, this lawyer said that he'd give me the money. Before we could shoot, he disappeared. I was sitting in my office and thought, "Well, to hell with that." Another lawyer came along. He had met me at a birthday party. I told him I wanted to shoot a little picture but I didn't have any money — the investor copped out. He said, "I'll give you the money, I was just thinking of doing something like this."

How long was the shoot?

We shot the thing in a weekend. It would have been a great movie if we'd spent more money on it. It was the introduction to Jennifer Welles' film career. She went on to be a producer in porn movies. Shelly Ables was also in the picture, before she was known as Georgina Spelvin. And that's how I emerged. The film played around. Carl Peppercorn and Irving Wormser, who distributed the film, said, "Make SEX BY ADVERTISEMENT." Incidentally, people are offering $3,000 for that print. Nobody can find it today.

I'd love to see it.

That's the one to find. I shot it in a weekend. I was running over to use everybody's apartment for it. Shelly Ables was in that one as well. She was the head of the film department at J.C. Penny. She was a housewife with three kids. She came over and we shot her scenes in two hours. She was saying, "Oh, my God, look at this terrible ad! This is a dirty old man who wants school girls." You know, she's sitting there saying, "Good evening doctor, good evening doctor." There were these awful ads — 'Have these people really satisfied their lust?' I played five characters in the movie; I was the dirty old man. I was also a male hustler — a stud. We shot it on 35mm, I bought old stock. The lab bill was around $5,000. My brother Elliott and I came up with the money. He's a big shot in television now; I don't talk to him anymore. But he did a lot of work on that film. He was the camera man and producer. The trouble with those pictures was that they were too mild. We couldn't go hardcore with them. A major studio wanted to shoot CAREER BED over in colour.

A lot of exploitation legends were working at that time.

Well, that was way before porn. And I met all those people — Rick Sullivan, Jerry Denby, practically everybody. Jerry Gross was doing GIRLS ON A CHAIN GANG. Barry Mahon had the original CUBAN REBEL GIRLS and MODELS INCORPORATED. I met him and he said, "Go see MODELS INCORPORATED on 42nd Street." It played at the Grand Theater, which was the only Theater that would play this type of picture. I went in and didn't see any MODELS INCORPORATED. I complained to the manager and he said, "The print ripped, the print ripped! You saw a tit, why are you bothering me?" I said, "I came here to see MODELS

INCORPORATED." He said, "Nobody comes here to see MODELS INCORPORATED!" So, Barry showed it to me. Those were the days where they actually showed two shots of a girl's breast.

Joel at Sardi's

How long did these films usually play in the theatres?

They ran for years. On 42nd Street, they just let them run.

Were they ever retitled and re-released?

I don't think so. They just let them run because they got the tourists in. There was the whole thing addressing the outside of the Theater. It was all hype. You walked in and thought you were going to see a great piece of porn, and it was nothing.

When hardcore porn became chic, it had a pretty big impact on the softcore sex film industry. Did everybody just try to jump on the bandwagon?

Oh, yeah. Not me, but everybody else jumped on the bandwagon. People made sex films for millions of dollars. In the very beginning, any hardcore picture made a lot of money. The mob was originally involved with these films. In the first six months, if you made anything, you made a fortune.

Victor Kanefsky was the editor on several of your films. How did you meet him?

51

I met Victor way before I started doing movies. He was a mutual friend of a guy named Dale McCarty. Dale introduced me to him. I couldn't afford him for the first couple of films. He started with WIT'S END.

WIT'S END was later retitled GI EXECUTIONER. How did that film get started?

By accident. I was in the lobby at Movielab, and I met this guy, Marvin Farkas. We started talking. He was there to find out some prices; he was going to shoot a film in Singapore. I said, "I'm going to show a picture." I think it was SEX BY ADVERTISEMENT. So Marvin saw it. He said, "It's brilliant. I need some advice on my picture in Singapore." He had this script that would cost about today — how much did they spend on TITANIC? Well this would cost more. It had ocean liners blowing up, temples blowing up, a million extras. He already had a director, but I gave him some advice. A little while later, he called me from Singapore. He said, "I'm having trouble with my director, David X. Young. He's down in the Village and he won't come back. He rewrote the script and we paid these guys $25,000. He took all of the money and spent it on pot." I went to go see David on Canal street. That was in the hippie era, so he's down there with hair down to his knees. He said, "Marvin? Fuck that piece of shit Marvin!"

We got into this conversation, and he said, "I want to hire Bradley Cunningham." Bradley owned a Jazz bar. He wanted to hire everybody from the bar to be in this movie. He told me to read the script. I said, "Well, Marvin hasn't even seen the script that you wrote." After four days, he gave me the script, and it was CASABLANCA. It was about this guy who owns this bar in Singapore...

Marvin flew in and we had a meeting. Marvin is sitting here, David is sitting there. Marvin said, "Tell David we'll give him a little extra money. Can we look at the script?" David said, "Tell Marvin I think he's a fucking piece of shit and I can kick him right in the balls!" After two hours, Marvin said, "Well, if David insists on doing this, we're going to have to fire him and hire you, Joel." That was a stupid thing to me, because I had a better deal going with a play. David said,

"That's the greatest idea, Marvin." He got up and walked.

So what did you do?

Well, this guy who lived in Singapore called me and said, "I have all the arrangements for doing the production management." I wrote him all these letters. I figured that the whole production was put together. The day I was leaving for Singapore, the bell rang at my apartment. It was this guy. He said, "I'm here, Joel. We're going to work out the production. I have all your letters but I haven't looked at them yet. We can start in six months when we go back to Singapore." I arrived in Singapore with nothing in place. We should have started with a new script. I was enticed; they gave me $7,000 up front. I could have done much better. We had Angelique Pettyjohn in that, who became sort of an idol in her own time. She ended up a porn star and a stripper in Vegas.

What was it like working with her?

I didn't hire her, my friend did. She came over to Singapore and I went into her hotel room. I said, "Hello, Angelique!" She said, "Smell my sweatshirt, my boyfriend came in it six times before I left." She threw it in my face. She was OK. I got along with her, she was very pretty. She told me about all the stars she fucked; Kirk Douglas was one of them.

Where did Tom Keena come from?

He's out on the coast now, he was the star of WIT'S END. Some agent sent him over. One of the guys from a big soap turned us down. He had this asshole agent. We took the second guy, Tom. He was OK, I still talk to him.

Tell us about the music from WIT'S END.

Elliot Chiprut did the music. He had a couple of hits in the Sixties, like SIMON SAYS. I guess Victor Kanefsky came up with him. Once in a while, I run into a couple of the oriental girls from that film. They're grandmothers now.

What was BLOOD BATH?

That was a picture that I shot for Cannon. It was an episodic horror film with three or four parts. Jerry Lacey was in it along with Doris Roberts. We had a lot of well known people in that one. It was actually very mild.

I guess it's time to move on to BLOODSUCKING FREAKS. Are you surprised that the film has such a cult following?

Well, when I made BLOODSUCKING FREAKS, there were things that would have been different if I had complete control of it. I wanted to open it as a cult film. There was some Theater down here that played midnight films and I was setting it up. The guy who was responsible for putting up the money said he wanted to open it up on Broadway in the Cinerama Theater. The original title was HOUSE OF THE SCREAMING VIRGINS and then he changed it to THE INCREDIBLE TORTURE SHOW. He spent almost $100,000 opening it up as a full-scale big feature. Everyone walked in, and half the women walked out. And then we had a big sale going in Japan that never happened and everyone thought it was a drop-dead situation. At that point, the original midnight Theater place in New York closed. I had to go into litigation to get the picture back. Unfortunately, the film went to Troma years later and they didn't do very much for it. But a critic for one of the East Village papers saw it on 42nd street and gave it rave reviews. It went into

midnight showings at the 8th Street Playhouse. It would have run forever if Troma didn't go for publicity and call up Women Against Pornography, saying, "How can you allow this?" Then they came down to picket and there was a clause against pornography. They were trying to evict this guy, Steve, who owned the Theater, for years. He had to throw it out. But later, it started to play the midnight shows and I started hearing from people. It played in Allentown Pennsylvania for a year and a half, and it played up in the Harvard circle.

Still, are you surprised that it generates so much attention?

I don't know. It might lead to something one day. I've been doing very well financially with multi-media and software, but I'd like to get back into film. I have a new project that I want to get going, so who knows. Somebody threw a big party for me and flew me out to LA a couple of years ago. BLOODSUCKING FREAKS played for two nights at one of the film clubs over there. I think the film's coming of age now.

Did living in New York City have anything to do with the kind of films you were making?

No, I don't think so. I didn't want to make BLOODSUCKING FREAKS. That came about totally by accident. I made that film when I was putting together a picture named TEEN DEMON, which was based on an Oliver Onions story, THE BECKONING FAIR ONE. It was about a guy who moves into an old house. He's either a writer or a painter and he starts hearing a woman's voice and music coming out of the walls. He starts breaking in the walls and he finds an old diary. Then it feels like

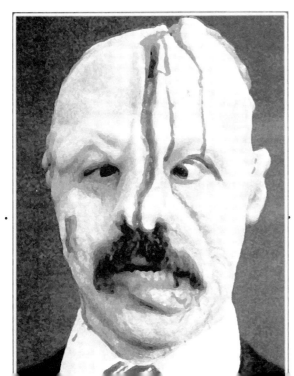

Ed French created this makeup for a BLOODSUCKING FREAKS poster campaign of the early Eighties (see page 49), bearing no relation to the film itself.

there's a woman in his bed. He's going crazy about this woman that comes around every night, so he sets up this trap for her. Everybody thinks he's totally insane. His girlfriend comes to help him and he kills her and walls her up. Well, I had a conception of doing this story as guy who moves into a much more modern house. In my case, he was a writer. He hears late Fifties rock and roll coming through the walls. He finds that someone has gone into his kitchen and taken the milk and the cake out of the refrigerator without putting it back. He's got a teen-aged demon from the late Fifties that's just driving him crazy. It turns out in the story that she was going to go to an early rock concert and her father shaved all of her hair off so she killed him with the scissors. Anyway, the writer falls in love with her, and he's having a terrible life. In the end, the police surround the house and they kill him. And in the last scene, there's a '56 Chevy coming up the highway and there he is with this hot little girl. I wanted to do that, I was pushing the story around. I met my partner, Alan Margolin, who was on the board of directors for the Paul Taylor dance company. He passed the script around. We were discussing at that time putting together $3- or $4,000 to do this movie. And at the moment, this agent called me up and said, "You've got to see this naked S&M ballet company downtown on Green Street. So I went down, and there was this guy, Gyles Fontaine, and a bunch of girls, totally nude. But it was ballet dancing, pretty off the wall. I came back and was at a dinner for the American Ballet Theater or something, and I said, "I saw this freaky ballet down on Green Street." Everybody said, "Let's go see that. Can you get tickets?" I told them I didn't think they wanted to see it. But I took them all down there, and they said, "Joel, forget about this TEEN DEMON movie, do a movie about a Theater like this." So I wrote a script, and half of the things in there came from other people. These were very big names. I did the script in a week or so, and of course these other people didn't put a nickel into it. It just happened that this was at the end of the year, and this tax lawyer called me up. He said, "If I send you a check for $75,000, you can make a movie, any movie." So he called me

up on a Tuesday and said, "Your check's sitting here." And that's how the movie got made. We shot in Gyles Fontaine's actual Theater. It was a little place down in Soho.

Is there anything that you wrote or filmed that was cut from BLOODSUCKING FREAKS?
No. Just a shit eating scene.

What was the attitude like on the set?
Everybody was cold. I think we shot it in February. But they were still all in good spirits.

The film owes a lot to HG Lewis.
Well, I hope not. I'd never heard of his pictures until many years later. And I saw BLOODFEAST and all of those things.

BLOODSUCKING FREAKS has the reputation of being one of the most tasteless films ever made. Did you ever get the feeling that you were making film history?
I had no idea. I just wanted it to be funny to myself. I didn't know Herschell Gordon Lewis existed. And then I became a cult figure. All these little kids started running over to my house with video tapes. You know, "Meet me in the Village to see THE CORPSE GRINDERS." People would call me on the phone and quote me the lines. I used to have quite a few memorised.

Tell us something about the score.
Michael Sahl did the music. I think that guy won a lot of awards for opera. He was an opera composer.

The film can almost be profound at times. Were you actually trying to say anything with Viju killing the critic in front of a roaring audience?
Well, I hope the film has its moments, but I just liked to put weird things together. I wasn't making a statement. That's what Fred Astaire said, "We're just trying to make a living here."

Let's go into some of the some of the people involved with BLOODSUCKING FREAKS. What happened to Seamus

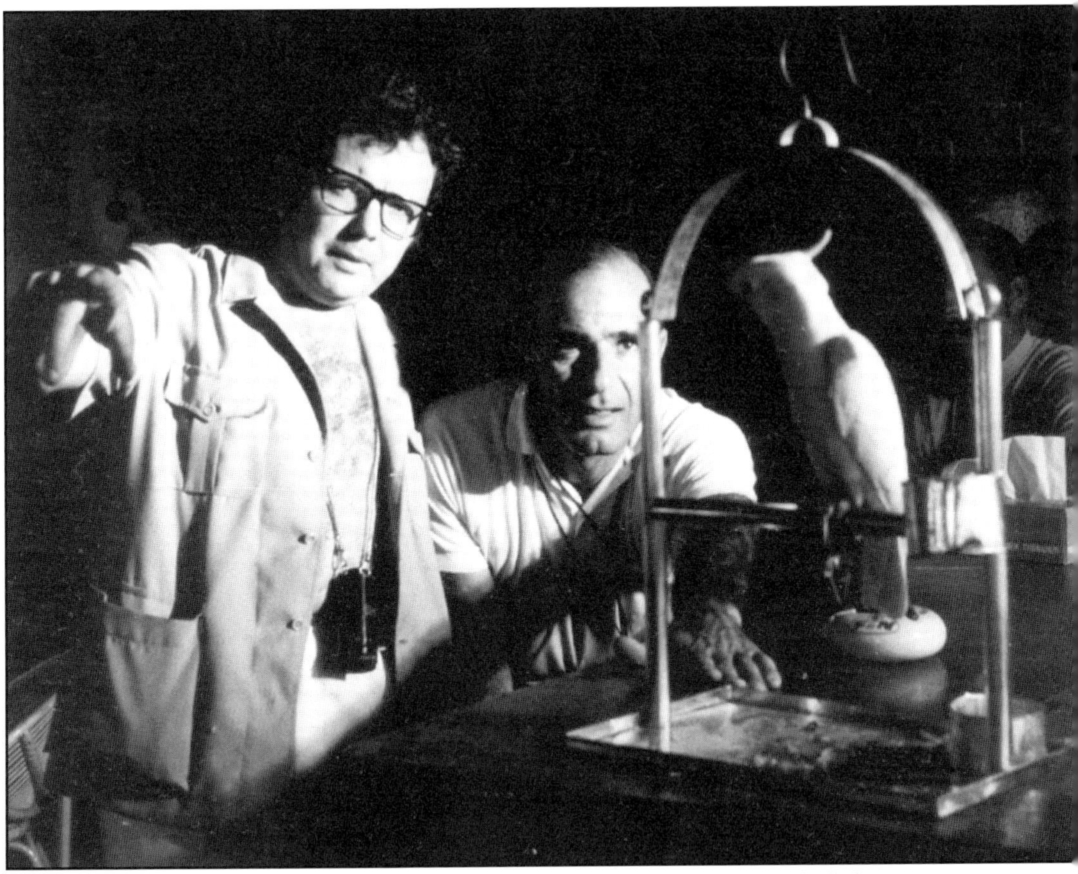

Joel shooting WIT'S END in Singapore with Marvin Farkas.

O'Brian?

Seamus got murdered right after that. I went to his wake and his funeral.

Did you know him prior to shooting?

No I didn't. He just came around. He was a wonderful guy.

How was he killed?

I don't know the true story. Some say he came home to the East Village and there was this guy sitting on his steps who stabbed him. Another story is that there was a burglary at his apartment. But he was a great guy. He played in THE FANTASTICKS for years. He was in MARATHON MAN. Ninety percent of BLOODSUCKING FREAKS was his; he helped me direct all of those weirdoes.

How's Alan Margolin doing?

Alan's still a friend of mine, he's in the construction business now.

What's Gyles Fontaine up to these days?

I don't know. Gyles used to do that kind of stuff, you know; the girls in his ballet were his actual slaves. I didn't use any of them in the movie. I had Viju Krem. She came over to try out and was around three hours late, which was typical of her. We were having dinner. I said, "Viju, you're going to have to be naked in this picture." She went into another room and came back totally nude. I said, "I think you've got the part, sit down and finish dinner. But don't put your clothes on."

Was she a model before that?

I'm not sure. She was married to a Saudi-Arabian prince who paid her 10 million dollars to get his children back. She wrote a book called THE VIJU KREM DIET.

55

I've heard she went to jail after BLOODSUCKING FREAKS.

Yes. She went to the clink after that. She married this ex-con and got involved in a stock swindle. She came over to my house and asked if she could move in with me for a couple of months. I told her no, which was a very good decision. The FBI was looking for her. They caught up with her and she went to jail. Later, she married this 87-year-old guy, a millionaire. I know she recently spent seven years in jail in Mexico, where she was raped 16 times.

She was in a Gerard Damiano film with Louis DeJesus called LET MY PUPPETS COME.

Yeah. She was banging him on the set as well. I think he was called the Anal Dwarf. There's a funny story about Louis. Herve Villechaize was hanging around from FANTASY ISLAND. We were going to use him for Ralphus. He was pretty big on getting laid. He said, "I can't get laid in New York, I've got to go to Paris to get my tube lubricated." This was before we had any money. Alan finally got things together and we called Herve in Paris. He said "You've got to send me

400 bucks to get back to New York." Within 45 minutes, Louis walked in. What's the difference between one perverted, demented dwarf and the next?

Herve would have done the film otherwise?

Yes. He was nothing at the time.

Where'd you get Louis from?

The circus. He lived on 8th Ave. I saw him the first time he fucked Viju. We had a cast party for everyone involved with BLOODSUCKING FREAKS. Viju came in with someone she claimed was Rod Stewart. I suspect that it was this Rod Stewart impersonator that was hanging around at the time. The party was at the house of a multi-millionaire. One end was devoted to the freaks, with a lot of cocaine. I walked into the freak room before Viju got there and Louis was rolling around on the floor. Everyone was ramming everybody. I was promising to do all the girls there. So Viju walked in with the fake Rod Stewart and said, "Were getting married. What's upstairs?" I told her that it was the freakier part of the party and advised her not to go there. She went up anyway. I walked up to get her out, looked down, and there was Louis doing Viju. Kind of strange. He had a dick about a foot long. Just then, the Rod Stewart impersonator came up behind me and said, "Did you see my fiancée?" There was like a pile of six people on her. It was very interesting. There was this one guy in the group that worked on my film that said, "You must have my girlfriend."

"I think the girl went to jail for murder and kidnapping shortly after this picture was taken" —Joel.

Left **A caricature of Joel by Joe Kaliff.**
Right **Joel in front of the Kaliff wall of
fame in Sardi's.**

I said, "OK." So a few years later, he said, "Come on over to my house. I'm married, meet my kids." I went over, and his wife walked in. I said, "Oh, God!" He told me to forget about it.

Let's hear some more about the girls from BLOODSUCKING FREAKS.
I think Oliver Stone was over at the casting call. I know he brought some girls over. There was one who I met at the William Morris Agency. She said, "I know what you want to do to me. You want to shit all over me and grind me into dust." We started fooling around and she demanded to be whipped. Her fantasy was a lot of S&M. She was really a freak. I'm not into hanging people up and things like that. One day, she came up to me and said, "Don't touch me, I've got a good shrink." She's actually doing very well in TV these days. She's a grandmother now.

Where did you get the women in the cage?
Most of them were Columbia University students. My brother found them; he put an ad on the bulletin boards at Bernard College and Columbia.

Did you get a lot of responses?

Yes. All the girls came down. I think outside of Arlana Blue, who was a porn star, the rest of the girls came from the university. One girl was running around there naked and her boyfriend was there to protect her. I said, "Get this fucking guy out," so she left. She's in one of the cage shots, but not the rest. I don't think I ever fucked any of the girls in the cage.

Any other stories about the girls?
Well, here's something about one of the girls in the backgammon scene. She left her honeymoon to be in the film. Around ten years ago, my friend went to get a job at Reader's Digest International. He walked in the office and had the interview. He noticed that the woman conducting things had the poster for BLOODSUCKING FREAKS hanging up. She was the vice-president. He asked her about it. It turns out that she was the girl from the backgammon scene. She was proud of the fact.

What's the story with the girl who had her head cut off?
That girl was Illa Howe. She was in Robert Rossen's LILLITH with Warren Beaty. She was a patient in the mental hospital where they shot it. She said that Arthur Penn and Warren Beaty

57

fell in love with her. They gave her the second lead in the picture. She became a great friend of mine. She's involved with Jodie Foster now. I think she's partners with her.

I've read something about BLOODSUCKING FREAKS 2.

Troma has the rights to that. I won't do that picture now. The copyright expires next year and I'll renew it. I might do it when I own it.

What's the film about?

Well, it's not really a sequel, but it's similar. It's about a 15-year-old girl whose father is the current candidate for President. She's a perverted freak who needs discipline, so he sends her to an academy where they train young girls to keep their virginity.

It sounds good. Let's go into NIGHT OF THE ZOMBIES.

That was originally called GAMMA 693. It was another horror movie. Lorin Price, the Broadway producer, used to hang out at this bar. He produced it. The only reason I did it was that he gave me the money.

You went over to Munich to shoot it, right?

That's right. We were supposed to shoot it in Asia with Japanese zombies, but I found out I could get air fare to Munich for a lot less. We also shot a portion of that in upstate New York.

How did the film do?

Lorin ended up paying everybody. It played around, it did very well in Germany. It's on television every once in a while. I don't even remember what happened to it.

What was it like working with Jamie Gillis?

He was a wonderful guy. He's got a doctorate from Colombia University. He was a nice Jewish boy, he almost went to dental school. He has certain perversions, but that's the way it goes.

Can you tell me anything about the CIA guy in the camera store? I think his name is Alphonso.

He was also in BLOODSUCKING FREAKS. He was married to a beautiful young girl. He committed suicide right after NIGHT OF THE ZOMBIES. He went back to New Jersey and got stuck in a turnstile. He was too fat to get through. They had to cut him out. He went home and shot himself.

NIGHT OF THE ZOMBIES was made on the cusp of the gore era. Why didn't you push it to an extreme?

Like I said, this was a picture I made to get the money. It could have been great if we had better make-up on the zombies — they look too young and healthy. I shouldn't have put in gore. It would have been a great picture. Incidentally, you know the hooker who answers the door? She went out with Lorin Price for 30 years after that. He also played the priest in the film.

What kind of guy was Lorin?

Well, Lorin and I were partners, but was the most obnoxious person in the world. I could clip him for money, but he was an asshole. He could sit down next to an old woman and clean her out for $20,000. But any time I needed money, I got it from him.

Were your films union pictures?

I always dealt with union recognition. I'd go with the teamsters.

I have to say that the highlight of NIGHT OF THE ZOMBIES was your performance as the Nazi.

Oh, it's awful. I'm going to be a real stud, I'm going to be the senior citizen Leonardo DeCaprio. You think I'm only kidding (laughs). You see, you have an authentic interview at Sardi's, the hot showbusiness spot. Watch as we retrogress with Joel M. Reed, he's the old geezer. He doesn't go down to the Bowery bar with the hot 16-year-old models because this is his era, the era of the Fifties, the Sixties. He lived through it all

DIRECTED BY JOEL M. REED
Career Bed (1967)
Sex By Advertisement (1967)
Wit's End aka *GI Executioner* (1968)
Blood Bath (1974)
Bloodsucking Freaks (1978)
Night of the Zombies (1979)

from garter belts to panty hose and back to garter belts.

Is there a reason that you didn't ever go into hardcore porn?

I don't know. I used to hang around all of those guys. I knew Gerard Damiano. I've been on their sets. It doesn't mean anything to me. I've actually worked on, in various capacities, several major porn films. I find them very boring. I used to hang around with Sharon Mitchell. I met her on a Damiano picture. I don't know, I like it when it's funny. But the reality of the people is... I think they're being abused. There were one or two major porn films that I thought were OK — THE OPENING OF MISTY BEETHOVEN and DEEP THROAT. Actually, women are more in tune to things like that. I've been to maybe 50 to 100 porn film sets. It's not erotic. There is a slice of life there, but I can't do that.

Have you written any books?

I've written a number of books. I wrote a bunch of dirty novels. I used to get $5,000 a pop for them. I started writing them around ten years ago, just to get the money. I wrote a series of semi-porn film books called the CHINA BLUE SERIES. They were about this kung-fu girl who goes to this temple in China where they not only teach you fighting, but the pelvic exercises as well. She was totally undefeatable. She would throw these guys down and get on top of them... and crush them. And then, I got $60,000 to write a book on Donald Trump in four days. I made everything up, it was all lies. I also have a new book out called PRIVATE SCHOOL GIRLS. I'm actually talking to the guys from BAYWATCH about that. They might do it as a series. It's very erotic, if you're 12-years-old. Judy Blume writes porn novels for 12-year-old girls. This is a spoof of her work, a spoof of things that she's writing about seriously. She gets all these educational awards for getting 12-year-olds hot.

Have you done any plays recently?

I'm involved with two or three Broadway plays right now, just to stay in the action. One of my plays is being done. THE LAST DAY OF THE WAR — a Vietnam thing. I hung around in Vietnam to-

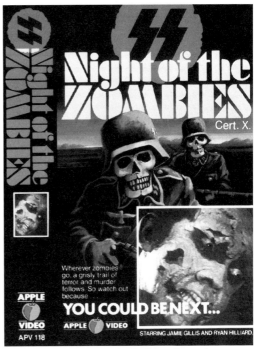

British video sleeve for
NIGHT OF THE ZOMBIES.

wards the end of the war.

What's your software business all about?

I'm doing a lot of multi-media for people. I'm actually more well known for that than for my films. Nobody knows about those, I have to explain them to people. I have a lot of deals, I'm doing a lot of MBA; some investment banking stuff. I'm doing consulting and things. My problem with film is that I've never been aggressive about it. I'm never aggressive about anything unless I see some hot teenage girls.

Give us some advice about women.

Well, I don't think anyone should be old film fans. I think they should be out getting laid all the time. I don't have any fantasies, I've lived through all of them. I've had all of the young girls in the neighbourhood, but they start saying things like, "Pay my tuition." I say, "I'll buy you some CDs at Tower Records," and they pick four baskets. I say, "What the fuck are you doing? How much do you think you're worth?" Six CDs, ten CDs, not 80. They threaten to squeal on me, but they're not getting $800 worth of

59

l'abécédaire chimerique
by Progeas Didier

AEROPHONISTE: gueulard céleste qui seme les fausses notes et perturbe les vents.

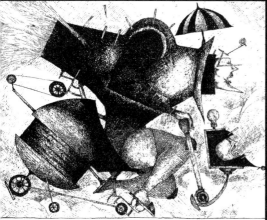

BICEPHALOPEDE: cyclophile émérite qui pratique l'ascension sur courants d'air

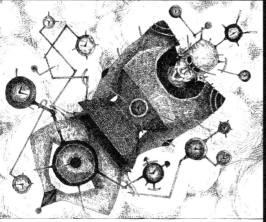

CHRONOLINGUISTE: polyglotte anonyme qui parle et traduit tous les decalages horaires

to be continued...

CDs. I'd rather pay their lab fee. So that does it, it's not very romantic. It's fucking awful. God has fucked you in the ass from the start. But you know, I met a hot little Italian girl here tonight. She's at least over 22. You're fucked if they're not legal.

What about older women?
If I went for older women, I'd be living in the south of France right now. You've got to realise that older women want dick. And you have to produce for them. Women are not much different than guys.

You said something about a new project.
I'm working on several new projects now. I have a couple of meetings with the majors out on the coast. I have a comedy called TEENAGE SPACE GIRLS; I have some pretty big projects going.

Have you been to the west coast recently?
The American Film Institute threw me a party in LA a few years ago. I went out there and all these old ladies were running out and hugging me. They were all in BLOODSUCKING FREAKS. I went out with Ron Jeremy over there and he brought me a girl. He said, "She's all yours tonight." The problem with her was that her face was all pierced. He got the girl that I really liked.

What's TEENAGE SPACE GIRLS about?
That's a funny romp about girls in space that don't have any men. I might do that as a book. But I want to get back into film. You know why? I just got rejected by this hot little thing. I said, "I want to cuddle with you." She said, "Get the fuck out of here!" The last girl I took home from professional childrens' school was on television. She's now 37-years-old. That's how long it's been since I've scored with one of those girls.

That's why you want to get back into film?
Yes. Because all of the girls in the neighbourhood say, "My mother can't pay my tuition." They ask for money. Joe here, [the bartender] notices that I sometimes talk to young girls. But you don't do baby pussy without asking the mother. Otherwise you end up in Poland with Roman Polanski.

Serial Killing Down Under

Anthony Ferguson

The topic of serial killing has been very much in vogue in film and literary circles over the past decade. Just check the number of slasher films lining the shelves of your local video store or the number of bookshops that dedicate entire shelves to True Crime. Most of us are familiar with American and British serial killers who have attracted world media attention—Bundy, Dahmer, Sutcliffe, etc—but I thought HEADPRESS readers might be interested in the situation vis-à-vis serial killing down under, both in a historical and contemporary context.[1]

61

I should point out that before starting research on this topic I assumed that the general mood of Australian society was not overly conducive to serial killing. Aussies are generally a pretty laid back, relaxed type of folk, and I thought most 20-40 year old middle class white males would rather sit down and watch the footy with a few tinnies than lead the police on a wild goose chase for several months following a bizarre string of murder mutilations. In addition Australia has a comparatively small and sparse population, with a current average of 2.3 persons per 10 sq. km.

However, on reflection the 200 plus years of colonised Australian history have evinced a reasonably substantial number of serial killers to date. Perhaps it stands to reason. White Australia began with a convict population, and random killers aside, our history is littered with sundry other violent incidents.

Much of the information which follows is rudimentary and forms part of an ongoing research project. It is likely that there may be even more serial killers lurking in the annals of Australian history yet to be discovered by your narrator.

The first prominent mass killer in Australian history may well have been **FREDERICK BAYLEY DEEMING** aka Albert O Williams. Readers with an interest in this subject may know the name Deeming as one of the individuals suspected in some circles of being Jack the Ripper. Rather than go into detail here I would refer you instead to further discussion on Deeming as Ripper suspect in other texts.[2]

Deeming was a seafarer who murdered two wives and four of his children. He was also loosely suspected of several murders in Johannesburg and New York. The Australian newspapers referred to him as "The Jack the Ripper of the Southern Seas", following a supposed confession by Deeming to the Ripper slayings while in custody in Perth, Western Australia, in March 1892.

Deeming's modus operandi was to bury his family members under concrete in the floor of his respective dwellings. This he did to a wife and four children in Rainhill, east of Liverpool, England, and again to his next wife at Windsor in suburban Melbourne.

Deeming was hanged in Melbourne on 23 May 1892.

Shortly after this, in the beautiful Blue Mountains rural setting of NSW, a prospector by the name of **FRANK BUTLER** executed three companions by gunshot to the back of the head between the months of August and November 1896.

Butler would place advertisements in the popular press of the day asking for a mate to accompany him on a bogus gold digging expedition, or in one case answered a similar advertisement himself. Whatever the catalyst the expeditions all ended in the same manner, with Butler requesting his companion to dig a small channel in the earth whereupon they were shot in the back of the head.

Butler's murderous shenanigans were brought to an end when he was found out by associates of his third and final victim after trying to pass himself off as the unfortunate man, a former ship's captain. By this time he had earned himself a passage on a ship bound for San Francisco, where he was arrested as soon as it docked.

Frank Butler was hanged at Darlinghurst Gaol in Sydney on 16 July 1897.

MARTHA RENDALL was a cold blooded

Ripper suspect Frederick Deeming.

sexual sadist who rejoiced in the slow suffering of her child victims. Between July 1907 and October 1908, she tormented and murdered three of her five stepchildren at her house in Perth, Western Australia, and had started on the fourth before she was found out.

When the fourth child fled the house and informed his real mother of his suspicions, the authorities exhumed the corpses of the three dead children. It became evident that Rendall had been 'treating' the children's sore throats with spirit of salts — diluted hydrochloric acid. She had first administered the substance in small quantities in drinks, then applied it in a regular throat swab (on doctor's orders, *sans* acid), causing great pain and suffering.

A neighbour came forward and confessed he had often peered through the family's windows on hearing the screams of the children, to witness Rendall standing in front of her screaming victim, rocking back and forth as if in ecstasy.

At her trial in September 1909, the prosecution contended that she was a sexual sadist motivated by the sheer pleasure she derived from her victims' agony. It transpired that she totally dominated the children's' father. At first he was also tried for the murders but was eventually acquitted. But he maintained her innocence to the end, such was her hold over him.

Martha Rendall became the last woman hanged in Western Australia, when she went to the gallows in Fremantle Gaol on 6 October 1909.

In 1930 came the strange case of the Murchison Murders, perpetrated by **JOHN THOMAS SMITH**, aka Snowy Rowles.

In late 1929 a well-known contemporary thriller writer named Arthur Upfield took a position on a remote cattle station in the sparse Murchison district, north-west of Perth, Western Australia, in order to study outback life for the setting of his next book.

Mountain Murderer Frank Butler.
Inset **Arnold Karl Sodeman**.

There he met a stockman named Snowy Rowles and shared with him his plot motif for committing the perfect murder. Unbeknownst to Upfield, Rowles was already wanted in Perth for theft and was a prison escapee. When Upfield returned to the city, Knowles went about translating the novel into fact, murdering three men in the latter months of 1930 for what would seem little reason.

The perfect murder? Well it involved shooting the victim, burning the body, sieving the ashes for all metal parts and dissolving those in acid, pounding the unburnt bones into dust, then burning a kangaroo or two on the same spot to divert suspicion. However, Rowles was nowhere near careful enough and he was convicted by his placement in the vicinity of each victim, by fragments of bone and metal found at the first murder scene, and also by the corroboration of Arthur Upfield and his 1932 novel, "Sands of Windee". He was only ever convicted of the first murder, but there was little doubt he committed the other two as well, even though the bodies were never located.

Rowles was hanged in Perth on 13 June 1932.

Between 1930 and 1935, **ARNOLD KARL SODEMAN**, a labourer/road construction worker, strangled four girls between the ages of six and sixteen in Melbourne, Victoria. He carried out the crimes in his local vicinity, was thought to be a good man by his neighbours and was generally respectable and happily married with a daughter he regarded with great affection. He was 30 years old at the time of his first murder.

It transpired (following an autopsy) that Sodeman suffered from a brain condition known as leptomeningitis, which caused inflammation of the brain tissues when the sufferer consumed alcohol, thus rendering him uncontrollable. Indeed, Sodeman had enjoyed substantial public support after his conviction from a group calling themselves 'Justice for Sodeman', who maintained that the killer should have been found insane at the time of his crimes.

Nevertheless, despite the possible mitigating circumstances, Sodeman was found sane, convicted on four counts of murder and hanged on 1 June 1936 at Pentridge Gaol in Victoria.

In the Western Plains district of NSW between 1938 and 1939, an itinerant drifter named **ALBERT ANDREW MOSS** murdered three men in a killing spree that came to be known as the Narromine Bones Case.

Moss, aged somewhere between 54 and 61, had a long criminal record dating back to the age of 17 on charges of forgery, theft and attempted rape. He had also been institutionalised in asylums on several occasions, although it is suspected that he regularly feigned insanity to make the authorities go easy on him.

Moss was found in possession of several items belonging to three missing men in the Narromine area and was placed in the company

Top **Sexual sadist Martha Randall.**

Main Picture **John Thomas Smith aka Snowy Rowles.**

64

L–R **Eddie Leonski, the Brown-out killer; Caroline Grills; John Balaban, the Rampaging Rumanian.**

of the men by other witnesses. However, he was only ever charged with one of the killings, when incriminating remains were found in a fire Moss had used to try and burn the body. It was never ascertained how Moss carried out his killings, but a clue was given by a report from another drifter that Moss savagely assaulted him one night with fists and boots, and was only dissuaded by a severe blow to the head from a wine bottle.

When taken by the police to the crime scene Moss tried to pull the insanity act again, plucking thistles from the ground and claiming they were lettuces, and pointing in the opposite direction to Macquarie River and exclaiming, "There's the River." It didn't wash — Moss was sentenced to death. However, the sentence was commuted to life imprisonment and Moss died of cancer in Long Bay Gaol, NSW, on 24 January 1958. Interestingly, at the time of his conviction there were six individuals missing in the vicinity of Moss's crime(s), and it is said in some circles that while in prison he claimed to have murdered thirteen men.

Next in line came another imported serial killer. 24-year-old **EDWARD JOSEPH LEONSKI** was a private in the US Army stationed in Victoria during the Second World War. He bashed and strangled three women, aged between 31 and 43 years, from 2–18 May 1942 on the streets of Melbourne, in what came to be known as the 'Brown-out Killings'. That being the term given to war-time Melbourne's lesser version of London's Black-outs.

Leonski was generally quiet and a loner except for when he was drunk, then he became quite gregarious and willing to make an exhibition of himself. When given leave from base camp he would invariably go off on his own to frequent hotels and brothels. It wasn't long before he moved on from womanising to murder to get his kicks.

However, Leonski left the body of his third victim too close to the base camp and was challenged by an Australian sentry on duty when returning to camp that night. The authorities soon put two and two together. Leonski pleaded insanity and offered the unusual motive that he had just wanted to hear the women's "soft voices".[3] The court-martial disagreed with his plea, finding him sane and he was hanged on 9 November 1942 at Pentridge Gaol in Victoria.

In another war-time case which could be read as a bizarre reversal of the Leonski murders, 34 year old ex-Australian Army serviceman, **FREDERICK WILLIAM EVEREST**, conducted a one man rampage in Brisbane against American servicemen, who he was convinced were out to get him.

Everest was a bread carter who had been discharged from the army after a psychiatric examination revealed he was suffering from schizophrenia. Between 11–24 January 1945, he gunned down two American servicemen, the latter victim living just long enough to identify Everest's red bread truck, which the police lo-

65

cated shortly afterwards.

At his trial, Everest expressed the fear that all Americans were out to get him so he wanted to make sure he got them first. The jury was eventually discharged and Everest was committed to an asylum.

Between late 1947 and early 1949, smiling grandmother **CAROLINE GRILLS** murdered four people with rat poison and attempted to kill three more in Sydney, NSW. She had used a commercial preparation to treat rats in her home which contained thallium, a chemical which was undetectable in the case of human poisonings until 1952. Grills was 62 at the time.

At her trial the prosecution alleged that while the first two poisonings were committed for obvious financial gain, the latter cases were perpetrated just for the thrill Grills enjoyed from her victims' suffering. This certainly contrasted from her public persona of a kindly old woman who spent her time caring for others, but there was little doubt she was a serial poisoner from the moment she was caught administering the poison in a cup of tea by suspicious family members.

Grills was convicted and given a life sentence in Sydney's Long Bay gaol, where she was known to her fellow inmates as 'Aunt Thally'. She died from peritonitis on 6 October 1960, outliving her last victim by four years.

Between the months of December 1952 and April 1953, 28 year old Rumanian migrant and cafe owner, **JOHN BALABAN**, murdered a prostitute and three members of his own family within the migrant community in Adelaide, South Australia.

The prostitute had her throat cut on 5 December 1952, while Balaban's wife, mother-in-law and stepson were battered to death in the early morning of 12 April 1953. During his trial Balaban also confessed to murdering a woman in Paris in 1946, a case which the French authorities were still trying to solve.

Balaban was hanged in Adelaide on 26 August, 1953.

Moving on a decade, we come to **LEONARD KEITH LAWSON**. An artist, Lawson was convicted of the rape of two teenage girls in NSW in 1952. He was originally sentenced to death but the sentence was later commuted to life imprisonment. He was released on parole in 1961, and soon after strangled and stabbed a young portrait model to death after she refused his sexual advances. The following day Lawson inadvertently shot a 15 year old schoolgirl to death during a struggle with the headmistress who was trying to disarm him. Lawson was holding the students hostage at the time.

Again sentenced to life imprisonment for the murders, the still living Lawson is now eligible to apply to the Supreme Court for a fixed sentence. However, while in prison he also tried to kill another woman in 1972.

Lawson claimed that a demon which possessed him made him commit his sex crimes. Although he only actually perpetrated one sex killing, there is no doubt that left unchecked he would have continued to attack women. There is also some speculation that Lawson committed a necrophilic act on his victim. The police at the time let the matter slide on the grounds that they already had their man, and that the girl's family had suffered enough.

Over on the west coast in Perth, the most isolated capital city in the world (the place where I grew up), lived **ERIC EDGAR COOKE**. Cooke was a truck driver who moonlighted as a petty criminal and murderer. He raped and strangled one woman and shot another woman and four men between 27 January and 10 August 1963.

Cooke had a long history of voyeurism and breaking and entering. At the time of his conviction he claimed to have broken into around 250 Perth households over an 18 year period.

He was only apprehended by chance, when an elderly couple discovered his discarded rifle hidden in some bushes. The police staked out the area for several days, and sure enough Cooke returned to the scene to retrieve the weapon. His explanation was that he wanted to hurt people.

Like many serial killers Cooke had experienced a tremendously unhappy childhood and progressed from petty criminal offences toward violent crime. On the surface he remained a happily married father of seven children.

A jury rejected Cooke's defence of insanity and he was sentenced to death. He was hanged at Fremantle Gaol on 26 October 1964.[4]

A contemporary of Cooke's back on the east coast was **WILLIAM MACDONALD**, aka Allan Brennan, aka Alan MacDonald. The homosexual killer MacDonald was dubbed "The Mutilator" by the press and had a penchant for slicing off his (male) victims' genitalia and throwing them off the Sydney Harbour Bridge.

MacDonald, an English migrant from Liverpool, stabbed and mutilated four male vagrants in 1961–62 in Sydney. He actually strangled a prior victim in Brisbane — but was never convicted for that crime. The Sydney murders were characterised by extreme violence and accompanied by extensive mutilation of the genitals. He was caught when one of the bodies was identified as Allan Brennan, which came as a big surprise to an ex-workmate who saw him walking around in Sydney some months later.

The exceptionally paranoid MacDonald had fled to Brisbane after his last killing, storing the body under the delicatessen he had run under the alias of Allan Brennan. When the badly decomposed corpse was discovered in the boarded up shop several months later, identification was near impossible, and it was assumed the nice shopkeeper himself had died by misadventure.[5]

If the Mutilator had not had the compulsion to return to Sydney to kill again and been spotted by a friend, he may well have got away with it. When the full story came out, the press labelled it "The Case of the Walking Corpse".

The jury ignored MacDonald's defence of insanity and found him guilty. While serving a life sentence in Long Bay Penitentiary he attacked and almost killed a fellow prisoner. Following this he was confined to a mental hospital.

Shortly after this we come to one of our nation's few unsolved suspected serial killer cases. A series of unexplained killings which came to be known as the **WANDA BEACH MURDERS**.

The bodies of two 15-year-old girls were found buried in a shallow grave in January 1965 at Wanda Beach, Sydney. They had been brutally bashed, stabbed and sexually violated. Despite witnesses providing descriptions of several possibly suspicious males present on the beach on that day, the case has never been solved.

Eric Cooke.

Right
Leonard Lawson.
Previous page
Albert Andrew Moss, the homicidal hobo.

Eighteen days after the Wanda Beach murders the body of a 57-year-old woman was found in Piccadilly Arcade in Wollongong, NSW (some 50km south of Sydney). She had been strangled, viciously bashed, mutilated and possibly sexually assaulted. Four days later, the body of a 27-year-old woman, a known Kings Cross[6] prostitute, was found near Lucas Heights, south of Sydney. She had been strangled and repeatedly stabbed.

The authorities were eventually to reveal that there were striking similarities between all of these murders. All of them were committed in a frenzy. In every case the body had been dragged along the ground. There was no genuine attempt to conceal the bodies. Sexual molestation occurred in all the killings but only after death. However, the murders remain unsolved to this day.

In a bizarre twist of fate, a subsequent link has been drawn between the Wanda Beach murders and Australian-born killer **CHRISTOPHER WILDER**. It was previously thought that Wilder committed all of his murders in the United States.[7] However, there are claims that the two unfortunate teenage victims were seen in the company of a young man matching Wilder's description on the dunes that day. He would have been almost 20 years old at

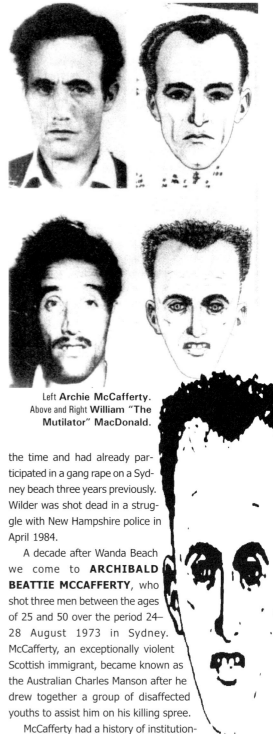

Left **Archie McCafferty**.
Above and Right **William "The Mutilator" MacDonald**.

the time and had already participated in a gang rape on a Sydney beach three years previously. Wilder was shot dead in a struggle with New Hampshire police in April 1984.

A decade after Wanda Beach we come to **ARCHIBALD BEATTIE MCCAFFERTY**, who shot three men between the ages of 25 and 50 over the period 24–28 August 1973 in Sydney. McCafferty, an exceptionally violent Scottish immigrant, became known as the Australian Charles Manson after he drew together a group of disaffected youths to assist him on his killing spree.

McCafferty had a history of institutionalisation and criminal behaviour before the accidental death of his infant son sent him on a bizarre murder rampage. McCafferty claimed

that the spirit of his infant son had appeared to him at the graveside and had spoken to him repeatedly, imploring him that if he wanted the boy to return he had to kill seven people to avenge the death.

It didn't help much that McCafferty was an extremely aggressive misanthrope who consumed as much alcohol and hard drugs as he could get his hands on. During his trial, at which he threatened to cut off the head of one of his co-accused's barristers, McCafferty informed the packed gallery that nothing would stop him killing four more people to avenge his son's death and bring him back.

McCafferty was given three life sentences. While imprisoned McCafferty wrote an autobiography titled "Seven Shall Die" and was suspected of killing a fellow prisoner in 1982. Aside from that he was a model prisoner. McCafferty continually applied for parole and was eventually granted his wish. He became eligible for release in August 1993. Against his wishes (and against Scottish authorities' wishes) he was deported to his native Scotland on 1 May 1997.

A short time after McCafferty's rampage, in Adelaide, **JAMES WILLIAM MILLER** (a petty thief and loner) and **CHRISTOPHER WORRELL** (a rapist just released from prison and who was subsequently killed in a car crash) were perpetrating a series of murder rapes which would come to be known as the "Truro Murders". Over a seven week period in the (Australian) summer of 1976–77 the bodies of seven young women aged between 15–26 were dis-

covered around the area of Truro, near Adelaide.

Miller and his accomplice picked up the victims, most of whom were hitch-hikers, and subsequently raped and murdered them. Miller was found guilty of six of the seven crimes. It appeared that all of the women had been strangled, often with the use of a nylon cord, though there was a suspicion that the last of the victims had been buried alive.

Although Miller accepted his life sentence and never applied for parole, he vehemently denied perpetrating any of the crimes. Miller, a homosexual aged 42 at the time of the killings, claimed he was totally devoted to the much younger and more attractive Christopher Worrell, then aged 23. The two were lovers for a short period and Miller stated he merely drove the car while Worrell picked up the girls and raped and killed them.

Miller claimed he would always go for a walk while Worrell committed his crimes, and that he would often try and dissuade the younger man from killing the girls. It was only Worrell's threats of violence toward him and his undying love for the younger man which made him complicit in the crimes.

Miller subsequently claimed that if Worrell had not died in a car crash one week after the seventh and final murder, the killings would have continued unabated. He said Worrell was his best and only friend in the world, and he would never have "dobbed him in".[8]

Staying in sunny Adelaide we come to the still unsolved case of the **ADELAIDE MUR-**

Above **Allegedly the only photograph of suspected Truro serial killer Christopher Worrell.** Right **Adelaide Murders suspect Beven von Einem.**

Left and main picture **David and Catherine Birnie**.
Below **Child killer Michael Laurance**.

DERS. Between 1979 and 1983 the bodies of five young men (between the ages of 14–25) were discovered in Adelaide. They all had similar types of wounds and were sexually mutilated; several were washed and dressed and their bodies were disposed of in similar ways. While the victims were not necessarily homosexuals, the authorities were certain that the crimes were sexually motivated.

It has been suggested that there are links between the five murders and a group dubbed the "Family", which had allegedly picked up, drugged and sexually assaulted numerous young men. One of the group, Beven von Einem, was eventually convicted of one of the murders, but unfortunately much of the evidence linking him and several other men to the crimes was eventually proved inadmissible in court. Von Einem for his part maintains his complete innocence to this day.

Shortly after comes the similarly unsolved case of the **TYNONG MURDERS**. Between 1980 and 1983, the bodies of two teenage girls aged 14 and 18 were discovered without any clues left for the authorities in Tynong, Victoria.

In 1989 an anonymous letter was sent to the mother of one of the victims, possibly from the killer, in which the writer boasted of four other cases of murder carried out in South Australia and New South Wales. However, the other bodies have not been located and the case remains unsolved to date.

A charmer by the name of **MICHAEL GEORGE LAURANCE**, a labourer from Griffith in NSW, drowned three boys (aged 11, 12 and 8) in a bath tub between 1984 and 1986 after luring them to his home, where he tied them up and raped them over a period of time. It was later discovered that Laurance had molested more than 200 boys since the age of 15.

The killer told the arresting officers that the murder of the children had given him a thrill.

In a similar vein is "**MR CRUEL**" a paedo-

70

phile who is strongly suspected of being a serial killer. He has been linked to the abduction of five girls since 1985. The first three were released alive, but since April 1991, two more girls have been abducted and murdered. He apparently displays a knowledge of forensics and has gone to great lengths to ensure that he does not leave a trace of evidence on his surviving victims.

The case remains unsolved.

In the latter months of 1986, the husband and 'wife' pairing of **DAVID AND CATHERINE BIRNIE** abducted, drugged, raped, photographed and murdered three women and a teenage girl in Perth, Western Australia. David Birnie was a near insatiable sexual deviant with a drive to find ever more violent outlets for his cravings. His common-law wife, Catherine Birnie (she changed her name by deed poll) was described at her subsequent trial as a totally dependent personality.

During October and November 1986 Catherine helped her lover abduct five women at knifepoint in their vehicles. The women were bound, gagged and chained to the bed of the Birnie's rented home where David Birnie repeatedly raped them while Catherine licked his anus and genitals. Thereafter Catherine looked on while David slowly garrotted the women to death, and in one case, bludgeoned a woman to death with an axe. Catherine Birnie strangled the second victim herself at David's bidding. The murders occurred in the Birnie's bedroom or in a secluded pine forest after the pair had satiated their lust.

However, a fifth victim managed to escape and raised the alarm. After a lengthy interview David Birnie led police to the graves of the four women. Both defendants were sentenced to life imprisonment, where, despite their pleas, they have been refused permission to ever see one another again.

At the beginning of 1989, 58 year old English migrant, **JOHN WAYNE GLOVER**, soon to be dubbed the "Granny Killer", began a year long series of killings around the lower North Shore area of Sydney. Six elderly women (one was 60, the rest were between 81–92 years old) died as a result of bashing with a claw hammer and

Left **Granny killer John Wayne Glover**.
Right **Gun fanatic Ivan Milat**

ritual strangulation with their pantyhose, tied in a bow. The victims skirts were pulled up over their heads, the legs were splayed and their shoes were placed neatly alongside the bodies.

Glover had a problem with female authority figures, stemming from his relationship with his own neglectful mother. Psychoanalysis later revealed that the victims "represented" both Glover's mother and mother-in-law, although he also hated "Mosman Matrons" (a close translation of which would be 'wealthy old women'). He specifically blamed his mother-in-law for his actions.

All of Glover's victims were strangers, except the last one, a woman with whom he had been having a 'relationship'.[9] He was also charged with attempted murder, indecent assault, robbery with wounding and assault and robbery. Glover had a long history of teenage delinquency, lying, stealing and voyeuristic activity as well as assault, both in the UK where he grew up, then in Melbourne where he worked, before moving to Sydney.

Glover struck everyone as being quite normal. He was an average family man, married with two daughters. He was sentenced to six terms of life imprisonment, never to be released. His family completely disowned him.

Between May and July 1989, 28 year old Sydney rock climber **PAUL GERARD MASON** murdered two women with one of the tools of his hobby, a pick-axe. He also strangled the second victim's infant child with an electrical chord.

The killings occurred on a rural property at Geary's Gap, near Canberra in the ACT, and in the NSW south coastal town of Pambula Beach

71

respectively. There was no apparent motive for the murders other than that the two women were known to the killer on a social basis.

Mason had also tried unsuccessfully to smother the first victim's one year old child with a blanket. He told arresting officers the murders were thrill kills. While being held in custody at Goulburn Gaol to await further court appearances, Mason hanged himself with torn bedsheets tied to the steel bars of his cell. He left a suicide note apologising to his family, but made no mention of the two victims' families he had ruined.

In the early to mid 1990s, 51 year old migrant Australian **IVAN ROBERT MARKO MILAT** perpetrated what came to be known as the "Backpacker Murders". The discovery of seven bodies (five women, two men) in the Belanglo State Forest in New South Wales was made in September 1992. The murders occurred over a two and a half year period (December 1989 to April 1992). The skeletal remains indicated that most victims had been variously strangled, stabbed and shot numerous times, although one was decapitated with a sword.

All of the victims were hitchhikers, who had at some stage stayed in backpackers' hostels in Surrey Hills or Kings Cross, Sydney. Five were European travellers and the other two were locals. Where partners were involved they had been separated.[10] All of the bodies had all been laid out in the same way (face down with hands crossed, parallel to a log with a canopy of sticks and ferns to conceal the body). Backpacks and other personal items had been souvenired, and the murder sites were marked by remnants of a campfire ringed by stones in a near perfect circle. The places had been carefully chosen, all on the perimeter of the pine forest.

Ivan Milat was found guilty of seven counts of murder and one of attempted murder relating to a hitchhiker who escaped after accepting a lift in Milat's car (an English tourist). Many of the weapons used in the killings and the souvenired items were found at Milat's home and at his mother's home.

On 17 May 1997 Milat and another prisoner, a convicted drug trafficker sentenced to life imprisonment, were thwarted in an escape attempt. The following day the drug trafficker was found hanged in his cell.

Finally, bringing us right up to date...

The "**CLAREMONT SERIAL KILLER**" perpetrated an as yet unsolved trio of murders in Perth, Western Australia between the months of January 1996 and March 1997. The West Australian State Government posted a A$250,000 reward on 18 March 1997 for infor-

Rodney Cameron is taken into custody.

REFERENCES & RECOMMENDED READING

The Australian newspaper, 1-2 September 1998

Australian Criminology Database
URL: http://www.lib.flinders.edu.au/resources/databases/local/cinch.html

Bouda, S. *Crimes that Shocked Australia*. Bantam Books, Moorebank, NSW 1991

Brown, M (Ed). *Australian Crime: Chilling Tales of our Time*. The Book Company International Pty Ltd, Sydney, NSW 1993

Crime stopper sites
URL: http://www.netasset.com/crimestoppers/others.htm

Dacey, P (Ed). *An Australian Murder Almanac*. Nationwide News, Canberra, ACT 1993

Kidd, P B. *Never to be Released: Australia's Most Vicious Murderers*. Pan Macmillan Australia Pty Ltd, Sydney, NSW 1993

Main, J. *Murder Australian Style*. Unicorn Books, East Melbourne, Victoria 1980

Murder Casebook 90- "Eric

The unnamed Perth
serial killer suspect
leaving work.
THE AUSTRALIAN,
1 Sept 1998.

mation leading to the arrest of the unknown killer. The killer is believed to have abducted three women from Claremont (Perth, Western Australia) night-spots since January 1996.

To give you some sort of social context, Claremont is the Western Australian equivalent of the Kings Road. Sloane Ranger territory. It's a place where one goes to be seen. The patrons of bars in the area are generally all from well-to-do families. Because of this, it has been suggested that the killer possibly resents the social status of the victims, or that he spent his youth being rejected by them. Public empathy was not encouraged when a news item following one of the killings featured a local female resident of similar age commenting along the lines of (I'm paraphrasing from memory here) "...Oh my God, like, it's not like it's just some prostitute or something. It's one of us!" However, that should not detract from sympathy toward the families of the victims, or lessen the horror of the crimes.

In subsequent developments, in the two years since the last murder there has been no arrest. However, in the past six months it has become an open secret that the Perth police have a major suspect in their sights. In a bizarre development that could probably only happen in Australia, everybody knows who the suspect is. A middle aged public (civil) servant who perfectly fits the stereotype has been staked out constantly by police, news media, fascinated work colleagues and neighbours for several months now. The individual has failed a lie detector test but the police still don't have enough

---

Cooke: Australian Nightmare". A Marshall Cavendish Weekly Publication. Marshall Cavendish Ltd, London 1991

The Serial Killer Info Site http://www.serialkillers.net/text.htm#reviews

Sharpe, A. *Australian Crimes*. Ure Smith, Sydney, NSW 1979

Warnock, S. "I've Killed Four More" (Rodney Cameron Confesses). Ralph Magazine, ACP Publishing Pty Ltd, Sydney, NSW, Feb 1999.

NOTES

1   I am indebted to Ron Mack's police web page for many of the chronological listings. Unfortunately, the site appears to have now gone offline.

2   See for example J S O'Sullivan's "A Most Unique Ruffian" or Frank Clune's "The Demon Killer".

3   As quoted in Simon Bouda's " Crimes that Shocked Australia" p.68.

4   Fremantle Gaol closed down in 1991 and the inmates were transferred to a new prison. The old Gaol is now a museum. I visited it recently. It can be hired out for parties and weddings, although it is said to be haunted.

5   MacDonald had gone into such a frenzy in killing this victim, that he had blunted the knife when it came time to remove the genitals. Instead he made a futile incision at the base of the testicles and a few stab wounds in the

evidence to make an arrest.

The suspect and his mother (with whom he lives) have subsequently given several interviews to news media denying his involvement in the killings. The suspect's mother claimed in the media that the fact that her son frequented the Claremont night-club district regularly in the early hours of Saturday and Sunday mornings and followed or circled young women in his vehicle, merely reflected his concern for their well-being — but she has warned him to stay away from the area in future.

It is noticeable that there have been no further attacks by the killer since March 1997, given that the suspect has been under 24 hour surveillance since then. However, the evidence to date is apparently inconclusive and there is some conjecture that the authorities may be accused of utilising the media to pressure the suspect into confessing.

POSTSCRIPT

As I was rounding off this piece, news broke down under that another killer had claimed from his prison cell that he had committed four more murders than originally been convicted for. If his claim is true it would take his total to eight, conveniently making him Australia's most prolific serial killer.[11]

RODNEY FRANCIS CAMERON made his startling claim in an article featured in the men's magazine "Ralph" (the Australian equivalent of "Loaded") in February 1999. Cameron is known to have murdered three people between January 1974 and June 1990 (two women, one man). He is most remembered for the last killing, following his release from a Victorian prison in November 1989. He befriended a lonely 44 year old woman he met through a Melbourne late-night radio matchmaking program and subsequently murdered her by bashing and strangulation. Before fleeing, he showered the body with carnations, thereafter earning the sobriquet, the "Lonely Hearts Killer".

In 1992, Cameron was also charged with murdering another woman around the same time of his original killing spree in 1974, an accusation which he denied and which was never proven. He now wants to claim that victim, as well as another four as yet unknown victims.

However, while examining Cameron's claims the authorities are treating them with a pinch of salt. Experts in forensic psychiatry have suggested that life sentence-serving serial killers sometimes have nothing better to do than bolster their egos by big-noting themselves as the most prolific killer in an effort to compete with each other. 💀

---

penis. When the corpse was eventually exhumed and thoroughly re-examined, police knew they were onto the Mutilator.

6 Kings Cross, an inner suburb of Sydney, is our equivalent of Soho. It is a seedy town where underage prostitutes, drug dealers and criminals congregate. It also has some nice cafes, pubs and clubs and it's a cool place to hang out for a short time.

7 There's a shot in the arm for economic rationalism. Aussie serial killers, we not only employ them, we breed and export them too. Quality serial killers delivered straight to your market. Guaranteed to increase electronic and print media sales tenfold.

8 As quoted in Paul B Kidd's "Never to be Released", p.114.

9 Not consummated though, as Glover was sexually impotent due to prostate problems following a mastectomy. Very rare in the case of men. His mother had died of breast cancer, and to Glover it was as if she was tormenting him even after death.

10 There is still some conjecture as to whether Milat was working in conjunction with an accomplice for some or all of his deeds. His is a case where more information may come to light.

11 Australia's most prolific known serial killers to date are Ivan Milat and Miller/Worrell, with seven victims each.

SIFTING THROUGH THE WRECKAGE

Simon Collins

Simon Ford is a curator working at the National Art Library of the Victoria and Albert Museum in London. He has recently produced his second book, <u>WRECKERS OF CIVILISATION</u>, a definitive history of the groundbreaking Seventies industrial band Throbbing Gristle and COUM Transmissions, the performance art group that evolved into TG. I first met Simon Ford on May Day this year, at the Royal Festival Hall, where he was signing copies of his book before the 'Time's Up' Psychic TV comeback gig, and I mentioned my own interest in TG — I had given a short paper on them at a three-day symposium called 'Rethinking The Avant-Garde' in Leicester last autumn. A few weeks later, I was back in London, and I arranged to meet Simon in the august precincts of the V&A. The following is a condensed version of the lengthy conversation that took place.

HEADPRESS Could we start with some information on yourself, your background and work, and on how you got interested in writing this book?

SIMON FORD I come from Devon and I started out as an artist. I did a Fine Art degree in Exeter. I then went into librarianship, and that's basically what I do now. The book began as a proposal to the Courtauld Institute for a PhD thesis, and the initial topic was quite broad. It was about avant-gardism in Britain in the Seventies, and my interest in COUM came about because I needed an interesting case study. I've always had a general interest in alternative and underground culture. I'd just written a book on the Situationists, THE REALIZATION AND SUPPRESSION OF THE SITUATIONIST INTERNATIONAL, and I'd been actively collecting alternative publications for the library and myself, so I had quite a broad knowledge of this area.

Throbbing Gristle

THE LAST LIVE PERFORMANCE OF TG

So your primary interest was in COUM Transmissions and not in Throbbing Gristle?

Yes, the focus was initially on COUM, because that was an under-researched area. I had a few TG records, and I remember buying 20 JAZZ FUNK GREATS (the first album I bought by them) just for the cover. My interest in them was more intellectual than musical. I appreciated the music, but I was never an obsessive fan.

Reading the book from a TG fan perspective, I found the stuff about COUM rather less interesting than the later stuff on Throbbing Gristle. I feel that, with hindsight, Throbbing Gristle were much more significant than COUM Transmissions. Would you agree?

I don't think you would have got TG without COUM Transmissions... COUM was important in trying out strategies, and there's a lot of precedents for what TG did in what COUM had done before. TG, though, was more focussed. COUM was very amorphous, there were a lot of people involved, but TG, once they got the membership sorted out, and the area that they were interested in working in, namely music, once that focus was there, I guess they did have a greater impact than COUM.

COUM now seem much more dated than TG though, more predictable in terms of the kind of avant-gardism that surrounded them, whereas Throbbing Gristle really stand apart from their cultural milieu. Do you think that's fair?

COUM and TG were always very good at reflecting their times. There are many imitators of TG now — there is a lot of music that sounds similar to theirs — but I still think they were very much of their time. They related to that moment in the late Seventies when there was a turn away from the Sixties permissiveness. COUM as well. I mean, they might have looked like hippies, but they were more coming from the 'Yippie' and freak culture.

When you say freak culture, do you mean something like the Motherfuckers in New York? Something more hard-edged?

I wouldn't say they were that obviously political.

But they were very provocative?

Yeah, and they predicted many things that happened with punk. Gen was wearing ripped clothing and chains and safety pins for COUM actions in the early Seventies. So, anyway, I would disagree that TG transcended their historical moment, but I would agree that they've been much more influential and imitated. There are still performance artists who do similar things to what COUM were doing, but for me they're not so interesting.

There's an archive here at the V&A of COUM and TG material. Was it just convenient for your purposes that it was here, or did its presence inspire your decision to write the book?
If I hadn't had access to these archives, I probably wouldn't have chosen COUM as a subject, so it was a significant factor. It was because of my interest that we acquired the archive of Harley Lond, the editor of a defunct American avant-garde art magazine called INTERMEDIA. This gave me access to a lot of COUM material. My personal interest also meant that I acquired an archive from Jonas Almquist of The Leather Nun. This gave me access to a lot of material on TG and Industrial Records [who released music by The Leather Nun]. Together they laid a foundation that I could build upon, and after that initial research I felt more confident about approaching individual members of the band.

There's another ICA archive at the Tate, I believe.
I had a look at that and I didn't find that much interesting material. There's a lot of press cuttings that have got mixed in with the Carl Andre 'bricks' cuttings, but there's very little that I could find about the ICA's internal problems with the 'Prostitution' exhibition. There's no minutes of their meetings, for example. There is, though, lots of mail from Gen in the David Mayor/ Beau Geste archive there.

In my paper on TG, I argued that the 'Prostitution' scandal at the ICA forms a convenient bridge between the bricks at the Tate and 'God Save The Queen' in 1977. There's art becoming music, as COUM became TG, and all three events inspired great public outrage.
I feel that the difference between Carl Andre and COUM has more to do with institutional re-

actions. Andre was an established artist with powerful institutional supporters; he was supported in the press, and he was rewarded with an exhibition a couple of years later at the Whitechapel by Nicholas Serota. Whereas after the COUM exhibition at the ICA, they were ostracised by art institutions, specifically the Arts Council. It was a much more volatile controversy, because it involved sex and morality. There was also a whole array of problems in 1976 connected with the political situation, especially the unstable Labour government and problems with borrowing money from the International Monetary Fund. I'm interested in how these two scandals, Andre's bricks and COUM's 'Prostitution' show, are looked at historically. If you count the amount of contemporary press coverage they're very equal — if anything COUM has more — but because the bricks are associated with the Tate Gallery and the whole question of minimal art, it comes up again and again, whereas the 'Prostitution' scandal was more or less buried until quite recently.

Is that because the controversy about Andre's bricks fed into the discourse on minimalism, which became a more dominant art-historical discourse than that on performance art?
I haven't really thought about it in those terms. My perception is that if artists drop out of the

20 JAZZ FUNK GREATS album cover.

art world like COUM did, then they also drop out of art history. It's the opposite with Mary Kelly, also from that period. There was her 'nappies' exhibition ['Post Partum Document'], which still gets written about quite regularly. It gets written about as a major scandal, but the press reaction was minimal. There was a reaction, but compared to 'Prostitution' and the bricks, it was minimal. People look back on history and concentrate on particular aspects, depending on what kind of contemporary concerns they have.

Could you tell me about the TG night at the ICA (26ᵗʰ November 1998), which was also a launch party for WRECKERS OF CIVILISATION?
The TG night was meant to coincide with the book launch, but the book got delayed. We had three DJs playing contemporary music with a TG influence, and two slide projectors showing slides from my archive and Gen's archive, images that people had rarely seen. We had a dummy copy of the book, so people could see what it would look like, and we showed a couple of TG films in the Cinemateque. The book was finally launched on 1ˢᵗ April 1999 at Salon 3 with live music from Male Nurse.

I've got a couple more structural questions about the book. You wrote this book with extensive co-operation from all the ex-members of Throbbing Gristle?
Yeah. I did a first draft, and sent everybody a copy so that they knew I wasn't just messing about, and then I arranged to interview them,

Gen with Psychic TV at the Royal Festival Hall, 1ˢᵗ May 1999.

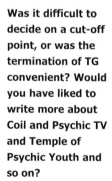

and periodically sent them drafts, so that I could get their comments.

Do you think this makes it an official biography?
No, not at all, because I tried to keep in all the disagreements and differences of opinion as to what really happened.

Is there still a lot of bad feeling then?
I think they've all got their own lives to live and they're getting on with them. I think they were interested in my approach because it was quite straight and academic. I wasn't taking sides and they appreciated that. They were interested in seeing somebody write something about their work that wasn't polemical or trying to push a particular angle on the group.

Was it difficult to decide on a cut-off point, or was the termination of TG convenient? Would you have liked to write more about Coil and Psychic TV and Temple of Psychic Youth and so on?
I always knew I'd stop at 1981. I was interested in TG as a group, and as the members split off into their various different projects it gets more difficult to see them as being connected. Psychic TV really needs its own book, and so does Coil, and so does Chris and Cosey.

Do you see any connection between the Situationist International and Throbbing Gristle, given that you've previously written about the SI? I can see obvious points of connection in the engagement

Photo © Simon Collins

with banality and everyday life, and in the way that TG had a self-conscious avant-garde fine art sensibility and subversive agenda and applied them to a popular medium.

I always shy away from trying to make connections between the Situationists and other groups. I've written a bit about how annoying it is hearing people make references to the Situationists without thinking through whether there really are any connections ('Pseudo Situationists', in ART MONTHLY, Oct 1997). My initial thoughts would be that they were very different. I see the Situationists as quite a tight theoretical group, whereas TG were more interested in spontaneity and improvisation. The Situationists were also hardcore leftists, and TG certainly weren't. I think they did share avant-garde characteristics in that they were into subverting all forms of establishment authority.

It also seems to me that there's a distinct Baudrillardean influence on Throbbing Gristle.

They wouldn't have read him, but I guess if you look at it broadly, TG were into upsetting the idea of the spectacle and consumer culture, as dictated by corporations and big business.

'Tesco Disco.'

Right. So there are probably connections there, but I wouldn't say there was any direct influence. During the Sixties, Gen was into radical politics, and Situationism was part of the wider radical discourse around at the time, and I think, like the Motherfuckers and so on, that it was just the kind of thing that people read about in OZ magazine.

Gen must have been aware of the events in May '68 in Paris, which was probably the Situationists' most public moment.

Yeah, although at that time he was in Solihull and he was only 18, still at school. It'd be difficult to know what information he was getting then, but subsequently he did immerse himself in alternative Sixties culture and he's still very much interested in it. I think that period is the key to his whole attitude.

It seems that in Psychic TV and latterly, he's been much more willing to own up to that. He's more openly interested in engaging with rock history than he was at the time of Throbbing Gristle. TG were always very concerned to present themselves as outside of rock history, as not owing anything to anybody, with the possible exceptions of Captain Beefheart and the Velvet Underground. But subsequently Gen's had this infatuation with Brian Jones and so on.

Some of that could be down to the fact that TG was a group project and it wasn't just his baby. They all contributed, and I think that's why TG is interesting. They were very focussed, and much of it was about what it was like to live in Hackney in the late Seventies, and apparently it felt like it was under siege. So they had this survivalist instinct, wearing camouflaged urban clothing and turning their house into a bunker.

There's definitely a hardening of attitudes from the Sixties. What about the connections between TG and punk rock? Obviously, they were fairly neatly contemporaneous in terms of punk rock in Britain, and there are clearly parallels between bands like the Sex Pistols and the Clash and Throbbing Gristle, but there are important differences too, and TG frequently stated that they weren't a punk band.

Punk has been so heavily focussed on, that its historical importance has become really disproportionate to its importance at the time. It was a significant moment, but there were other things going on. TG was closely involved with particular characters in the punk scene, like John Krivine [of Boy clothing] and Mark Perry. Gen was very close to them, and Malcolm McLaren employed Sleazy to photograph the early Sex Pistols.

And the Banshees wanted them to support and so on.

Yeah. It's not that big, the music scene in London, so they knew what was going on. I think the major difference was TG's attitude to the production and distribution of their own music, and their attempt to be independent and autonomous from the music industry.

There was a do-it-yourself ethic in punk. Which TG took on, but they took it a bit further. They were their own managers, marketers and their own distributors.

Can Throbbing Gristle be seen as a missing link between Sixties freak culture and punk rock, in much the same way as Malcolm McLaren took Situationist imagery and ideas from 1968 and applied them to his marketing of the Sex Pistols?
I don't really perceive history in that kind of linear way, as if you need a link between two points. I think

a lot of punk carries traces of freak and Situationist influences. Graphically, it's quite different, but a lot of the ideas and attitude come from alternative and oppositional culture that has existed through the ages. It just takes on a different form at each moment. I think TG was post-punk before punk even started. They had a longevity that punk never had.

TG are acknowledged as the pioneers of industrial music, but they also defined an industrial sensibility. The topics that they engaged with — deviant sexuality, mass murder, mind control techniques, weapons technology — what's the common thread here? You mentioned survivalism earlier.
It's difficult to talk about these issues because they are quite imprecise. I think it's to do with opposing the dominant ideas that control society. TG were looking at what authority figures are afraid of, and systematically working through those subjects to see what happened. But what was significant about TG was that they didn't dwell on these topics. They explored them and then moved on, and that's different from a lot of the later industrial bands, many of whom

PEOPLE WHO READ HEADPRESS
WRECKERS... author,
Simon Ford.

WRECKERS OF CIVILISATION
The Story of COUM Transmissions and Throbbing Gristle
Simon Ford
£20 350pp approx. (see below), London: Black Dog Publishing, 1999

In the autumn of 1968, young Neil Megson left Solihull to study Social Administration and Philosophy at the University of Hull. A little over a year later, he had dropped out of his course, joined and then left a radical arts

commune called Transmedia Explorations, founded his own performance arts group, COUM Transmissions, and, perhaps most importantly, met a young woman called Christine Newby. They were to become famous (and notorious) during the Seventies as Genesis P-Orridge and Cosey Fanni Tutti , working together first in COUM, and, from 1975 to 1981, as half of the trailblazing industrial quartet Throbbing Gristle. The details of how and why this happened are exhaustively and authoritatively set out in WRECKERS OF CIVILISATION, a definitive new study by Simon Ford.
    As many of the wider issues surrounding TG and COUM are discussed at length in the above interview with Simon Ford, this review will be less discursive than it might otherwise have been, and I'll confine myself to remarks on the book itself. Ford, coming from an academic and art-historical

background, has produced a rigorous and admirably dispassionate account of the career of this seminal band which is a million miles away from the average rock star 'biography', i.e. a cut-and-paste job assembled in a fortnight by a jaded alcoholic music hack with more pictures than words in it. This is not to say that WRECKERS... is short of pictures — on the contrary, it has many, including a lot — particularly of COUM actions — that have rarely been seen before. This in itself would make it an essential purchase for any TG enthusiast. But we are also treated to a great deal more information about what actually *happened* whilst TG existed than has ever been made publicly available before, not least because Ford managed to secure the co-operation of all the ex-members of the band for this project, including P-Orridge, who categorically refused to discuss

Photo © Simon Collins

never really developed. I mean, once you've done one song about a serial killer, what's the point of another?

TG had an aura of wickedness about them that they achieved with a really elegant economy of means, and someone like Marilyn Manson, for instance, has much to learn in this respect. They really didn't have to try very hard to come across as very disturbing.

There was a lot of variety in TG's work. People picture them mostly in the combat gear and Genesis shouting "Discipline!" and acting shamanistically, but they also had very lyrical moments. My interest in TG is based on this variety and contrast in their work, rather than just a penchant for unrelenting hardcore noise.

Could we discuss the visual presentation of the band? The most familiar images of Throbbing Gristle display a really deliberate lack of glamour. Mostly, they don't even look like they're trying to be punk, or anti-fashion. They wear pullovers! Has that kind of detachment from trendiness helped to prevent them

from seeming dated?

Definitely. If they had all dressed like punks, then they would be fixed in that historical moment. They were always very conscious about image, even in the sense that they were consciously anti-image. Also, coming from their art background, they knew about constructing identities, and there is very much a sense that they were playing characters when they were posing for photographs, especially Cosey. She was very aware of how you can construct an identity through wearing particular clothes and striking particular poses.

She talks about that, I think, on the TIME TO TELL solo CD — which is an excellent package, but hard to find. Do you have any comments on Cosey's sex work, the porn modelling and stripping, and the fact that she was doing this with a self-conscious and art-focussed attitude (as well as it being a convenient source of income!). Her work in these areas prefigures the current discourse from post-feminist pro-porn women writers, talking about female empowerment through display of sexuality.

· ·

Throbbing Gristle with anyone throughout the Eighties. I already knew, for example, that Cosey left Gen for Chris Carter — what I hadn't realised, though, was that this had already begun to happen by the time they were working on DOA, the second album.

In addition to the main text, WRECKERS... comes equipped with a useful chronology, discography and bibliography. The discography is, by Ford's own admission, not exhaustive on the matter of bootlegs and 'posthumous' unofficial releases, or indeed on the subject of 'associated' recordings, though the book does helpfully direct you to the most useful websites where the real completists hang out. A lot of information is given on all the official releases, though, right down to the various messages inscribed around the run-off grooves of different pressings of albums. What really limits the book's usefulness

as a research tool, however, is the lack of an index. And, whilst the book is handsomely designed, some aspects of it seem over-designed at the expense of utility — for example, the pages are tiresomely numbered within chapters rather than over the entire length of the book, in the manner of a technical manual. This has two effects — it becomes difficult to assess the overall length of the book (hence the 'approx' page count noted above), and it would make any index that did exist cumbersome and unwieldy. Also, the sans-serif font used for the main body of the text is not particularly easy on the eye over an extended period, and this is a serious problem with a text of this density and length — it would be fine for a magazine article, but WRECKERS OF CIVILISATION is a pretty large book. And, whilst we're on the subject of largeness, £20 is a fairly hefty

price-tag to put on even a *large* paperback — this isn't an oversize coffee-table book, it's about the same page size as HEADPRESS, and there's no interior colour. Maybe you can find a discounted copy (Mute are selling it for £18, and I got mine in a special promotion at the Royal Festival hall bookshop for £16).

All these cavils aside, however, WRECKERS... really is a marvellous book, and anyone interested in Throbbing Gristle on any but the most superficial level (and TG fans, after all, tend to be obsessive rather than dilettante) will not rest easy until they lay their hands on a copy. TG were a serious and important band, and their faith in the intelligence of their audience has been ultimately vindicated by the appearance of this book — it's a great deal better than anything that most bands ever get written about them. **Simon Collins**

I've written about this in MAKE magazine, discussing Cosey specifically in the context of artists like Cindy Sherman, this idea of the feminine image being a constructed image, and the idea that the woman artist can regain control of her own image through a form of masquerade. I was interested in presenting Cosey's work to a contemporary audience, because she contradicts artists like Mary Kelly, and their concept of the representation of women being a taboo subject, which has been a dominant idea in feminism. But recently there has been an explosion of interest in women artists who make work about their own bodies. Just like Cosey had been doing since the mid-Seventies.

Not only artists, but also theorists and activists like Camille Paglia, Pat Califia, people in the SM communities, Suzie Bright, Tuppy Owens and so on.

Cosey's work is not only underrated, it's still pretty much unknown. It's just a question of academics writing the articles and younger artists doing some research and finding these things out — and that is beginning to happen. I know Cosey gets lots of approaches from student artists who have discovered her work and are interested in finding out more. She's exhibited more in the past couple of years than she has done for quite a while.

To return to the subject of TG band photos, you see the same ones again and again.

There's not that many photos of them, when you think about it. They were quite anonymous in the sense that 20 JAZZ FUNK GREATS was the only record they allowed themselves to feature on. Chris Carter appeared in the shower on the cover of the 'United' single, but that was uncredited. They wanted to present this kind of neutral corporate/terroristic identity. And of course Peter Christopherson was working for Hipgnosis at the time, and he was totally sick of doing over-the-top album covers. They realised that doing something apparently banal and straight would make TG stand out. It was a strategy that Factory Records later adopted. The look of the photographs is very much of its time and

Gen with Thee Majesty at the Royal Festival Hall, 1st May 1999... exuding ectoplasm!

you can tie them in with the conceptual and photo-text artwork that was happening then, for example artists like Stephen Willats, who was photographing tower blocks and suburban estates. The style of photography also related to their interest in the genre of documentary. They also saw their music as a form of documentary.

I think the covers of the singles in particular are brilliant, but in general the cover art for their recordings stands in such contrast to what Sleazy was helping to produce at Hipgnosis, which is very much what we think of as typical Seventies cover art — Yes, Pink Floyd...

It was a way of differentiating yourself in the market. A lot of the covers are meant to look quite amateurish.

The austerity of them, and the deceptive banality, is remarkable.

Yes, the singles and that repeated corporate style

and the camouflage bags are really design classics now... As I said earlier, I bought 20 JAZZ FUNK GREATS just for the cover. I still can't get enough of looking at it!

What about the way that TG were ahead of their time in their promotion of, and engagement in, body art — tattooing, piercing and so on? It makes them seem bang up-to-date. In the Nineties, there's been this whole 'transgressive' culture, embracing not only the industrial culture issues we already discussed, but also body art and altered states of consciousness produced through body manipulations.

I don't think that relates to TG particularly. Gen and Cosey got their first tattoos when they were in Hull and working with COUM. They were into body modification and cutting themselves up (or applying stage make-up to look like they had), they were doing all that with COUM, but it wasn't really a big part of TG's image. It was probably the Psychic TV period when he really got into that area, and started promoting it.

In the MODERN PRIMITIVES book.

Yeah. But, having said that, a lot of his interest in that area stems from his interest in using his body as an art object, which related to his early work with COUM.

Across the TG albums released whilst they were still extant there's a growing interest in the occult, in religious ritual, and one of the most exciting things, I think, about TG, is the dynamic opposition of futurism and atavism in their work. Certainly, post-TG, Psychic TV were much more occult-focussed and more body art-oriented.

Those interests were there with TG, but they weren't really made explicit. Because TG was very much a collaborative project, you couldn't really take one member's obsessions and promote that through the group. Probably Gen's interest in this area was growing, and it was one of the reasons why the band split. Later, he could take them to their logical extreme without conflict with the others.

What's your take on the fact that Gen was recently back in Britain, playing with Psychic TV at a prestigious venue like the Royal Festival Hall?

It was great for the promotion of the book! It was also interesting to see what his latest manifestation looked like, because he's continually reinventing himself.

In fact he played two sets on the night, one with his new band, Thee Majesty, and then again later with Psychic TV, and in the earlier set he was at pains to point out that it wasn't Psychic TV. He said that several times.

It's good that he can come back and work, and hopefully he'll be back again soon.

It's nearly 20 years now since TG split, and they've never really gone away. Why are people still interested? Does it have a lot to do with Daniel Miller and Mute bringing up their back catalogue?

I think there'd still be interest even if the albums weren't available. Although TG did produce stunning music, it's more what they represent than the actual music that people find fascinating. I think they've remained significant because there hasn't been anything that's come along since that's been remotely as interesting!

Across the whole spectrum of popular music?

Yeah, and the art world too.

That's quite a bold claim!

Maybe that's because of my particular interests. Everyone looks back to the period when they were adolescents, and the late Seventies and early Eighties was my period. But the younger generation still appreciate them. A lot of it is built on myth. People are interested in all the stories that circulate around the group, and they want to check them out and know more.

There's a resurgence of interest right now, what with the publication of your

83

book, Mute bringing out all their CDs on mid-price, Gen back in the UK, the interviews with him in mainstream newspapers, and so on. Do you think this will lead to a critical reassessment of Throbbing Gristle, or are they always going to enjoy cult status?

I think critical reassessments take a lot of time. It needs people like you and me, who are writing papers, who have got the time and the interest to reassess them. The press coverage around the Royal Festival Hall event and reviews of my book have been very much just repeating the myth rather than saying something new. That's the nature of journalism, though. It takes time, in-depth research and reflection for people to start reassessing historical events. It's coming to that moment though, when you get that historical distance. Now researchers can start writing academic papers on them and as we know, the more you write about a subject, the more people disagree and the more the discourse expands.

Many seminal bands have tarnished their myths by ill-advised reunions, for instance the Sex Pistols and the Velvet Underground. A Throbbing Gristle reunion — possible or desirable?

It'd be interesting just to see them all in the same room together, let alone playing together! I don't think it's on the cards, or even desirable. They were never in it for the money, and they're not in it for the money now, so they would only reform for artistic reasons, and I think they're all pretty much fulfilled in their own projects at the moment.

I think that part of their appeal precisely is that they happened some time ago and had their moment in history.

Definitely. That's another reason for stopping the book in '81. It's a definite end to what they were doing, and the postcard they sent out is an excellent illustration of that — 'The Mission Is Terminated'.

It was a very deliberate way to end.

Yes, and it's a very good way of packaging what you're doing. The story of TG fits very well into the chapters I've created. It's almost as if they were writing the book as they were going along. You know, they were thinking about how is someone going to read this in years to come. One album per year for four years and then finishing. It wasn't necessarily a totally planned project, but they knew when it was over. They did the right thing by making a clean break.

It would have been embarrassing to have, say, Gen leave and the others carry on — like the Velvet Underground's albums after Lou Reed went, or the Doors' two post-Morrison albums.

Everybody likes a neatly framed picture, and that's what you get with TG. It's a bit confusing now with all the bootlegs floating around, which is why I don't really discuss them in the book, but the way I present it and they created it, the story — like all the best stories — has a neat beginning, middle and end.

SUGGESTED FURTHER READING

Dwyer, Simon. 'From Atavism to Zyklon B'. In Dwyer, Simon (ed), *Rapid Eye*, Rapid Eye, 1989.

Ford, Simon. *The Realization and Suppression of the Situationist International: An Annotated Bibliography 1972-1992*, AK Press, 1995.

Ford, Simon. 'Subject and (sex) Object', in *Make* magazine, No 80, Jun-Aug 1998.

Ford, Simon. *Wreckers of Civilisation: The Story of COUM Transmissions and Throbbing Gristle*, Black Dog Publishing, 1999.

P-Orridge, Genesis and Paula. 'G. and P. P-Orridge', interview in Vale, V and Juno, Andrea (eds), *Modern Primitives*, RE/Search, 1988.

Vale, V and Juno, Andrea (eds). William S. Burroughs, Throbbing Gristle, Brion Gysin, RE/Search, 1982.

Vale, V and Juno, Andrea (eds). *Industrial Culture Handbook*, RE/Search, 1983.

OF CULT RELIGIONS AND CARS THAT FLY

a look back at the future that never came

Jack Stevenson

WELCOME SPACE BROTHERS 2001

AS THE NEW MILLENNIUM approaches, 'the future' — a concept and creature quite separate from the mere recorded progression of time — has returned to haunt us in all its fantastic and frightful glory.

As the clock ticks down on the final days of the second millennium, it's time to take stock of some of the more extraordinary ways in which this chimera, the future, has taken shape and substance on film.

In a post-war America flush with optimism and prosperity, the specific and quantifiable commodity known as the future was born. It was a password to fabulous luxuries and comforts to be had in a space-age world of all things possible, a world cast in new miracle materials — many of them recently developed for military purposes — and draped in new fabrics. The future was fashionable, and one never grew tired of it because it never actually arrived.

But it did eventually end, or at least our love affair with it ended in the early Seventies when economic and environmental crises brought us all back to earth. An earth of finite resources and fragile balances. Technology became the devil, not the saviour. The concept of 'future shock' was introduced in a book by Alvin Toffler and a documentary film of the same name hosted by Orson Welles.

The golden age of the future then, as it existed in a distinctly American context made possible by post-war prosperity and privileged isolation, spanned from the late Forties to the early Seventies. Within this period a series of 'futurist' styles in fashion, architecture and consumer product culture were born and faded away. This type of consumerist futurism, distinct from the formal artistic movement, became an end in itself: it was the act of foretelling the future in some marketable, new creative expression that mattered, not the accuracy of the prediction. The styles produced by this movement, transitory by definition and wholly imaginative, dated rapidly.

Of course innumerable science-fiction films — by nature 'futurist' — have visualised the future for purposes of dramatic entertainment. But this genre of feature films, so often addressing bold and profound themes and reaching a zenith of sorts in the Thirties, was basically escapist, while the future discussed in this article was consumerist and born in the post-war period. If a portable jet pack was involved here, it was so a man could fly to work, not to Mars.

From a sociological perspective then, it's more interesting to set aside consideration of science-fiction feature filmmaking and concentrate on the depictions of the future as they were mani-

85

fest in the typical short, 16mm, non-commercial films of the 'parallel' cinemas. This encompasses a largely unheralded body of work produced by educators, religious groups and industry to be screened in classrooms, church basements and at employee training conferences.

Here in these secret corners of exhibition the illusive concept of the future took form in some of its most unusual variants.

FUTURISM FOR PROFIT: CONSUMERISM UNBOUND

DREAMING ABOUT THE FUTURE WAS A LUXURY few Americans could afford in 1940, as the country entered a war that the Allies were in the process of losing, but that didn't stop the General Motors car company from producing a 22 minute film entitled NEW HORIZONS which promoted a concept dear to the auto industry: personal — not mass — transportation. The film depicts a Sixties style futurist landscape centred around the automobile.

Although he had different ideas about the future world order, Hitler was on the same page with General Motors here. His backing of the Volkswagen, or 'people's car' which ideally every German could afford to own, was a concrete manifestation of this philosophy.

Following the war, industry was retooled to produce consumer goods, and this trend was reflected in films like the 1947 promotional, LOOKING AHEAD THROUGH ROHM AND HAAS PLEXIGLAS, which demonstrated how Plexiglas, used extensively in airplane cockpit canopies during the war, could now be used in the manufacture of paperweights, toys and vases.

The film also depicts a bizarre 'Dream Suite', a room appointed wholly with Plexiglas materials. Such wildly impractical visions were created by advertising executives training consumers to 'dream', not by designers or engineers concerned with the practicality of everyday use. 'Dream' was the key word in this era of all things possible, and in a style sense, the strange and almost surreal excesses of the products and lifestyles envisioned made them unique.

The Detroit-based Jam Handy film company — named after founder, Jamison Handy — made both of the aforementioned promotionals and stood as the most prolific and influential producer of industrial informational films until into the Seventies. Jam Handy worked with almost every major industry to promote everything from coloured telephone sets and new refrigerators

A scene from THE ARRIVAL
by the Unarius Academy.

86

to the construction of the Interstate highway system and the first major American suburb, Levittown. Its films read like a roadmap to the future as it unfolded in the Fifties.

At the heart of the future lifestyle existed the white, middle-class nuclear family which enjoyed unlimited consumer consumption and leisure time. Ad execs were not troubled by as yet non-existent issues of race and class, exploitation of the environment and unfair distribution of wealth and natural resources. The Fifties were bounded only by the limits of the ad man's imagination as he sat in front of his sketch pad and... dreamed.

"Nuclear engines, radar, retractable wings, a pressurised, water tight body?", speculated a late-Fifties promotion for the auto industry. "Perhaps by 1964 these features will be standard — your family sedan will fly and swim too. But one thing is certain: Detroit will never compromise with the sound functional engineering that has made American cars the envy of the world."

As impractical, as impossible, as doomed (and arrogant) as these consumer-driven dreams appear in retrospect, they added up to create a strange and coldly beautiful world, a modular, prefabricated and pre-assembled world that lacked only living, breathing people... people who would spring to life in films like DESIGN FOR DREAMING that featured a couple dancing around futuristic night-time cityscapes.

The idea of the future was embodied by that

Top **The FX-ATMOS, a future experimental car model designed by Ford in the 1950s. Note the tail fins that indicate the car might be able to swim or fly.**

Left **Artist's conception of life in the future that appeared in an American magazine of the Fifties.**

87

Images this page taken
from THE ARRIVAL.

most coveted of consumer commodities, the automobile, which one in every five American workers would be in some way contributing to the production of. It was here that the common man could own a piece of the dream. Automobile design is stressed in many films, one of the more extraordinary being Jam Handy's 1958 film for General Motors, AMERICAN LOOK, in which futuristic 'dream cars' are displayed alongside other futurist consumer products.

Reality was now intersecting with the dream. The common man would never get his hands on a dream car prototype which might only be displayed at an auto show, but he could buy a 1958 Thunderbird with its exaggerated tailfins and an aerodynamic design that suggested it really could fly.

A TOUCH OF MAGIC, produced in 1961, again by Generals Motors corporation, unspools as something of a 'cooled down' version of DESIGN FOR DREAMING. "All we see in A TOUCH OF MAGIC", notes industrial film historian Richard Prelinger, "are the new 1961 car models — where have all the dream cars gone? Could it be that the future has finally arrived?"

Not according to the Ford-Philco Corporation, who produced the 25 minute YEAR 1999 A.D. in 1967 to commemorate their 75th anniversary by envisioning the lifestyle of the 'family of the future'. Although a futuristic automobile makes a striking appearance at the start, the film concentrates on the more mundane accoutrements of domestic family life.

Starring popular TV game-show host Wink Martindale as the father, the predictably white family of three in YEAR 1999 A.D. sport hairstyles and social attitudes that are straight out of the Sixties. The film introduces technologies already then in the developmental stage, and accurately predicts modular home construction, home computer shopping, and the use of video monitors for surveillance. Other 'innovations', such as a closet that shakes and steams clothes clean while still on hangers, are simply absurd, while references to the 'central home computer' where the family's collective 'vital information and its "secrets"' are stored seems downright sinister.

The film attempts to present all these advances as liberating, but the overall impression

Top **Uriel, Cosmic Visionary**.
Bottom **A scene from FOR TIME OR ETERNITY**.

is of a lily white family isolated by its wealth, controlled by its computers and imprisoned in a sterile environment by supposedly beneficent technology.

FUTURISM FOR SPIRITUAL SALVATION

WHILE THE FUTURE APPEARED TO HOLD OUT the promise of boundless material gains and comforts, in its imponderable vastness it also held the key to our spiritual awareness and salvation. A very different and more complicated kind of future is depicted in the films of religious organisations as diverse as the Church Of Latter Day Saints (Mormons), The Paulists and The Unarians.

FOR TIME OR ETERNITY, a 25 minute drama directed by Wetzel Whittaker for the Morman church in 1970, visualises Mormon concepts of pre-existence and immortality where souls, not products, are the coin of the realm. Characters in Romanesque robes and Sixties flip hairdos debate spiritual issues in a cushioned and pillared state of 'pre-existence' that translucent superimpositions imbue with an aura of otherworldliness.

Whittaker's film is as woodenly moralistic as

the Jam Handy pictures are coldly if stylishly manipulative. Unburdened by any pretensions to great art, both kinds of filmmaking, however dissimilar in philosophy, deliver their messages in terms so amateurishly straight-forward that they attain a kind of uncanny sincerity. One is entering the realm of the true believer.

In 1977, the Paulist media production group in Palisades, California, produced CHRISTMAS 2025 — a half-hour episode of their INSIGHT TV series which starred many of the top actors of the period in hard-hitting dramas that sought to address the topical moral issues of the day in a relevant, modern style.

This episode, directed by Douglas Meredyth, plays out as an absurdly low-budget take on NINETEEN EIGHTY-FOUR and stars a young James Cromwell as a Christ-like figure named George in what must be the most bizarre performance of his career.

We see the soulless, frightening world of 2025 where individualism is subservient to the new God, National Efficiency; where the utterance of words like 'love' and 'Christmas', or the display of any human emotion, is punishable by death. When tempted to express natural feelings, citizens are instructed to stare into a 'reality gauge' in which their reflection appears as a skull.

The most ambitious attempt to depict the future in a spiritual context is found in a one-hour film from the mid-Eighties entitled THE ARRIVAL, a 'space saga' made by the Unarius Academy Of Science of El Cajon, California which, among other activities, offers courses in past life therapy.

"This is a true story of reincarnation", we're informed in the Academy's publications cata-

89

logue, "…inspired and re-enacted by individuals relieving their past on the continent of Lemuria 156,000 years ago. Zan, an aborigine, is contacted by an immense spaceship. In telepathic conversations with the Space Brothers, he is awakened from his psychic amnesia to become aware of the reasons for his mental frustration and discontentment with life.

"Zan relives his past as a spaceship commander of an Orion battle cruiser, at a time 200,000 years previous, when he helped to destroy an entire civilisation of people!"

Despite drawbacks like the hypnotic acting style, the use of poorly concealed skinhead wigs and a sub-STAR TREK look to the space cruiser, the film delivers its message with a naïve sincerity that is strangely effecting, and the special effects are stupendous. 'Cosmic Visionary' Ruth Norman, one of the founders of the Academy, appears in space amid sparkling blasts of colour as a kind of Good Witch Of The East from space.

PREDICTING THE FUTURE WILL CONTINUE to remain a participant sport for amateur inventors and religious proselytisers alike, and their predictions will consistently prove to out-do what finally arrives in ways both oddly compelling and wholly revealing.

We don't have to wait for the future itself to experience the strangest extremes of futuristic styles, attitudes and products, and we don't have to wait for the future to come to find salvation within it. As we've seen, all this already exists, captured on the archaic medium of celluloid 16mm wide that's clipped onto a clanking old-fashioned movie projector whose beam flickers back into the past… to take us into the future.

A future that never came.

Unarius films and literature is available from:
UNARIUS ACADEMY OF SCIENCE, 145 S. Magnolia Avenue, El Cajon, CA., 92020-4522, USA
Fax: 001-619-447-6485
Email: uriel@unarius.org

Burn, BRANDO, Burn!

Anthony Petkovich

hey hate him for being overweight. For turning down Oscars. For siding with Native American causes, shameless skirt-chasing, criticising the Jews, receiving truckloads of money for walk-on roles in films... and, sometimes, simply for having the name 'Marlon Brando.'

But, of course, such criticisms only make Brando that much more fascinating a figure.

So much has been written about the guy (the public conscience basically viewing him over the years as 'that reclusive fat fuck who eats bricks of ice cream somewhere up in the Beverly Hills') it's hard to know where to begin discussing him. Yet after Brando's appearance on The Larry King Show on April 5, 1996, and all the media attention — mostly negative — it generated because of his views on Jewish control of the Hollywood movie system, I knew some personal commentary was necessary. I had to flush this thing out of my system like a bad case of the squirts. The problems with such a venture, of course, are the controversial, unending,

unanswerable issues which inevitably revolve around any discussion of Brando... namely, race, sex, class, and — the umbrella covering it all — politics (sex obviously having become more and more a political issue as we've progressed — or regressed — from the anal-retentive Eighties into the "politically correct" Nineties).

But I especially wanted to write something about the 75-year-old Brando before he dies (...or I die, for that matter). And, as a consequence, before all the articles and spotlights about him start pouring out from every pore of the media with as much profusion as the double speak oozing from the rubbery lips of Bozo Bill Clinton. (Nixon's nose, like Pinocchio's, grew vertically, but Bill's shnaz over the last eight years seems to

91

have extended horizontally — have you noticed? — moving from golf ball to cream puff.)

Okay, so what *fresh* angle to take on Brando? *Is* there one? Well, in terms of media figures, especially the ones who, at one time, achieved megastar status, I've always been fascinated by that period in their lives when they were in a slump, down on their luck. William Shatner, for instance (after his salad days as Captain Kirk on the original STAR TREK series), making all those exploitation films back in the Seventies like THE DEVIL'S RAIN, KINGDOM OF THE SPIDERS, and (the brilliantly sleazy) IMPULSE. Elvis during his fat-Vegas days. Orson Welles ever since he'd been blacklisted for making CITI-

Faces of Brando #1.
MORITURI promotional art.

ZEN KANE. OJ Simpson after beating the murder rap for his double-billed slashing of Brown and Goldman. The rapid decline of Mike "the cannibal"/rapist Tyson.

And Brando in the Sixties.

That is, Brando in the Sixties, as well as the period immediately *prior* to his 1972 "comeback" with THE GODFATHER, and even some films *afterwards*, in which he made it brutally clear that, while he was now earning suitcases of money through top-billed 'guest' appearances in blockbusters like APOCALYPSE NOW and SUPERMAN, he just didn't give a rat's ass about the Hollywood system anymore. All he was interested in now was stuffing the insides of his baggy pockets with millions upon millions of greenbacks to figure out "what the hell (he) was going to do with the rest of (his) life," as Brando's stated in many an interview.

But it was during the Sixties, specifically, that Brando was considered "boxoffice poison." Such a slump is said to have stemmed from the 1962 MGM remake of MUTINY ON THE BOUNTY. The

filming of BOUNTY went on for almost two years in Tahiti — months fraught with seemingly unending production problems — at a final cost of close to $30 million, a staggering price at the time, though now a mere drop in the bucket. MGM ultimately blamed Brando for the film's jinxed production, claiming he was difficult, if not impossible, to work with. As a direct consequence, Brando had a hard time getting roles in big-budgeted features for quite some time, due to what he in essence called MGM's scapegoating tactics. And his public image took a nose dive, as well.

As Brando told Lawrence Grobel in a 1977 PLAYBOY interview conducted on Teti'aroa (the 13-island, South Sea atoll which the actor purchased in 1966):

You could see it in the faces of the air hostesses; you could see it when you rented a car; you could see it when you walked into a restaurant. If you've made a hit movie, then you get the full 32-teeth display in some places; and if you've faded, they say, 'Are you still making movies? I remember that picture, blah blah blah blah.' And so it goes. The point is... people are interested in people who are successful.

During this period, however, Brando starred in some of his most provocative features. Action-packed (MORITURI), political (BURN!), sexual (THE NIGHTCOMERS), these largely overlooked movies warrant a second — if not a first — look. A couple of post-GODFATHER films (THE MISSOURI BREAKS and THE ISLAND OF DR MOREAU) also contain some of his best yet — albeit for whatever reason — critically dumped-on performances.

Underproduced (MORITURI, BURN!, THE NIGHTCOMERS) or overproduced (BREAKS, MOREAU), these films may represent "low points" (definition supplied by Hollywood critics) in the actor's extensive career. Yet each is relevant since — as the politics of acting, money, activism, and Hollywood inevitably creep into most all of Brando's performances (starting perhaps with ON THE WATERFRONT) — looking at these films may give us the reason(s) why Brando made the seemingly disparaging comments he did on the King Show circa '96. Moreso, these unusual-to-bizarre flicks might also tell us why Brando, as senior citizen, is still one of the most controversial people in Hollywood.

FAT!
—gay blade, Franklin Street, SF

BRANDO?... IS HE STILL ALIVE?
—78-year-old barber, San Rafael, CA

HOW COULD A MAN DO THAT TO HIMSELF? IT'S DISGUSTING.
—drunken female, Original Joes Restaurant, SF

OH, I LOVED THE WATERFRONT THING...
—toothless bartender, Mission St., SF

LOVED THE GODFATHER... AND ON THE WATERFRONT.
—60-year-old hippie, Emeryville, CA

WELL, HE MADE IT BIG WITH ON THE WATERFRONT, RIGHT? THAT WAS HIS BIG ONE. AND THE GODFATHER.
—middle-aged male porn star, LA

MARLON BRANDO? HE'S BEEN OUT OF CONTROL FOR WAY TOO MANY YEARS!!
—out-of-control magazine art director, Emeryville, CA

Morituri
dir: Bernhard Wicki, 1965

With Brando, unfortunately, there's always this GODFATHER/ON THE WATERFRONT thing to live down. These two films, at least to the more mainstream public, are considered his best. Why? Probably because they won him Academy Awards, the ultimate symbol of achievement (other than an outrageous actor's fee) in Hollywood and, thus, the ultimate seal of approval to the easily brainwashed masses. ("The point is... people are interested in people who are successful.") Brando, as we all know, accepted his first lump of metal in 1955, yet turned down a second one in 1973.

But I was curious: What do people think of Brando these days? So I decided to conduct an experiment. Nothing fancy. Simply, when I went out with various friends to a bar, or bumped into someone on the street, I'd ask them — if the opportunity properly presented itself — "What do you think of Marlon Brando?" (trying my best to stress an immediate, instinctive response by, subtly, not allowing them to dwell too long on their answer). Here are some of the replies I received [highlighted, left]...

So, is that what he'll be remembered for? — being overweight? — for lines like, "Make 'im an offah he can't refuse"

93

and "I coulda' been a contendah, Chahlee"? So it seems. Take a look, for example, at his 1994 appearance on The Larry King Show. King could *not* stop talking about Goddfaddah/Wadduhfrun. Even if you jammed a .37 Magnum into his fish face and threatened to blast it off, the king of Kings just wouldn't shuddup already about Goddfaddah/Wadduhfrun. It all goes to show you how the American public is obsessed with perfection and success, which, again, are perfectly symbolised by 'Oscar.' But I'm equally guilty. I've made comments about Brando slopping down buckets of ice cream up in his secluded Beverly Hills reservation. Hey, it's easy to slam someone. And fun. But my feeling is that Brando's been hammered *so* many times by the media, without complaining or suing for libel/slander, it's obvious that he avoids reading such rubbish and/or has acquired a sense of humour and deep stoicism about it all.

But as a result of 'Oscar,' an interesting film like MORITURI will always remain in the shadows of Goddfaddah/Wadduhfrun. I mean, c'mon, Brando as a *Nazi*? How could you resist such a treat? Of course, he'd already done it 1958's THE YOUNG LIONS, and he'd do it again as American Nazi George Lincoln Rockwell in the US television series ROOTS 2 during the mid-Seventies. Which leaves his 1965 role in MORITURI neatly sandwiched — and all but forgotten — in-between two decades. The question is *why* did Brando chose to play a Nazi (other than for money, that is)? More specifically, in two films (YOUNG LIONS, MORITURI), why did he approach his Nazi roles from a generally more sympathetic angle?

As he writes in his 1994 autobiography, SONG MY MOTHER TAUGHT ME:

I thought the story [of THE YOUNG LIONS] should demonstrate that there are no inherently 'bad' people in the world, but that they can be easily misled... Hitler propagated the myth that Germans were a superior race and the Jews were inferior, but accepting the reverse of this is equally wrong; there are bad Jews and Germans, and decent Jews and Germans. I decided to play Christian Diestl as an illustration of one element of the human character — that is, how, because of their need to keep their myths alive, people will go to enormous lengths to ignore the negative aspects of their beliefs... In THE YOUNG LIONS I wanted to show that there were positive aspects to the Germans, as there are to all people...

In MORITURI Brando returns as a 'good' Nazi in a thoroughly gripping, downbeat action thriller. Brando plays Robert Crain, a German-born, ex-demolitions expert — and pacifist — living (or, rather, hiding out) in India during WWII. Crain is blackmailed by British intelligence officer Colonel Statter (played with memorable despicableness by Trevor Howard) into posing as a full-blood Aryan SS officer in order to sabotage (yet also save for the Allies, rather than blow up) a German freighter containing a vital shipment of rubber. The twists and turns in the plot are terrific. All the crew think Brando is a hardcore SS officer; some are SS party members themselves who defend him, while others are political prisoners who — though essentially on Brando's side — want to snuff him out because they wrongly, yet correctly, think he's a Nazi. Throughout the film, Crain creeps about the grimy ship, trying to locate the scuttling charges. As he gradually finds one charge after another, Crain breathlessly disarms them, trying his best to also avoid detection. Director Wicki's build-up of tension and suspense here — and throughout MORITURI — is superb. The film also has a gritty, all-male, industrial edge to it. Steam-filled engine rooms. Rusty metal. Oily machinery. Bitter-cold sea weather. Hard, leathery characters.

It's a grey, bleak world in MORITURI.

But perhaps the most amazing scene takes place when Brando is not even on the screen — during the American prisoners' gangbang of a young Jewess named Esther (played by the fetching Janet Margolin). After a load of American POWs and Esther (most probably on her way to the death camps) are brought on board the German freighter, Crain is intent on somehow getting the GIs to help him take over the ship. But there's no way of getting a message to the well-guarded prisoners... except, perhaps, through the much-hated Jewess. Crain quickly concocts a reason to have her sent down into the hold with the prisoners. But before having her incarcerated — as well as trying to reinforce his cover as a Nazi — he brutally slaps her in the face. "I don't wish to interfere," he tells another Party member, as he wipes the Jewess' 'scent' off his hands with a handkerchief," but this is... disgusting." Here we have a perfect example of Brando showing the need for humanity by playing a thoroughly ugly, inhuman character.

Once among the POWs, the Jewess tries her best to convince them to storm the Germans. But they refuse to do so. Instead they're far more interested in having it off with her.

"You can have it," she tells the Americans, "Just promise you'll help [Crain]."

We really don't find out what the POWs' decision is, until later, when Crain finds Esther in a corner of the ship, alone; her clothes are on, but she's totally spent. It's obvious that the Americans took her up on her offer. Now how often was *that* sort of thing even *implied* in other Hollywood movies around this period? Was it? Did I miss something?

Yet despite all the good things going for MORITURI, Brando recalls little of it.

"I enjoyed a picture called SABOTEUR: CODE NAME MORITURI," he states in SONGS, "because my pals Wally Cox and

Billy Redfield were in it." Brando also remembers co-star Yul Brynner teaching him the importance of lighting on the set... but that's about it.

What's most interesting about MORITURI is that, moralistically, it's not a black-and-white film. Yes, the Jews are viewed here with sympathy. But so are a good number of Germans who resist Hitler's regime. It's actually the Americans (gangbanging the Jewess) and the Brits (blackmailing Crain) who are depicted as equally cold and treacherous as the Nazis.

But as time passed, Brando's would make his political positions on other peoples' suffering — not just the pain endured by the Jews in WWII — dead clear through various other movies.

Burn! (aka Quemada!)
dir: Gillo Pontecorvo, 1968

Basically a spaghetti western cleverly disguised as a political action film, BURN! contains what Brando believes is some of his finest work. And he's right. His portrayal of British mercenary Sir William Walker is so low key, you almost miss it if you aren't paying attention. But watch, for instance, how his face contorts into a vicious snarl when he calls a Negro slave a "black ape."

BURN! takes place on the fictional Caribbean island of Quemada, circa 1845. The island — made up of 200,000 inhabitants, of whom only 5,000 are Europeans — is, for the most part, economically supported by sugar-cane plantations, which are controlled by the Portuguese but worked by the black slaves. Sir William Walker is an agent who, by Her Majesty's (satanic) request, must elbow the Portuguese out of Quemada, and thus secure control of the sugar cane industry — at whatever cost. Franco Solinas and Giorgio Alorio's well-thought-out script has Walker's mission broken up into three parts (courtesy of

95

the video boxcover's liner notes): "...Trick the slaves into revolt, grab the sugar trade for England, then return the slaves to servitude." Walker's major pawn in this game of revolution is José Dolores (Evaristo Marquez), a simple-minded plantation worker who, at first, is a naïve puppet enlisted to create civil unrest and chaos amongst the natives. Yet once his hands are soaked with the blood of his own people, Dolores realises that the new boss — Britain — is no better than the old one. Only the accents have changed. Much to Walker's chagrin, Dolores wages a bloody guerrilla war against the arrogant white colonialists. In turn, Walker must now destroy the 'monster' he created in Dolores.

Most critics no doubt dump on this film simply because it's dubbed. That, of course, is one of the reasons why I love it. I mean, how many spaghetti westerns has Brando made? Exactly. So what's not to love about BURN!?

Yet aside from the engaging story — and the wonderfully atrocious dubbing — Brando's unpredictable, dynamic characterisation of Sir William Walker thoroughly carries the film. So many of Brando's politically based films have failed due to dry storylines (THE UGLY AMERICAN, where you have to wonder *why* they didn't stick to the first-rate novel by Lederer and Burdick), uninteresting characters (the bland cardinal in CHRISTOPHER COLUMBUS), and heavy-handed political statements (the embarrassingly self-conscious approach to South African apartheid in A DRY WHITE SEASON, though it's rewarding seeing Donald Sutherland and Brando in a film together). Sir William Walker, however, is one of his most fascinatingly contradictory characters, in what you'd think would typically be a dull political (is that redundant?) film. Gentleman and lout, revolutionary and scoundrel, instigator and coward, Walker is nothing if not a

dual-faced opportunist. He dresses impeccably, with pastel scarves, wide-brimmed hats, and flashy coat tails. Yet his scheming eyes shift at the most unexpected moments like an opium addict. At one point, over cigars and brandy, Walker suavely tries to seduce a Quemada council into rebelling against the Portuguese. He cleverly incorporates the "impertinent metaphor" of the wife and whore when comparing the constricting laws, vetoes, and taxes imposed by foreign (i.e., Portuguese) domination to that of a totally independent state.

"Gentlemen, which do you find more convenient?" Walker artfully inquires...

A wife?... or one of these mulatto 'girls'? I'm speaking strictly in terms of economics: What is the cost of the product? What does the product yield? The product in this case being love... purely physical love since the sentiments obviously play no part in economics... A wife must be provided with a home, food, with dresses, medical attention... But with a prostitute, it's quite a different matter, isn't it?... she's yours only when you need her, you pay her only for that service... and you pay her *by the hour*. Which is more important?... and more convenient? — a slave or a paid worker?

Yet in the following scene, the unpredictable Walker may very well be beating a slave's face raw with the back of his hand, hammering him, forcing the poor sap to call his own mother a "whore."

Interestingly enough, Brando was fighting his own private little war with director Gillo Pontecorvo throughout the filming of BURN!, shot over a period of six months in the humid, tropical city of Cartagena, Columbia. The working conditions were not only physically draining, according to Brando, but "wild," as well.

In SONGS he writes,

Everybody smoked a strong variety of marijuana called Colombian Red, and the crew was stoned most of the time. For some reason making a movie in Cartagena attracted a lot of women from Brazil. Dozens of them showed up, mostly upper-class women from good families, and they wanted to sleep with everybody. After they went home, some told me, they intended to see a doctor who would sew up their hymens so that when they got married their husbands would think they were virgins. The doctors in Rio must have made a lot of money from that movie.

But it was the off-screen tension between Brando and Pontecorvo which nearly culminated in a much larger blood burst.

"Gillo's superstitions knew no bounds," Brando recalls.

If somebody spilled salt, Gillo had to run around the table and throw more salt on the ground in a certain pattern dictated by him; if wine was spilled, he made the guilty party dip a finger in the wine and daub it behind each ear of everyone at the table... I began doing things to irritate Gillo... once I opened the door of my caravan, shone a mirror on him and yelled, 'Hey, Gillo, *buon giorno*,' and then smashed the mirror. In Gillo's eyes breaking a mirror was a direct invitation to the devil to enter your life. Once he raised his glass at lunch in a toast and said, 'Salute.' I raised my glass while everybody drank, then spilled my wine with a flourish on the ground, which to Gillo was the supreme insult. [Gillo eventually] got a gun and stuck it in his belt, and I started carrying a knife. Years before, I'd practised knife-throwing and was fairly accurate at distances up to about eighteen feet, so sometimes I took out my knife and hurled it at a wall or post a few feet from him. He shuddered slightly, put his hand on his waist, rested it on the butt of his gun and then eyed me sternly, letting me know that he was ready for battle, too.

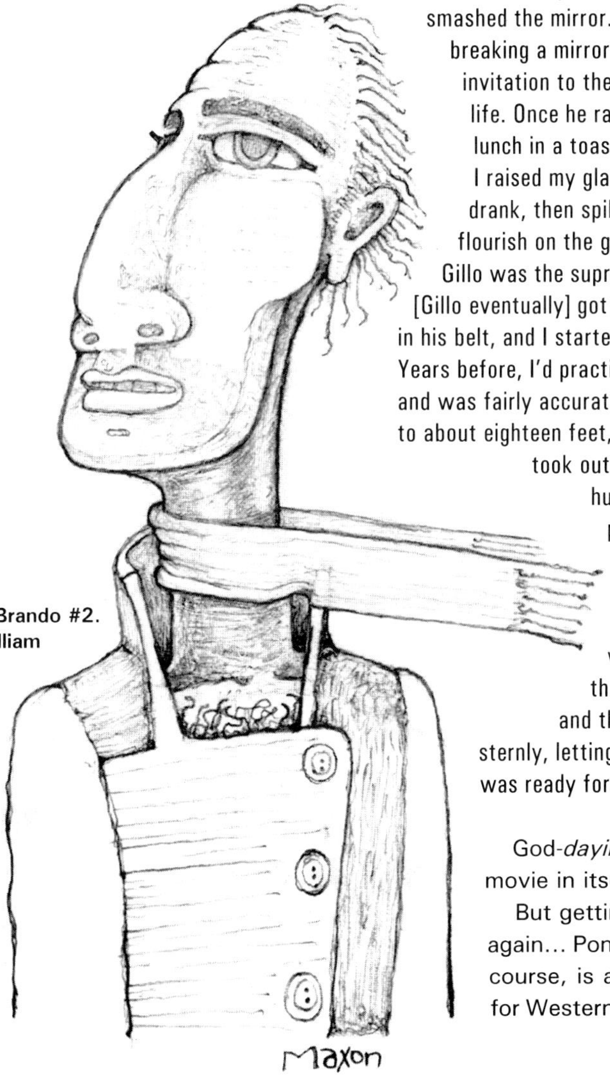

God-*dayim*! Sounds like a movie in itself, doesn't it?

But getting 'serious' once again... Pontecorvo's film, of course, is a slap in the face for Western imperialism. The

Faces of Brando #2.
As Sir William Walker in BURN!

© Maxon Crumb

Maxon

97

slaves of Quemada are merely metaphors for those non-white foreigners (past and present) oppressed under the self-righteous arm of the Westerner, in this case the British and Portuguese. Consequently, the victims in BURN! could very well have been the North or South Vietnamese during the Sixties and Seventies, Native Americans during the European settlement of the US, or black slaves in pre-Civil War America. The white European in Pontecorvo's sweeping saga is the harbinger of all that is corrupt, gluttonous, and evil. Personally, I've recently seen the same thing happening in Southeast Asia, though on a far less bloody scale (for now, that is). Non-Governmental Organisations (NGOs), backed by Western dollars, are trying to 'improve' centuries-old cultures by wiping out prostitution and what they claim is "sexual slavery." It's the same ol' crap: the world *must* be identical to that of the Westerner, who represents all that is 'civilised,' 'decent,' and, heaven help us, 'modern.' And if you've ever seen these NGO representatives in 'action,' you'll know that they drive around in the best cars, eat at the finest restaurants, buy the most expensive foods from the most exclusive supermarkets (food which their native 'subjects' most probably have never tasted, let alone seen), have pampered work hours slanted towards a life of leisure rather than charity, and — understandably when you take all these perks into consideration — are very secretive about their organisations, obviously not wishing to blow the 'good life' based, almost exclusively, on the Western taxpayer's money.

Getting back to BURN!, however, Pontecorvo's film is also important in that it shows Brando's shift away from the Jews and towards other peoples' suffering: again, the Vietnamese ("The soldiers," he writes in SONGS, "who massacred the villagers at My Lai were no

more inherently evil than the Germans soldiers who committed atrocities in World War II... "), the blacks during the Civil Rights Movement, and the modern Native American. Oddly enough, I know various people who would *like* to openly appreciate Brando's films, but refuse to do so because of his politics.

But Brando seems an almost self-admitted failed liberal.

As he explains his involvement with the Civil Rights Movement during the late Sixties in SONGS:

> I was hungry for information about the [Black] Panthers and still trying to understand what it was like to be a black man in America... At Bobby Hutton's funeral, I began... to understand... that I was an outsider... Those Panthers made me realise how protected my life had been as a white person, and how, despite a lifetime of searching, curiosity and empathy, I would never understand what it was to be black.

Duh!

Why does Brando even *want* to be black? Similarly, why would a *black* man want to be *white*? Either way, it ain't gonna happen... not in this lifetime at least. (Ironically, Brando cut off all ties with the Black Panthers before he'd finished filming BURN!)

But Brando becomes *really* corny at the end of the same chapter, wherein he fully unloads a wheelbarrow of pity for African-Americans.

> It is not the racism of the Ku Klux Klan, which everybody recognises is a ship of fools, that debilitates blacks, but the subtle, insidious racism that robs black children of pride and self-esteem so that they never have a chance.

Brando is right about the KKK, but he's syrupy and embarrassingly naïve in his appraisal of black and white relations.

To me, there's no bigger racist and hypocrite than a white bastard/cunt who treats blacks better than whites simply because they're black. Where's the equality *there*? I've met scores of decent black people, but I don't treat them as if they're special. I treat them the same I would the other guy, be he/she white or black. But, call me a hypocrite if you will, I'm also cautious when hoofin' it through those parts of Oakland and San Francisco densely populated with blacks. I don't have bodyguards (as do armchair liberals and black ass-kissers like Warren Beatty, Mick Jagger, Jimmy "Puff Daddy" Page, Steven Spielberg, and, yes, Brando) protecting me from the urban elements. Yeah, I do my best to take blacks on an individual basis, but I've also been conditioned from bad experiences (muggings, robberies) to take them with a good dose of awareness when, again, surfin' their turf.

Not to say that I can't get along with blacks.

I'll give you an example...

It happened about a year ago in San Francisco, on 7ᵗʰ and Market Streets. My friend Nick and I had been editing an amateur film all day. Finally, after about twelve hours of non-stop work, we decided to call it a night. It was around 11:30 PM. Not terribly late, but we were fried, dead on our feet. The editing wasn't going too well, either, and I was frustrated as hell. And now I had to drive (what seemed at the time) a fairly long distance to get to bed.

Nevertheless, what Nick and I wanted now was a drink.

So we headed into a nearby liquor store. The area, by this time, was crawling with plenty of nightlife. But I'd become pretty numb to it all.

Or so I thought.

As I walked into the store, a short black guy in his late forties was walking out. I was too tired to even eyeball the dude (sometimes, as we all know, it just takes a simple look to set people off). Still, he gave me a hideously contorted look and literally spat out at me, "Kill all white people!"

Well, that was it. I'd had it.

I didn't even bother turning around to confront the nutso black bastard. I just let him walk on his merry way. Instead I went into the store… and blew my cork.

"That's right!" I said "Kill all white people. KILL all white people! Kill ALL white people! Kill all WHITE people!" The street folk in the store — all of them black — quietly, nervously moved out of my way, as if I was some kind of raving, rabid lunatic. Which, of course, I was.

"Sick," one black guy said, shaking his head as he looked at me and stumbled out of the store with his quart. Oh, so *I* was sick. But what about the black prick who initially spat out, "Kill all white people" at me? *He* wasn't sick?

It didn't matter at this point. Call me "sick." Call me what you will. I just kept barking as I rummaged around one of the refrigerators looking for something to drink. "Kill all white people! That's right. Kill all white people!"

Ultimately, it was a pair of black dudes in their late twenties who brought me back down to earth.

The two guys had no idea what wavelength I was on, just that I was speaking some sort of strange truth — "Kill all white people!" — which they probably believed.

Then one of them spoke up. "Kill all black people," he said, chuckling to his friend, who likewise chuckled.

I paused. Thought for a moment. And chuckled, too.

That was it! A meeting of minds — through mutual frustration, anger… and insanity.

White man: "Kill all white people!"
Black man: "Kill all black people!"
Total equality. Total understanding.
Now, I ask you, how often have you

99

seen an inner-city black say, "Kill all black people"? Better still, how many *white* folk do you know who've been *able* to get blacks to say that?... of their own volition? Thank you.

But that's not all.

Afterwards, when I went outside the store and had a smoke with Nick, both of us calmly stood right next to the two black dudes, who were also casually smoking. I didn't bother them. And they didn't bother us.

Equality and understanding, on the street level. It was a Kodak moment.

But, looking back at your more phoney liberals in relation to race in America, I had a white manager who once told me that "we whites" have to accept centuries of "bad karma" for what we did to the blacks during the days of slavery in America. That's funny. How is it that *I* am responsible for what some Southern cotton plantation owners did over 200 years ago? I flat out told the fool that I've been robbed and attacked by blacks without provocation, and yet I've never robbed or attacked a black myself. So, I asked him, are these episodes of violence, therefore, examples of "bad karma" reaped by yours truly for those actions perpetrated by Americans before the Civil War, even though I

Faces of Brando #3.
As Peter Quint in
THE NIGHTCOMERS.

DoGGER
'99

consider myself a fairly responsible citizen? My slob-of-a-manager was tongue-tied. I'm sure he would have loved to respond in the affirmative. But he couldn't. Either way, his argument was lame, ridiculous. C'mon, get over it, bub. Time for a reality check.

Okay, okay... back to Pontecorvo's film...

Like the issue of politics in MORITURI, BURN! is not a clear-cut movie when it comes to the subjects of race and heroism, making it all the more interesting. Yes, the white man cannot stomach the black man's rum, and, likewise, the slave finds his master's whiskey repugnant. But black conservatives in the film raise arms against black guerrillas, as much as black slaves battle white imperialists. Also, there's the question of Sir William Walker: Is he hero or villain? Again, he's a bit of both. But, moreso, Walker is a hired gun caught in the crossfire. It's big business — in this case the sugar corporations — who represent the evil forces initiating, supporting, and ultimately profiting from large-scale battle, be it genocide of the Native American, or full-scale war in Vietnam, the Persian Gulf, and the former Republic of Yugoslavia.

Brando probably considers BURN! one of his best films because it's the closest his fiction came to imitating, to mirroring the reality of his life at the time, as well as his lifelong affection for the underdog. And the fact that it *wasn't* produced on Hollywood soil (which is surely why it received almost zero distribution) undoubtedly places it all the closer to his heart.

The Nightcomers
dir: Michael Winner, 1972

Best known as 'the film Brando made immediately before THE GODFATHER,' THE NIGHTCOMERS is a "sexy shocker" which not only contains one of the actor's most

unpredictable characters (the wild Irishman Peter Quint), but is also director Winner's obvious, yet effective, nod to class consciousness.

A clever prequel to Henry James' ghost story TURN OF THE SCREW, THE NIGHTCOMERS concerns the bizarre, unorthodox 'education' of two upper-class children (Miles and Flora) in an isolated English mansion. Recently orphaned, Miles, 12, and Flora, 13, are left to the care of the housekeeper Mrs Grose (played by Thora Hird) and the nanny Miss Jessel (Stephanie Beacham). The only man on the grounds is Peter Quint, recently demoted from valet to gardener. Quint, however, sets out to undermine the entire estate. He mocks Mrs. Grose, ravishes Miss Jessel, and toys with the childrens' emotions.

Difficult to pin down, Quint is a Jekyll-Hyde type whose ribald, at times twisted nature constantly makes him both entertaining and engrossing. He frequently acts like a big brother to the children, playing hide-and-go-seek with them, teaching them archery, kiting, telling them engaging anecdotes about Irish rogues and farting horses. Yet he's also a demon in disguise. Early on in the story, for instance, as a harmless 'joke,' Quint puts a cigar in a frog's mouth to amuse Flora and Miles. Yet the frog, unable to stop inhaling the smoke, rapidly inflates and bursts. Flora is horrified while Miles is fascinated; both terror and titillation being the emotions which seem to motivate Quint. He also feeds the childrens' minds with thoughts of death, not realising the extreme extent to which they are truly impressionable.

"Ah," Quint at one point tells Miles and Flora in his heavy brogue, "if you really love a woman, you want to see her dead."

The children, in turn, taking Quint's words on face value, decide to murder him and his lover Miss Jessel — in the most gruesome fashions, typical of the vivid imagination of children — so that they might "be together" in the after-life.

Naturally it's Quint's sadistic, lustful antics with the submissive Miss Jessel which ultimately make THE NIGHTCOMERS — as the video boxcover so blatantly, yet correctly, labels it — a "sexy shocker." Actually, it's Jessel's outward prudishness in public which makes Quint's rough sex with her in those dark, shadowy quarters of the estate all the more erotic. During one such nocturnal tryst, Quint ties up Miss Jessel, binding her with rope her until she literally re-sembles a human box. He then forces her to suck him off. In the same scene, through an effective series of lap dis-solves, Winner shows Quint screwing the disturbed yet similarly excited Jessel. Beacham, who plays Jessel, was sup-posedly 21-years-old at the time... and a choice specimen, indeed. Tight, smooth, white skin. An angular, distinc-tive face. Long, flowing red hair. Large, fresh, swimmingly swollen tits with pert nipples. I only wish we could have seen more of her fantastic fanny ['Fanny' in the American context! —Ed.], which is unfortunately shielded in all the sex scenes, but most definitely a winning bumper, even when viewed beneath the thick cover of Beacham's long, Victo-rian-style gowns.

But in spite of Quint's dark side, what makes him a sympathetic character are the constant insults he endures from the harsh, class-conscious tongues of Miss Jessel and Mrs Grose.

Towards the start of the film, Miss Jessel tells her secret lover Quint — who is symbolically plucking a chicken behind the mansion — that he better run and say goodbye to the orphans' departing uncle/guardian if he wants to keep his job.

"Well, why don't ye come along with me then," Quint inquires.

"I don't want to be seen with you,"

Miss Jessel icily tells him. Yet, hypo-crite that she is, Jessel is more than willing to fuck Quint under cover of night, hence the film's title.

"You're scum, Quint," Mrs Gross also snaps at him as the beer-bellied Irish-man takes the liberty of trying on his dead master's ill-fitting clothes back in the mansion. "Why don't you go back to the stable where scum belongs?" she continues.

Quint is quick to point out, however, the singular grotesqueness of Mrs Grose, as he notices something crawling about in her greying mane.

"And there's a lice as big as me fin-ger in your hair," chuckles the down-to-earth Irishman. "Would ya' be rottin'?"

Grose also calls him, just for the record, a "bastard" and an "evil pig," which I guess is a step up from, say, the "scum-sucking pig" reference in ONE-EYED JACKS.

And in the movie's climactic love se-quence, when Quint tries his best to be a "gentleman" with Miss Jessel, he's unexpectedly slammed once again.

"I need you with me, Margaret," Quint tells Jessel; this time, however, he's well-dressed, perfumed, and — unchar-acteristically with Miss Jessel — gentle. "I need you to stay with me."

Yet Jessel is anything but romantic. "To live with you in your pig sty?" she coolly responds.

At this point, Quint goes bonkers, responding to her figurative slap in the face with literal ones, savagely beating her until she's black and blue all over. The question is: why did she bait him? Is Jessel properly conditioned to enjoy Quint's sadism? Is she living out a fan-tasy of being overtaken, dominated, and raped by a man? Or does she, as an Eng-lish governess, firmly believe that a woman will never marry a man like Quint, far below her station and social class? All such questions only make THE NIGHTCOMERS that much more curious a picture. What's also nice about Winner's film is that Quint appears throughout it, rather than in bits and pieces, as would become Brando's style after the enormous financial and critical successes of THE GODFATHER and LAST TANGO IN PARIS.

Fascinatingly enough, THE NIGHTCOMERS also gives us an example of life imitating art. For it was during the filming in England that the actor discovered, as he did with the Black Panthers in the late Sixties, the problems his profession had created in terms of his own social status. In SONGS he recalls how director Michael Winner had arranged a magnificent dining room — containing the finest linen, cutlery, and china — in a country mansion near Cambridge, where they were shooting. The room, he told Brando, was expressly reserved for the actor, his close friends, and Winner himself.

Brando writes:

I didn't find that type of class distinction appropriate, and wanted to eat with the other actors and members of the crew, but Michael said, 'Marlon, I am sorry to say this, but the crew do not wish you to eat with them. They are much happier in the next-door canteen eating on their own and not worrying about the overpowering presence of their employers and a major star.'
I left, and went into the canteen room, sat down at the table, and when the other actors and crew members entered holding their lunch trays, I held up my hand urging them to sit near me, but they all walked on. 'Marlon,' Michael said, 'it's no good waving your arms about; none of these people are going to sit with us. They'd all much rather gossip among themselves and they're terrified of you.' Apparently he was right, because no one would sit near me except him and my friends from the other room.

But, aside from the issues of caste —

both on and off camera — what's also noteworthy about THE NIGHTCOMERS is that it's often referred to as a "lurid" movie, no doubt because of the male-initiated and controlled sado-masochistic sex. Funnily enough, the much more technically pornographic, at times equally brutal, LAST TANGO IN PARIS is far more accepted by the art-house crowd. My theory is that TANGO is better-received because Brando's sexually aggressive character of Paul receives his 'just deserts' in the end (by taking a fatal bullet from co-star Maria Schneider). And, of course, because by then — 1973 — Brando was once again a big star (though he does put in one of his best-ever performances in TANGO). At the end of THE NIGHTCOMERS, on the other hand, Quint bites the big one, as well. But so does his lover Miss Jessel. Quint, therefore, might *not* be seen as getting what he 'deserves' as does Paul in TANGO. And, following through on James' TURN OF THE SCREW, Quint ultimately *returns* to the world as a tortured — yet torturing — ghost. So, in that respect, he doesn't really die, does he? But, then again, neither does Miss Jessel, who similarly returns as a haunting spirit.

In some ways, "lurid" is one of those words which is, generally speaking, worse than "pornographic" in that it implies all things ugly, seedy, ghastly. And, hey, there's nothing wrong with that. Actually, when I read one critic's description of THE NIGHTCOMERS as "lurid," I rushed out to find the thing. But how do you gauge something like luridness? It's so subjective. I mean, is shoving a stick of butter up a woman's ass and then sodomising her more or less "lurid" than tying her up and forcing her to blow you?

Well, either way, the 'sex' is there... in both films.

Actually, if you want "lurid," read the MUTINY ON THE BOUNTY chapter in Peter Manso's 1994 biography on Brando. Ironically, the actor states that "ersatz"

103

sex took place in front of the camera for both the sexually charged NIGHTCOMERS and LAST TANGO, yet in the more classical Hollywood production of BOUNTY, it was nothing but sex, sex, and more sex for male Westerners after they'd landed in Tahiti both on and — more entertainingly — off camera. Manso writes about the female Tahitian "vahines" ("voluptuous beauties, some no more than 16" years old) who constantly "invaded" the male cast members' quarters looking for sex; about Brando diving head-first into this sexual "free-for-all," telling friends lines to the effect of, "I can't talk to you until I get somebody over to give me a blow job"; about the many male cast members getting the clap... The debauchery on the exotic set of MUTINY is, to say the least, overwhelming... and a great read.

Yet it's Brando's complicated, non-'black-and-white' portrayal of Peter Quint in THE NIGHTCOMERS which truly makes the movie worthy of repeated viewings. And Brando obviously fell in love with the character, as large chunks of his wonderfully spontaneous Irishman would pop up only four years later courtesy of the weird killer Robert E. Lee Clayton in director Arthur Penn's first western since LITTLE BIG MAN.

The Missouri Breaks
dir: Arthur Penn, 1976

In some ways I think of my middle age as the Fuck You Years.
— Brando, SONGS, p. 337

THE MISSOURI BREAKS was definitely 52-year-old Brando's way of saying "Fuck You" to Hollywood — while obviously having a grand time in front of the camera.

Majestically shot by director of photography Michael Butler in the hot, boundless plains of Montana, BREAKS is a simple western — with, surprisingly, *no* connection to the issue of Native American rights. Set in Montana during the 1880s, BREAKS concerns hired killer Robert E. Lee Clayton (Brando) who is commissioned to liquidate a band of horse thieves (Jack Nicholson and motley crew). According to director Penn, the script wasn't finished when they began filming in Montana, which explains a number of abrupt cuts in the story. Consequently, actors like Nicholson, Harry Dean Stanton, and Randy Quaid ramble through their roles, idiotically smiling at each other as if waiting for the other guy to, quite literally, come up with the next line. The main problem is that Nicholson and the 'good guys' in BREAKS are not that terribly interesting... let alone likeable. Rather, they come across as a pack of unwashed, witless morons.

Brando, however, has a field day. Without the constrictions of pre-written dialogue, he lets his unorthodox ideas run wild, magnificently interpreting his character as a shrewd loony and a master of disguise. At one moment he's wearing a preacher's collar and reflectively singing "Life Is Like A Mountain Railroad" with trusty mandolin, while the next he's dressed up like Whistler's mother and hideously torching horse thieves as they sleep. His accent wildly fluctuates without warning — from Irishman to Englishman, from German to American — with Brando, as usual, delivering each and every tongue with flawless dexterity. His character — like that of Robert Lee Clayton's 'cousin' Peter Quint — crackles with charisma, cunning, and creepiness. Other moments of inspired lunacy include Brando's outrageous manhandling of a corpse packed in ice during a solemn wake, sticking a cricket in horse thief Randy Quaid's mouth as the latter sleeps, and Clayton's bizarre monologues with both his horse and mule(!).

© MGM Home Entertainment

MARLON BRANDO JACK NICHOLSON

THE MISSOURI BREAKS

Faces of Brando #4.
Promotional art for THE MISSOURI BREAKS.

"A search among the more than three thousand western movies made since the start of the sound era," writes Tony Thomas in THE FILMS OF MARLON BRANDO, "is not likely to turn up a character more bizarre than Robert Lee Clayton."

But despite this unique performance, BREAKS is considered a major "disappointment." As a teenager back in the Seventies I recall how United Artists transparently built up the promotion of BREAKS, claiming it would be the film of the year, starring two Academy Award-winning actors — Brando/Nicholson — in their first film together. It was like some spectacular boxing match with two world-class heavyweights pitted against one another. Brando was still flying high in the critics circle with LAST TANGO, as was Nicholson with ONE FLEW OVER THE CUCKOO'S NEST. But when the thing finally came out, few critics had anything good to say about BREAKS (which, of course, only made me all the more eager to see it). Leonard Maltin called it a "bomb" and "one of the worst 'big' movies ever made." Chris Hodenfield in his on-the-set article for the May '76 issue of ROLLING STONE magazine wrote, "THE MISSOURI BREAKS was not a movie, it was a business proposition." But, hey, aren't they all? Nicholson — second billed to Brando — received $1 million and a percentage of the film, while Brando received $1,250,000 and a similar percentage. These salaries were unheard of in 1976, but they're nothing now when compared to the $20 million which guys like Stallone, Schwarzenegger, and (Jim) Carrey have been known to pocket per flick.

Which, of course, only begs the question: Is "art" more important than the almighty dollar in world of the Hollywood actor? No, Brando makes it painfully clear in his 1977 PLAYBOY interview with Lawrence Grobel.

"In your heart of hearts," he tells Grobel, "you know perfectly well that movie stars aren't artists."

"But there are times," the reporter argues, "when you can capture moments in a film or a play that are memorable, that have meaning..."

"A prostitute can capture a moment! A prostitute can give you all kinds of wonderful excitement and inspiration and make you think that nirvana has arrived on the two o'clock plane, and it ain't necessarily so... acting is just hustling. Some people are hustling money, some power."

Brando was definitely hustling for both in BREAKS.

Not only was the actor's (then) exorbitant fee his way of 'sticking it' to Hollywood for a role which he whimsically made up on location, but, when he wasn't 'working' — much to the annoy-

BURN, BRANDO, BURN!

ance of producers and publicity folk — Brando, writes Tony Thomas, whittled away his time "examining the behaviour of grasshoppers, collecting stones from the Yellowstone River, playing his bongo drums in his trailer, studying solar energy, and attempting to reduce his weight, by this time close to 250 pounds."

Penn's film is a mess. No doubt about it. Much like 1966's THE CHASE (Penn's first feature with Brando), the story is muddled, and at times the scenes are painfully slow and dull. But, critics or no, it's a treat seeing Brando more than willing *not* to take himself too seriously in BREAKS, especially after his previous critical victories with GODFATHER and TANGO. And, when all's said and done, if BREAKS *is*, let's just say for the sake of 'art,' nothing more than an acting contest between Seventies monoliths Brando and Nicholson, then Jack most certainly lost, baby.

The Island of Dr. Moreau
dir: John Frankenheimer, 1996
The best thing Brando's done since THE MISSOURI BREAKS. Oh, he's memorable in ROOTS 2, SUPERMAN, and APOCALYPSE NOW. But his Moreau is just... insane. The critics, of course, panned it because they thought Brando at this point was an "anti-Semite." Which he wasn't. But we'll get to that volatile topic soon enough.

HG Wells' 1896 novel takes place on a remote Pacific island where the god-like character of Dr Moreau surgically carves humanoids out of animals (dogs, hyenas, leopards, apes, goats, horses) inhabiting the isle. Moreau ultimately dubs these pseudohumans his "Beast Folk." They speak English, walk as bipeds, and even develop their own religion, at the centre of which is, naturally, Moreau the "Father." But, as is the case with all Wellsian characters playing God

and vainly attempting to subvert and control nature through science, Moreau loses. The experiment goes awry, with the Beast Folk violently revolting against their 'creator' and inevitably reverting back to their natural, more primitive states.

Frankenheimer's 1996 film (did the producers know they were, in fact, celebrating the book's 100th anniversary?) brings Wells' tale up to date by having the good doctor fuse animals with human genes and thus create his man-beasts. Strictly as a Hollywood production, the end result is technically impressive, with Stan Winston's monster makeup reeking with creepiness, and the actors playing Moreau's "children" doing thoroughly believable jobs.

And Brando is as good here as he's ever been. Absolutely "out of control." If you haven't seen it, rent it. And if you have seen it, you know what I'm blabbin' about. Like a Fellini-esque pope, Brando's Moreau has his grotesque beings — or "Moreauvians" as I call them — carry him in a sort of mock popemobile; he also occasionally dons black goggles, lipstick, medicated white cream, and an insect net over his face to protect himself from ("can you feel it?") the heat; additionally, Moreau sports buck teeth; an affected English accent; is constantly accompanied by a gargoyle-like midget sidekick named "Majai" (Nelson De La Rosa, reportedly the smallest man in the world) who wears identical clothes; and, in one amazingly over-the-top scene, Moreau actually tries to teach a small group of his monsters how to play Schoenberg on the piano. Brando's performance stands up well next to — and independent of — Laughton's rendition of Moreau in ISLAND OF LOST SOULS, and positively blows Burt Lancaster's 1977 version off the fuckin' island. In fact, you're actually saddened to see Brando exit the film after he's offed by the monsters (just as he is in Wells' book)... his character is that captivating and fun. Yet Frankenheimer's taut direction — despite David Thewlis' overacting — keeps the film entertaining throughout, as does Val Kilmer's spaced-out rendition of Montgomery the "beast keeper," especially when Montgomery goes nuts after Moreau's murder and actually thinks he's *become* the doctor.

Though critics for the most part hated Brando's rendition of Moreau (THE S.F. CHRONICLE labelled his performance "tired Brando"), it's obvious that the actor had a blast drawing this over-the-top portrait of the mad, misunderstood scientist in exile. And the updated storyline fits in well with certain political issues (global warming and cloning among them) on Brando's agenda.

"It's true that I was attracted to this project," he said, "because it offered the possibility of putting into dramatic form the issue of genetics, its research and application, and its historical applicability to the course of development of mankind."

"[Brando] came up with ideas nobody would have thought of," said executive producer Tim Zinnemann. "When you first hear him talk about the direction he plans, it's so shocking and bizarre that you don't think it's going to work. Then after a couple of days you can't imagine how the character could have been played any other way."

Brando, by the way — the same crazy guy who wanted to play Superman's dad as a "large bagel"(!) — initially wanted to play Moreau as an Hasidic Jew? Can you imagine?

When I mentioned to a friend how I found it incredible that the Marlon Man didn't find his calling in horror film years ago — after, say, a feature like THE NIGHTCOMERS — he simply responded with, "Wasn't *every* film he did a horror film?" And if you look at many of his roles, you do find one strange anti-hero after another... some far more monstrous

than others, Stanley Kowalski perhaps taking the cake as his most heinous. Then there's Johnny the leather-clad rebel in THE WILD ONE, Sky Masterson the womanising gambler in GUYS AND DOLLS, Rio the revenge-obsessed gunslinger in ONE-EYED JACKS, Fletcher Christian the foppish mutineer in MUTINY ON THE BOUNTY, Freddy the con artist in BEDTIME STORY, Major Weldon Penderton the dangerously repressed homosexual in REFLECTIONS IN A GOLDEN EYE, Grindl the whacked-out guru in CANDY, Bud the ready-to-flip kidnapper in NIGHT OF THE FOLLOWING DAY, and Paul the tortured, sadistic Bohemian in LAST TANGO IN PARIS, to name a few.

But, taking it even further, can you imagine Brando in HORROR HOSPITAL? Oh, sure, Michael Gough was incredible in the role of Dr Strong. But Brando would have been absolutely nuts! Gough's sidekick, of course, in HOSPITAL was actually a midget (the memorable Skip Martin). So who knows? Maybe there was some influence there. And what about Brando playing in something like the underrated WOLF, maybe in the role of the old witchdoctor/lycanthropy expert? Or Brando in a Dario Argento film? Hell, Keitel did it in TWO EVIL EYES, and Marlon admits how talented "Harvey" is. So why *not* Brando in an Argento movie?

But MOREAU makes up for all Brando's lost time in your more purist sci-fi/horror movies.

Strangely enough, Frankenheimer's MOREAU was a ghostly example of art imitating life... namely, Brando's life. The film was originally written as an homage to Japanese ghost films from the Sixties. Cool. But as we all know, they rewrote the thing into a wonderful mess. And looking at the title character's life, we see that the actor patterned the doctor after himself. Brando, that is, lived on an island (like Moreau), upon which he tried to unsuccessfully build a hotel (as did Moreau's Japanese predecessors

107

on the fictional island in Frankenheimer's film), and Cheyenne, Brando's estranged daughter, wound up hanging herself (much like the Dogman hangs Moreau's daughter towards the climax of the picture). So it was Brando who was actually writing an homage to his own real-life ghost story here.

Life imitated art, as well, since Brando became known, after his comments about Hollywood Jews on the Larry King Show, as a sort of true-to-life Josef Mengele, which is the type of character he played in MOREAU.

"I'm very angry with some of the Jews," Brando told King...

> I am very goddamned angry at some of the Jews who have suffered terribly at the hands of the Russians, of the Germans, and the Poles, and all of the anti-Semitic elements in Europe, and it was a Godsend to come to America where they could be free... and they could do whatever they wanted. [But] Hollywood is run by Jews, it is owned by Jews, and they should have a greater sensitivity about the issue of people who are suffering. Because they've exploited... We have seen the nigger, and the greaseball, we've seen the Chink, we've seen the slit-eyed dangerous Jap, we have seen the wily Filipino, we've seen everything, but we never saw the kike. Because they knew perfectly well that is where you draw the wagons around.

In his reference to the Jews needing greater sympathy towards the "issue of people who are suffering," Brando is no doubt referring to more contemporary forms of genocide, as illustrated in the allegorical BURN! The deaths, as examples, of hundreds of thousands of Vietnamese during the Vietnam War; the extermination of three million Cambodians under the long arm of the Khmer Rouge; and the ethnic cleansing of tens of thousands of Muslims, Croats, and

Albanians during the war in the former republic of Yugoslavia.

The Jewish Defense League immediately responded to the King interview by calling Brando "a disgusting, fat, Jew-hating whore." They stated that his daughter Cheyenne killed herself because "she couldn't live with the fact that [he was] her father." Their Web site further proclaimed that Brando having photographed himself "giving oral sex to another man was the height of depravity," and that they *promise* to "make the rest of [his] life a living hell." Finally, the JDL presented a caricatured image of the back of Brando's head — in which he looked like a bloated version of Mr Clean — at the bottom of which read the caption, "Brando Without His Rug" (it's actually a pretty funny cartoon). But my question here is: if *that* wasn't a hate site (which your oh-so-politically-correct zombie is oh-so-adamantly against), what is?

Consequently, the JDL said it was "disgusted" by Brando's "latest debacle" when, on April 12, 1996, the actor, as a symbolic gesture of apology, visited the Simon Wiesenthal Center in LA. Afterwards he had a closed door meeting with a number of rabbis (including Rabbi Marvin Hier, owner of the Wiesenthal Center) during which Brando, supposedly, apologised for his King Show comments and also, supposedly, cried. Since, of course, it was a closed door meeting, we'll never know what really transpired. And the JDL was quick to jump on that fact.

"If Marlon Brando wants to apologise for the hatred and lies he spewed to the world on the Larry King Show on CNN," they stated "then he should make that apology to the same audience who originally heard it. To do less is NOT acceptable."

I, for one, don't see where an apology is necessary. Brando merely criticised the Jews, he did not condemn them. In turn, I'm glad that, if he was going to make an apology, he did so behind closed doors. The truth, therefore, is left purely to conjecture.

Strangely enough, Brando spoke critically about the Jewish moguls in Hollywood twenty years earlier during his PLAYBOY interview.

"I was mad at the Jews in the business because they largely founded the industry," he said, continuing...

> You've always seen the wily Filipino, the treacherous Chinese, the devilish Jap, the destructive, fierce, savage, blood-lusting, killing buck, and the squaw who loves the American marshal or soldier. You've seen every single race besmirched, but you never saw an image of the kike. Because the Jews are ever watchful for that... They never allowed it to be shown onscreen. The Jews have done so much for the world that, I suppose, you get extra disappointed because they didn't pay attention to that.

In the same interview, Brando poignantly recognises how equality in America is not really about "brotherly" love... but self interest.

> ... The blacks are concerned about the blacks, the Indians are concerned about the Indians, the Jews are concerned about the Jews. In the United States, people are trying to look out for their own. The Puerto Ricans are not going to take up the Indian cause. The Indian cause is not going to be concerned about the injustice to the Japanese. Everybody looks at whatever's close at hand.

Consequently, when Grobel asked the actor if there were any major reactions in the movie industry about what he'd said in PLAYBOY — and in the past — about the Jews, Brando replied in the negative. So why the problem twenty years later on the Larry King Show? Just goes to show you, I suppose, the power of the more visual mediums — like television, video, the Internet — as opposed to that of the printed word.

Let's take, however, a recent example of Brando's point concerning the invisibility of the "kike" in American cinema. How about AMERICAN HISTORY X? Fine. The 'token' Jew here (played by the ever-annoying Elliot Gould) comes across as a passive high school teacher who suffers some horrible insults from the film's featured skinhead (played by Edward Norton), who calls Gould's character a "kike" whose only goal in befriending his family is to "stick his dick" in his widowed mother. Afterwards, the humiliated yet stoical Jew walks out of

Faces of Brando #6. Brando's Dr Moreau (here with Moreauvian sidekick) is regularly characterised in SOUTH PARK.

© Comedy Central

the skinhead's house, followed by the racist's apologetic mother. Gould's character simply tells the mother that her son's life — since the boy has decided to express his racism so passionately, in the most negative sense of the word — is "finished." Gould's character further states that he is "sorry" for the mother's imminent 'loss' of her son. Here we have the voice of reason. The knower of things to come. In turn, AMERICAN HISTORY X shows us negative stereotypes of all kinds. We see the violent, car-jacking, prison-bound "nigger"; the low-down, minority-hating piece of "white trash"; the uneducated, illegal "spic"; and the greedy, suspicious "gook." But, still, we do *not* see the stereotype of the manipulative "kike." Why? My impression is that those particular Jews who control a large portion of Hollywood do not have the capacity to look at themselves introspectively, to criticise their culture, to laugh at themselves or, more importantly, to laugh at themselves when *others* make fun of them.

Oh sure, AHX addresses the race issue. But what of the issue of social class? It's a subject, I believe, which is largely ignored here because, let's face it, AHX was most probably made by members of the upper echelon, i.e. the Hollywood movie system. AHX fuels white anger against blacks, and black anger against whites, yet wisely offers no solutions. Are there any? Not really, unless you get the hell out of the inner-city and "move to an island." If you can *afford* to do so, that is. The question one should ask here is, where is all this hatred and anger coming from? Some of it, as the movie points out, comes from parents who pass their conditioned notions of race onto their children. Some of it comes from other, outside human influences. Some of it comes from first-hand experience with other races. And some of it comes from the media... from

films like AMERICAN HISTORY X. Whether intentional or not, AHX shows the futility of American multiculturalism which, for some odd reason, the media keeps trying to shove down our throats. Frankenheimer, to some extent, points towards the failure of the multicultural experience in MOREAU. The man-beasts do all the grunt work on the island, fight amongst one another, while Moreau sits in his palace acting like God. As Jim Goad poignantly states in his book THE REDNECK MANIFESTO, "Skin privilege is largely a myth peddled by those who are made uncomfortable by the idea of class privilege."

Aside from AHX, wherein Hollywood fails to address the issue of race in relation to class, look at Warren Beatty in BULLWORTH. So now Beatty is playing a rapper, hmm? He's rubbing elbows with the bruthas 'n' sistas. Wonderful. How liberal of him. But is he, Warren Beatty, willing to *live* with the inner-city blacks? Is he willing to buy liquor from the same mom-and-pop joints as the blacks? If so, I'm sure Warren will have plenty of security agents to protect his beautiful white ass.

As a sidebar, when you've got an ultra-commercial gent like Beatty doing rap videos, isn't it high time hardcore rappers took a long, hard look at their medium and either (1) did some serious reinventing of the genre or (2) dropped it like a hot fucking potato and waited patiently for the next pop music movement to arrive?

Then again, one may well ask, "Why *should* Warren Beatty or Marlon Brando come down off the hill and hang with 'the bruthas'?" Good question. My answer is that, if they're not willing to make some effort on a regular basis to put their liberal spewings where there mouths are, then it's just armchair liberalism — talking about the problem from a distance, not experiencing it, not having to live with it, just paying lip-service to the down-and-out working slob in order to make themselves, i.e. the Hollywood actor, look all the more human, with-it, and cool. And that's okay, too. If, again, they're willing to recognise their own liberal shortcomings. In his experiences with the Black Panthers during the late Sixties, as well as with the British working class during the early Seventies, Brando did recognise the division his profession had created between him and Everyman.

Yet in terms of the 'convenient' inequality afforded upper-class folk, Brando's not gonna get out of this one so easily, either. Look, for example, at the near-royal treatment his murderer son Christian Brando received in 1990. After Christian had murdered his sister's fiancé, Brando was complaining to the courts that his son should be judged as a victim of a schizophrenic upbringing and *not* for being the son of Marlon Brando. But it was ultimately for *being* the son of Marlon Brando — a guy who could afford the legal services of super lawyer Robert Shapiro — that Christian got only five years in jail. If it was, say, Anthony Petkovich, or David Kerekes, or Johnny Strike, who killed Marlon *Brando's* son, what would happen is: (1) each of those three mentioned individuals accused of murder most probably *couldn't* afford the services of Shapiro, (2) they would be held accountable not for killing a human being but rather for killing the son of the great Marlon Brando, and (3) they wouldn't get five years in jail... they'd get at *least* 15! We saw the same circus happen with the criminal trial of OJ Simpson, in which it was a case of class (rich man killing waiter, i.e. Goldman) and gender (angry black man consistently beating on his "bitch" wife, i.e. Nicole Brown) rather than race. But it was the issue of race which made the headlines and ultimately helped OJ beat the rap. We also know that if OJ *had* gone to jail, it would have

ignited an all-out race riot in LA and other areas of the US.

Amazingly enough, Brando is willing to admit his own hypocrisy here, too.

"In the main cities," Brando told reporter Grobel, "when you can't walk out in the streets without getting mugged or being in fear of your life, something's wrong. All the rich people do is move farther and farther away from the areas of trouble."

"Until you finally come to an island?" Grobel is quick to question.

"Until you finally come to an island," Brando has no choice but to answer.

Good going, Larry. Nice touch.

Ben Stein...
Ben who?
Ben Stein...
Ben who?
Ben Stein (I don't *know* who he is, but), in his 1996 article for E! Entertainment, "Do Jews Run Hollywood?", vehemently acknowledges that members of his "tribe," as Stein himself calls 'em, do in fact run Hollywood to some extent. But let's forget about the obvious for now. The real icing on Stein's cake comes when he tries to pummel Brando for being a shivering, sweating paranoiac hiding out like a frightened warlord up on Mulholland Drive.

"The only reason," Stein writes, "why the question of whether Jews 'run' Hollywood is at all interesting is because there is some residual thought — apparently as was in the mind of Marlon Brando — that Jews are sinister and alien."

Correct me if I'm wrong, but didn't Brando *praise* the Jews during the King interview? "[They] are amazing people," Brando told King. "I think that per capita, people don't realise that Jews have contributed more to the best of American culture than any other single group."

Brando didn't even hint at, as Stein bizarrely insists, the Jews being "sinis-

111

ter and alien."

But now, since we're on the topic of control... why *haven't* we seen a film involving a fictional tale (repeat: *fictional* tale) of a *Jewish* conspiracy to take over the world? We've seen the Japanese (RISING SUN), Russians (RED DAWN), Germans (THE BOYS FROM BRAZIL), Chinese (pick any number of James Bond films), Koreans (THE MANCHURIAN CANDIDATE), Italians (The GODFATHER series) even aliens from outer space (INVASION OF THE BODY SNATCHERS and a slew of imitations)... all such races intent on ruling our small planet. But why not the Jews? I mean, *has* there been a film which tackles this notion? Please, if I've overlooked that particular flick, let me know... I'd love to see it. Hell, I'd love to *make* it! Whaddya think? Is Hollywood 'liberal' enough to hire me?...

And back on the subject of race...

Perhaps we should briefly *look* at the term "anti-Semitic." Like "sexist" and "racist," anti-Semitic is a description which is used far too loosely in America. I don't know what it's like in Great Britain, but in these here United States of America, if you simply say something that's critical — not hateful, not angry, not racist, but simply critical — of the Jews in mixed company, you're immediately labelled an "anti-Semite," which is equivalent to receiving a death sentence, equivalent to being made a social leper, to being labelled a maniacal, rabid Neo Nazi. Well, if a "great" country like America is so intensely populated by so-called "liberals" all cheering for First Amendment rights, freedom of speech, acceptance of the "individual," and — oh, boy, here we go again — "equality," then why can't a guy like Brando, or me, or whoever's read this fucking article this fucking far, *criticise* whomever he/she damn well pleases? Because we have the facade of political correctness, i.e. liberals who laugh at/condemn political correctness, yet who are themselves the paradigms of that horrifically fascistic universe which they've helped to both create and sustain, and who are no less insanely conservative than your most staunch, party-line obsessed Republican.

No nice, neat conclusion is really possible here. I mean, we can talk about race, sex, class, and politics 'til we're blue in the face — and probably be all the more in the dark about such. Nonetheless, *talking* about these subjects is perhaps healthy... a dollop of insight being *some* kind of start... I guess. We can't, however, overlook the fact that Brando has had the balls to speak out about those issues which others are too sheepish to even mention. And he's also willing to expose his own hypocrisy and shortcomings in the process. Films like MORITURI, BURN!, THE NIGHTCOMERS, MISSOURI BREAKS, and MOREAU are not only entertaining because of Brando, but they show the many sides of this contradictory hulk who's so difficult to figure out. And, hey, if Hollywood is so adamant about these films, so willing to trash 'em, eager for us to forget about 'em, eager for these 'lemons' to shrivel up and disappear, then you *know* they've gotta have *something* going for 'em, right?

Well, that's all there is to say I guess, except... let the hate mail roll right in, you Jew boys, Injuns, niggaz, cunts, 'n' queeyahs...

The Exotic Beatles

Fairground Organs

Police Choirs

Singing Cats

Jim Phelan

Get Back

David Kerekes

The Exotic Beatles ARE A SERIES OF CD ALBUMS FEATURING UNUSUAL VERSIONS OF **BEATLES** SONGS AS PERFORMED BY A WHOLE HOST OF PEOPLE AND BANDS DOWN THE YEARS. (SEE NEXT PAGE FOR EXOTIC REVIEW.) **JIM PHELAN** COMPILES AND PRODUCES THESE ARTEFACTS...

Headpress **What inspired THE EXOTIC BEATLES?**
Jim Phelan I had an idea a few years ago to do a compilation called VINYL CRIMES, which was to be celebrities doing songs... material by people who really shouldn't have gone into a recording studio but had been persuaded to by their agent. In this plethora of terrible songs I noticed a lot of Beatles covers. From there I started to collect albums which were exclusively devoted to Beatles covers or maybe just had one Beatles track on them. I licensed this material and put the first EXOTIC BEATLES album out. I thought that'd be it, I wouldn't find any more stuff. But I did, and people also started sending me stuff.

How difficult is it for you to track this material down?
Getting hold of a track — whether it's on tape, or DAT, vinyl, whatever — you've got your starting point. The real difficulty is finding out who actually owns the work. And then when you've done that you've got to licence it. The problem is that a lot of the stuff is owned by major record companies who don't even know they own it, or if you point it out to them they say it's not for licence. Often the ownership will have reverted back to the original artist and the companies don't have the paperwork together and just say 'no'.

An interesting track for me was the Velvelettes, the prog rock band doing 'It's For You'. I'm always looking around second-hand shops and record fairs for Beatles covers, and I came across a demo by this band called Springwell doing this crazy uptempo version of 'It's For You'. But it was on one of the major labels who claimed not to know anything about it. So I

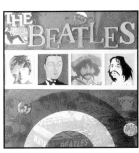

113

sent the demo to some friends of mine in Manchester and asked them to do a version of the song in the same style. And that's what they came back with.

Have any of the EXOTIC artists been in touch to say 'How dare you!'? Not really. Certain people actually asked if they could be on there, like Frank Sidebottom and Klaus Beyer. There are quite a few people who have done tracks and sent them to me in the hope of getting on, but there's a criteria I have: the track has got to be unique and quite different from any other version.

Are there any tracks you're particularly looking for and haven't yet been able to find? There's a legendary album that I've heard of called ODEON'S JUJU by The Beetles, which came out on Nigerian EMI. Now, what it is or how I get hold of it I've no idea. And then there are things like the Mrs Miller tracks, which I'd like to have on there but that's a licensing problem again. Similarly there's a whole album of Cathy Berberian stuff [REVOLUTION: AN OPERATIC FIRST] which Polygram refuse to licence, while not actually admitting whether they still hold the rights.

Do you have any personal favourites that have appeared? Yeah, it changes from week to week. Akiko Kanazawa's 'Yellow Submarine' was a favourite for a long, long time. And of course I like William Shatner's 'Lucy In The Sky With Diamonds'. And I think Arthur Mullard's 'Yusterday' is a fantastic version.

I have to confess that's one of my least favourites. It's funny... I work in the music business as a sleeve designer and if I meet someone in the pub and say I've just done this album for a new band and it's really good, nobody actually gets inspired to go out and buy the record. But if I say I've got Arthur Mullard doing 'Yusterday', it paints a picture, and people are up for it.

Have you had any reaction from Apple? Not from Apple, no. I know they're 'into it'. The one thing is if you use Beatles tracks and don't pay your MCPS [the society that collects royalties on behalf of writers and publishers] you're finished. So I

Arthur Mullard

THE EXOTIC BEATLES
Parts 1, 2, & 3
Various Artists; Pelé 3CD/7CD/14CD

These three volumes collect unusual covers of Beatles songs and intersperse them with various celebrities analysing, and denigrating, the music of the Fab Four.

William Shatner has recorded a notoriously bad Beatles cover, so it's no surprise to find him here along with police male voice choirs, singing animals and Moog synthesisers. But the majority of tracks are from unknown artists and for every gimmicky rendition of a Beatles song, there is a revelatory or truly demented number to compensate — art critic Brian Sewell reciting the lyrics to songs he claims never to have heard, for in-

. . . .

GET BACK
The Beatles' Let It Be Disaster
Doug Sulphy & Ray Schweighardt
£12.99 248pp; 1998, Helter Skelter, 1998
ISBN 1-900924-12-9

Covering the same ground as Peter Doggett's LET IT BE/ABBEY ROAD book [see: *Headpress 18*], GET BACK takes a microscopic, more clinical look at the rehearsal sessions that were a part of the disintergration of the Beatles. If it was debatable whether Doggett could have written his book without accessing some of the bootleg tapes that exist of the sessions, with Sulphy and Schweighardt it's not open to question — their book is *based* on these tapes. A quick recap: the

Beatles entered Twickenham film studios (and later Apple) in January 1969 with intentions to rehearse new material for a live concert and album. A film crew accompanied them in order to make a documentary of the band at work. The resultant documentary was officially released as LET IT BE, comprising only a miniscule part of the material that was actually captured on both audio and film tape. But pieces of unreleased material have been 'steadily' filtering through underground channels and onto various bootlegs ever since.

Sulphy and Schweighardt

stance, or an elderly Mae West thinking she's still a prick teaser in Day Tripper. Tsunematsu Masatoshi's Nowhere Man features some great acid guitar, while Balsara and his Singing Sitars reverse the clock on the Beatles' Middle Eastern influences for a straight sitar rendition of the early hit, I Want To Hold Your Hand. Then, of course, there's Margarita Pracatan applying her customary half-remembered lyrics and occasional bum chord change to From Me To You, Lol Coxhill leading a bunch of kids through I Am The Walrus, Shang Shang Typhoon doing an effervescent Jap version of Let It Be, and The Mirza Men's kaleidoscopic Eight Days A Week. They all add up to a world that is a little bit groovy and a little bit mad. These are songs we've known forever, and will be known afresh after you and I have shrugged off our mortal coil. With that thought, who can listen to the happy sounding 52 Key Verbeek Fairground Organ playing In My Life and not feel the cold fingers of death running up their spine?

have to make sure I get the legal side of it right. And I did get a phonecall asking certain details about the project. Nobody was saying what exactly it was they were after, but it was a surreptitious way of saying 'Have you paid all your dues?'

If you produce a version of a song that differs from how it was originally done — say you change the words around, or change the song so no one can recognise what it is — then you must go and get permission from the owners of that work. So I suppose strictly I should have submitted all the albums to Apple or Northern Songs... and then of course they would have said 'no you can't use any of it'. I just had to go with it.

Somebody once said the popularity of the Beatles is down to them writing songs that everyone already had in their head. What would you say to that? Probably true. But it's easy to say that in hindsight. I was a Beatles fan in the early Sixties. Then I got into 'harder stuff' and psychedelia, and didn't catch onto the second half of the Beatles career until later on, when I realised just how good this stuff was. When you've listened to 60 or 70 versions of say 'Hey Jude' — played on the harmonica, on the Jew's harp, the accordion, or whatever — you realise it is a brilliant song, and there's no one to match Lennon and McCartney.

It's interesting how most covers come from the Beatles' early career and there's little drawn from their later catalogue. There's something insane like 20,000 covers of 'Yesterday' alone. Some of the later material, like that which appears on the Double White album, I've only got three or four versions of.

Shonen Knife did a cover of 'Rain'. Yeah, I tried to licence that from them. That's funny because I thought they would be up for it, but their management said that it was a period of their career they didn't want resurrected. At the time I was trying to licence this stuff the band had just signed a new record deal and it looked like their career was going to bloom. They came back with a firm but polite 'no'.

· ·

have dissected and analysed every moment of tape that has become available. The chapters of their book are divided into the 20 days of the sessions themselves, with a thorough breakdown of the songs. However, while occasionally the band will make it through an entire number, these 'songs' mostly comprise of half-remembered vocal lines or stray riffs of a few seconds duration. While such minutae hardly makes for fascinating reading in itself, the conversation and arguments intercutting the songs are absolutely compelling in a thoroughly miserable way. (To the authors' credit, they sustain this aspect of the book without the use of any direct quotes whatsoever. Their reason for this is presumably a copyright one, but it's never made clear.) With the exception of McCartney, who exudes ambition and drive throughout, the members of the band arrive late for the sessions most every morning and count the hours until it's time to go home again in the evening.

The Beatles only call for the cameras and recording equipment to be turned off on a handful of occasions, and it becomes apparent that they've relegated the subject of disbanding to private discussion following a major flare up between Lennon and Harrison. Shortly after this, Harrison quits the group and when Lennon doesn't bother to show for rehearsals it looks like the Beatles are down to two men, with a live show imminent.

This, of course, is where the book gets really interesting…

Because of the many recording devices utilised (which include hidden mics and phone taps!), members of the band may be arguing in one corner of the massive Twickenham studio lot, while at the same time in the opposite corner sound engineers and crew may be commenting on the fact. It's a weird situation, more so given that it concerns the most influential figures in Twentieth Century popular culture. **David Kerekes**

ADAM • ANT

SEX • AND • PERVERSION
FOR • TEENYBOPPERS

Dr Mark Griffiths

I HAVE BEEN A FAN of Adam Ant's music for nearly 20 years, which might lead some people to conclude that I am a few tracks short of an LP. However, as someone who takes more than a passing interest in human sexual behaviour (I teach a whole course on it here at Nottingham Trent University), I would argue that Adam's music has covered more atypical sexual behaviours than any other recording artist that I can think of (e.g. sadomasochism, bondage, spanking, transvestism, voyeurism, body piercing, fetishistic behaviour etc). Anyone who has

followed Adam's career will recall that his music was billed in the late 1970s and early 1980s as "antmusic for sexpeople". **Adam's followers (according to the free booklet given away with early copies of the 1980 LP KINGS OF THE WILD FRONTIER) were the** "sexpeople" **who** "get off on sexual phenomena; people who like sexual imagery and enjoy being sexual".

116

here are very few songs in the Ant repertoire that are about what I would call 'straight sex'. Adam's most obvious songs here are *S.E.X.* where he proclaims in the chorus that

Sex is sex, forget the rest / The only one that's free / The only great adventure left / To human-kind, that's you and me

and *Beautiful Dream* where

Sex is emotion in motion.

For me this is very bland stuff which is also echoed in many songs from the 1983 **STRIP** album including the title track, *Baby Let Me Scream At You*, *Libertine* and *Navel To Neck*. "Straight sex" in the form of sexual promiscuity rears its head in third-person male account in one of Adam's own favourite songs, *Juanito the Bandito*, in which Adam (singing in a Latino-type accent) says

Young ladies he likes to ravish / He knows how to make them wet / And if he can't, he'll dig himself a hole / Or go looking for your favourite pet

I'm not quite sure whether that's some reference to a potential bestial act or just a bad rhyming couplet, but it's still pretty tame as far as I'm concerned. The more humorous side of promiscuity is also outlined in 1983's *Playboy* from the album **STRIP** when Adam asks

What do you wear in bed? / Some headphones on my head / What do you like to hold? / 'My breath' she said

Other types of "vanilla sex" include dressing up in sexy clothes (*Spanish Games*), and sex in aeroplanes in the shape of the non-subtle *Mile High Club*,

747 or a VC 10 / Winter, summer, who knows when? / Take off passion, fly away love / Mile High Club

There is also a whole song about sex in the bathroom (*Bathroom Function*) which makes lots of references to lathering and rubbing unhygienic places and soap-on-rope.

ADAM·and·the·ANTS

YOUNG·PARISIANS

Record sleeve of first single. Bondage imagery, whip, leather, and (back cover detail, previous page) voyeurism.

However, the lyrics make it hard to decide whether the sex in question is masturbatury or copulatory!

Very few of Adam's songs refer to homosexuality except when he is singing in the third-person. The two most striking examples of this appear on his 1989 album, **MANNERS AND PHYSIQUE**. One song *Bright Lights, Black Leather* is an observation of the gay scene in West Berlin,

There they go, the buccaneers / Hand in hand in leather glove / So fast, so crazy / With a creepy kind of love

The other song is about the rent-boy scene in Piccadilly (appropriately entitled *Piccadilly*). Another song where Ant takes a third-person view of a sexual behaviour is in *Cleopatra* (from the **DIRK WEARS WHITE SØX** LP) where he makes reference to the Egyptian queen's alleged penchant for fellatio. As Adam observes

Cleopatra did 10,000 in her lifetime / Now that's a widemouth / Cleo gave service with a smile / She was a wide-mouthed girl / She did a hundred Roman Centurions / For after-dinner mints

Many of Adam's songs make passing references to activities associated with the more extreme fringes of sex such as body piercing

She's got a little chain through her tit / And she doesn't seem to mind it

and tattoos

I've got a heart on my arm / It says 'PURE SEX' / It hurt / I mean it / I got it till I die / Or until I reach orgasmo [sic]

He also hints at bestial pleasures and clitoral stimulation in the 1982 song *Why Do Girls Love Horses?*

Is it 'cos they're round? / Or 'cos they're six feet off the ground? / Is it because they're on top? / Or the clippety-clop?

It is when we start to examine Adam's earlier output that things get far more interesting. Transvestism may have been covered implicitly in The Kinks' *Lola* or Lou Reed's *Walk on the Wild Side* but I don't know another song like *Greta-X* which includes the chorus

I'm a joyous glad TV / Why don't you come TV with me / I know a girl who likes to dress me / Up like this and then caress me

Some may claim that the "TV" here may not necessarily be about transvestites but the last verse clears up any ambiguity!

Underwear all tidied away / Thirty eight bust just for a day / Heels so high, my furs so fine / All a woman's things, they are mine

One of the most salient themes through

Above **Early badge; SM imagery.** Below **Early poster; "Breasts, Bottoms, Schoolgirl, Stockings, Suspenders, Spanking, Domination, Rubber, Squatting."**

much of Adam's early work is sadomasochism and bondage. Live favourites such as *Physical (You're So)* and *B-Side Baby*, being typical of the genre. An early stage favourite was *Beat My Guest* which would often disturb club owners:

Well tie me up and hit me with a stick Yeah, use a truncheon or a household brick / There's so much happiness behind these tears / I'll pray you'll beat me for a thousand years / Well use a truncheon or a cricket bat / A good beating's where it's really at

Their other early SM classic *Whip In My Valise* with the immortal chorus line

Who taught you to torture? Who taught ya?

was the first song that moved my Dad to question my musical taste! When you look at some of the lyrics, you can perhaps appreciate why my father was concerned about what his 13-year-old son was listening to.

118

When I met you, you were just sixteen / Pulling the wings off flies / When the old lady got hit by the truck / I saw the wicked in your eyes / You put my head into the stocks / And then went to choose a cane / But hey, your cat has got nine tails / You like to leave me lame

Very few of Adam's later songs return to these themes although there are exceptions including the self-explanatory *Human Bondage Den* and *Rough Stuff*, the latter of which was a big hit in the US. The world of rubberites is explored in another self-explanatory song *Rubber People*. Adam proclaims that

Rubber people are lovely people / They long for latex on their skin / A hole in the ceiling / A nice strong gag / Nicely wrapped and strapped

This again has strong SM overtones especially when references are made to being "bound to discipline" and spanking. Spanking only appears in one other Ant song — the aforementioned *Whip In My Valise*. Voyeurism with naïve SM overtones also appears in the early live favourite *Lady* when Adam sings

I saw a lady and she was naked / I saw a lady she had no clothes on / I had a good look through the crack / She had footmarks up her back / How did they get there?

Although Adam sings about many fetishistic behaviours, the only direct reference appears in the classic *Christian D'Or*. Adam reels off a whole list of fetishes and concludes there is something wrong with him

I've got a fetish for black / A fetish for green / A fetish for those arty magazines / I've got a fetish for Brando / A fetish for cats / A

fetish for ladies in Christian Dior hats / I've got a fetish and that means I'm sick / So very sick

The one song I have not been able to decide whether it is about a paraphilia is *1969 Again*. In this song Adam sings that

Oh how you make me wish I was a baby / Yeah, when you're playing Miss Swish / Knickers on — you're my big agony nanny / With your big towel protection

TRACK LISTING

1969 Again — 1995, **WONDERFUL** LP
Bathroom Function — 1978, **ANTMUSIC FOR SEXPEOPLE** bootleg LP
Beat My Guest — 1981, B-side of *Stand and Deliver*
Beautiful Dream — 1995, **WONDERFUL** LP
Christian D'Or — 1981, B-side of *Prince Charming*
Cleopatra — 1979, **DIRK WEARS WHITE SOX** LP
Greta-X — 1985, B-side of *Vive Le Rock*
Human Bondage Den — 1985, **VIVE LE ROCK** LP
Juanito the Bandito — 1982, B-Side of *Friend or Foe*
Lady — 1979, B-side of *Young Parisians*
Mile High Club from the 1981 **PRINCE CHARMING** LP
Punk in the Supermarket — 1978, **ANTMUSIC FOR SEXPEOPLE** bootleg LP
Red Scab — 1982; B-side of *Goody Two Shoes*
Rough Stuff — 1989, **MANNERS AND PHYSIQUE** LP
S.E.X. — 1981, **PRINCE CHARMING** LP
Spanish Games — 1983, from the **STRIP** LP
Whip In My Valise — 1979, B-side of *Zerox*
Why Do Girls Love Horses? — B-side of *Desperate But Not Serious*

To me, this looks like a song about infantalism (people who get sexual kicks from being big babies) but I could be wrong. There is also the reference to Miss Swish which suggests some spanking reference (SWISH was a spanking magazine in the mid-1980s) but maybe that's wishful thinking.

So there you have it. My own little trawl through Adam Ant's song catalogue. As a psychologist, there are lots of questions I'd love to ask him if ever I got the chance to interview him!

BETTIE PAGE vs TRACI LORDS

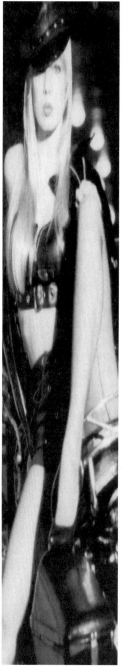

Traci!

Johnny Strike

AFTER A PERIOD AS A CHRISTIAN cultist, hearing voices and suffering from paranoid schizophrenia, Bettie Page began attacking people. Finally in Lawnsdale, Ca. in 1982, in a trailer park, overweight, age 59, she attacked another woman with a knife. The charge: Attempted murder with a deadly weapon. She pleaded not guilty by reason of insanity. Two doctors testified that she was indeed insane. At Patton State she underwent 'drug therapy'. In 1992, Bettie became an outpatient and today at 76, lives in quiet seclusion, and reports to be in good mental health.

April 22, 1923 Betty Mae Page was born in Nashville, Tennessee. Later she changed the spelling from Betty to Bettie. May 7, 1968 Norma Louise Kuzma, was born in Steubenville, Ohio. After various aka's, she settled on Traci Lords. Both Bettie and Traci were born under the sign of Taurus, which is ruled by Venus, the goddess of sexuality. Traci and Bettie each have 10 letters in their names. Both have their first names misspelled frequently. Ten years after Bettie Page's disappearance Traci Lords was conceived. There are an amazing amount of connections, similarities and synchronistic points between these two cult figures. Even their differences read like two sides of a coin, yin and yang, a female version of the Roman deity Janus; one face looking back, the other into the future.

Bettie!

SEX-O-RAMA! PONY GIRLS THAT ROCK!

Both Bettie Page and Traci Lords were trail blazers for sex. Irving Klaw guided Bettie through a collection of black and white documents that seem to have secured her title, 'Queen of Kink.' The likes of John Willie, Eric Stanton, and Robert Blue should also be acknowledged. Blue's pop-photo realism, reworking of the Klaw pictures even in the 1970s disturbed the art critics. In THE REAL BETTIE PAGE, by Richard Foster, Blue claims that if Bettie had not done the kink, she would have been just another pinup. I agree. The 'power' that Klaw developed and Blue talks about has inspired a mob of models and actresses who have tried unsuccessfully to emulate her. At least once a year your local bondage club will have the required Bettie Page lookalike contest. The last one I heard about in San Francisco was won by a guy.

Some may point out that Traci Lords has never really done any kink but they would be wrong. In 1985 she made a film entitled, PONY GIRL. In it Traci and other girls, after being captured by some men, are fitted with leather head-and-neck halters. Traci wears a leather corset as well. They're hooked up to a 'horse walker' and trained to walk, trot, and prance around a track. Traci finally escapes from the stable but is recaptured, eventually promoted to trainer, at which point she is pulled around by another pony girl. A rare collectors item. (It's rumoured that a PONY GIRLS VOL 2 may exist.) Bettie has said that the strangest thing she ever did was get up in a full-length pony-costume-with-head for one of Irving's customers. And really, Bettie's bondage stuff, with its whiff of nostalgia, is viewed today as almost charming. Bettie once turned down an introduction to Howard Hughes. One wonders how Traci

Pony girls. John Willie, 1946.

Art © John Willie

would have handled that one? In a Sadean world Bettie is Justine; Traci, Juliette.

Bettie Page's image has been portrayed as a devil by the artist Olivia. Traci Lords was the 'Devil' in the film NEW WAVE HOOKERS. Bettie's 'nature side' was explored by the 'camera club' gang from the cad era, as well as Bunny Yeager. What followed during the Fifties were studio shots, jungle themes, sun splashed, on sand and sea, and finally her walking through Miami's, Africa USA leading twin leopards on a leash. Traci Lords released her terrific exercise video, WARM UP WITH TRACI. In it she's wearing a yellow bikini, her body in most every position imaginable; perhaps her most suggestive role ever. The first version has Traci rappin' along with the workout. It includes such niceties as Traci doing the swim. One line goes, **"On your hands, on your knees, thrust your tummy, you don't have to ask your mummy."** More on this mummy business later.

Bettie has been in nearly as many fetish magazines as Traci has been in pornos. Both have appeared in ADAM, CELEBRITY SLEUTH, CHIC, DETAILS, ENTERTAINMENT WEEKLY, FEMME FATALES, GQ, HIGH SOCIETY, HUSTLER, INTERVIEW, LEG SHOW, OUI, PENTHOUSE, PLAYBOY (Traci clothed), PRUDE, and VELVET. And while Bettie appeared on the cover of SUNBATHING FOR HEALTH, ELLERY QUEEN'S MYSTERY MAGAZINE and FANTASTIQUE in the Fifties, Traci graced the covers of MUSCLE AND FITNESS, ADULT CINEMA REVIEW and FILM THREAT in the Eighties and Nineties. Paul Hugli, men's magazine expert, and author of the privately published TRACI LORDS, A PERSPECTIVE told me that only two models can substantially up the price of a magazine. That's right, folks — Traci Lords and Bettie Page.

Bettie's eyes as blue as Barbados, Traci's as

121

FREE BUMPER STICKER! SEE DETAILS INSIDE

FILM THREAT

THE OTHER MOVIE MAGAZINE

Issue 2 February 1992 $3.50 U.S. $3.95 Can £2.10 U.K.

HOW TO BE A STAR
IMMORTALITY FOR $4,800?

CRASHING THE TORONTO FILM FESTIVAL

EXCLUSIVE PREVIEW!
SAM RAIMI'S ARMY OF DARKNESS

ON THE SET OF **CRONENBERG'S NAKED LUNCH**

PLUS!
ABSOLUTELY NOTHING ABOUT STEVEN SPIELBERG'S HOOK

**Traci on the cover of
FILM THREAT.**

green as Tahiti. Raven-haired Bettie, Traci blonde, although recent sightings report her mane a reddish brown. Both ladies with enough curves to wreck a Maserati. Traci is mostly a pouter. Much has been made of her mouth. She supposedly 'feels' too much. Both Traci and Bettie appeared on the covers of a couple of smutty paperbacks. THE HOTTER DAUGHTER GETS, featured Traci, and Bettie adorned the cover of, SEX MERRY-GO-ROUND. Bettie once did a 'Dance Of The Seven Veils.' Traci appeared out of a bottle in the streets of Cairo, in another rare porno film. In 1951 Bettie appeared in a pair of fishnet black stockings, high heels, and twin telephone dials over her breasts at the Beaux Arts Ball. In the Nineties, Traci's picture was used for telephone sex ads: **"Phone Sex with Traci Lords"**, and **"Phone Phuk A Star"**, for two dollars!

Bettie has had many titles bestowed upon her: **"Americas Number One Pinup"**, **"Queen of Kink"**, and so on, while Traci to this day is still mostly referred to as the **"Former Porn Queen"**. During her stint in X-rated films she was referred to as, **"The Princess of Porn."** In 1992, HUSTLER named her **"Asshole of the Month"**, six

years after the (underage porn bust) scandal!

Bettie is mostly adored while Traci is still dissed. I interviewed a number of exotic dancers for their take on the two ladies, and most were Bettie positive, Traci negative. I think this reaction is the trickle down from the porn industry at large. And even today the mere mention of her name will send some pornsters into mindless, stuttering states of irrational anger.

There's the good Bettie/bad Bettie, but Traci Lords seems to have combined vice and virtue simultaneously. Even with the kink, Bettie was mostly smiling, and ardent admirers are quick to point that out. She remains the **"untouchable angel"**, and old timers refer to her as, **"Sweet Bettie."** To the fetish world she is strictly the Dark Angel of Bondage. Traci maintains her bad girl persona, seductive, sometimes even vulnerable. Does the 's' in Lords stand for sex and sin as rumoured? Bettie has said that she lacked ambition. Traci is just the opposite.

Both ladies have had their fill of hard luck. Both were married then divorced. Bettie miscarried. As a young girl Traci had an abortion. Bettie's first bad luck — or bad something — began in San Francisco in 1946 when she was found guilty of misdemeanour assault and battery. The following year in New York, she was forced to perform oral sex on a gang of guys. Traci was famous for orally doing two at once, and gave instructions on fellatio in the March '86 issue of VELVET. Traci and Bettie both endured FBI investigations. In 1954, a nitwit senator, Estes Kefauver, who wore a coonskin cap, and chaired a subcommittee investigating organised crime, rabidly turned to juvenile delinquency and comics like TALES FROM THE CRYPT. (Years later, Traci would play a scene in the TV TALES FROM THE CRYPT.) The Kefauver investigation led to harassment for Bettie, Irving and Paula Klaw, since CARTOON and MODEL PARADE were included in the crazed senator's mission. This episode also seemed to cast the die for Bettie quitting, disappearing, and eventually going off her ever-lovin' rocker. Traci, of course, is famous for her highly publicised, underage, porn bust in 1986. No one was actually prosecuted in either case. Who dropped the dime on the Lord's scandal is still a mystery, but one thing is certain — Traci conned the industry. And to her credit she never blamed the industry. The Meese Commission tried to add this case to their arsenal, but after one look at Traci, it was obvious even to those old fucks that this was not kiddie porn. After two years in semi-seclusion, Traci was back in 1988 with her exercise video, and a lead role in Jim Wynorski's remake of Roger Corman's NOT OF THIS EARTH.

The FBI came to see Bettie again when they thought that a person who was stalking her was a serial killer. He turned out to be only a juvenile delinquent fanboy. Traci would eventually play a number of roles that concerned serial killers. Both ladies were in John Water's film SERIAL MOM. A young punk in a red convertible ogles the pics in an issue of THE BETTY PAGES. Later Traci shows up in a cameo. Had Waters cast Traci in the lead, we may have had a memorable film.

Bettie tried out for beauty contests, and shilled as a faux Miss Tennessee for a comedian's act. Traci played a beauty contest winner in one of her obscure films, and has shown a comedic side. Both have at one time lived in Lawndale, California, and both have done stints as runway models. Today they both live in the futuristic city of Los Angeles. Olivia also portrayed Bettie as a mermaid. Traci played a mermaid in another porn flick. Both have had E! Entertainment Television 'True Hollywood Stories' devoted to them. In 1955, Bettie Page was PLAYBOY's Playmate Centrefold. In 1986, Traci Lords was the PENTHOUSE Pet. Years later Traci would turn down PLAYBOY, saying something like, 'Been there done that.'

Both Traci Lords and Bettie Page dreamed of singing torch songs. Traci actually did it in the movie UNDERWORLD, while Bettie admitted that she could not really carry a tune. Traci auditioned for part of Breathless Mahoney, the torch singer in the movie DICK TRACY. Madonna was given the role. After viewing the film, one feels that Traci would have been a better choice. Both have had country-flavoured, rockabillyish songs done in tribute to them: 'I Love Traci Lords', and 'Bettie Bettie'. Both were used for record cover art. Bettie most notably on Fats Waller's 'Ain't Misbehavin'. Traci on Sonic Youth's, 12"

DISAPPEARER. Traci Lords has gone on and actually pursued a singing career. Firstly, she sang back up on 'Little Baby Nothing' from Manic Street Preacher's (1992) GENERATION TERRORIST album. In 1995 she released her own techno-dance-trip-hop record, 1,000 FIRES. Her voice is not unlike Shirley Manson's of Garbage. One song she penned goes, **"Okey dokey, doggy, daddy, yummy yummy sugar, mummy."** This reminds us of her exercise rap about tummies and mummies, and porn veteran Jamie Gillis told Anthony (X FACTORY) Petkovich that when copulating with her, as a 15-year-old nymphet, even after the cameras stopped rolling, Traci moaned in his ear, **"Fuck your mommy."** Okey dokey, doggy, daddy! She has talked about a second LP with Radioactive Records, venturing into new musical ground, even a possible tour.

In cyberspace Bettie Page web sites outnumber Traci's, but Lords are strong. One of the latter's sites announces, 'Resistance is futile. Come and worship at the Temple of Traci Lords.' Browsing a Traci Lords Bulletin Board I came across this gem by 'anonymous,' **"It's cool that she started fuckin' in the pornos at 15! That's a good age for pro fucking!"** And from a fan named

Filthy, **"Traci rox my world! I could really care less about her roles in porn movies... but I love her real acting and her music is awesome."**

The selling of the Bettie Page image seems to be approaching something along the lines of STAR TREK Convention status. The merchandise using Bettie's image is astounding with new products (Zippo lighters, talking postcards, glow in the dark clocks) popping up all the time. A booking agent even asked Bettie if she would host Lollapalooza! Bettie, showing that she had indeed regained her sanity, declined. So did this agent then ask Traci Lords? Of course not. Lollapaloser! Traci's merchandise does not compare in volume, but Lords has her share of posters, calendars, comics, and t-shirts. The most interesting product was a personalised 'fuck me doll' which Traci and another porn starlet had marketed themselves. Understandably these are rare collector's items. Bettie's merchandising went sky high after the Dave Stevens' ROCKETEER comic and Disney's film of the same name. THE ROCKETEER shot the Bettie image machine into full-swing, giving birth to perhaps even Xena. Traci Lords has not been interpreted by any artists of note to my knowledge, which gives an indication of the sorry state of the art world. It's mostly her B-movie art (standees, posters, and the like) that are coveted.

Traci Lords and Bettie Page both wanted to become actresses. Both could use their body and face to convey emotion

and dialogue. Bettie studied the Stanislavsky method; Traci, Lee Strasberg. Bettie it seems was either too lazy or too unlucky to achieve an acting career. Traci continues to work within the industry. Witness the 1998 BLADE, in which she practically steals the film in just the opening moments. Later, when the other vampires show up, one laments that Traci was offed too soon.

Television. Bettie played a cigarette girl, a jailed illegal alien named Carmelita, and appeared on some variety shows. Traci made appearances on MARRIED WITH CHILDREN, HIGHLANDER, PROFILER, MELROSE PLACE, WISEGUY, to name but a few. And word is, a show being developed around her is in the works. Bettie Page's foray into 'films' is also limited. She played an exotic dancer, bathtub bather, maid, and kink girl. TEASERAMA, VARIETEASE, and Klaw's Bondage loops Vols 1 and 2 sum it up. Traci Lords, on the other hand, has played a private eye, detective, police science expert, KGB agent posing as a call girl, escort, dope stealing prostitute, Kung Fu-ing jewel thief, exotic dancer, devil hooker, lingerie and stocking model, sexy maid, beauty queen, secretary, round girl, high fashion photographer, night-club singer, country singer, punk rock singer, rock band manager, implant subject, lab tech, future voyeur, alien, mind reader, interactive VR babe. Should I go on? Okay... a genie, mermaid, nurse (three times!), valley chick (twice), ball-busting domineering bitch, sexually naïve housewife,

Above **Dave Stevens' 'Betty' in a panel from THE ROCKETEER.**

Swimsuit competition.
Traci (left), **Bettie** (right).

rich bitch, hot teenager, car hop, dragstrip girl, chain smoking bitchy dyke, Drape gang member, teenage runaway, **"Mati Hari of the fast food business"**, herself (in a black-and-white short lampooning Universal Studios — along with other Hollywood luminaries including the Universal Studios JAWS shark), disfigured survivor of a serial killer, serial killer's assistant, gang member's junkie girlfriend who is also a scream queen in horror films, carnival owner, mayor's ex-wife-turned-fashion-model, post office supervisor-turned-zombie, physical fitness advocate, vampire raver and, ahem... a pony girl. Note: This is not a complete list, but damn close.

Traci Lords is certainly an actress. For three years she convinced the Adult entertainment industry that she was a different age. **"I've al-ways been acting,"** Traci has said. And as we're beginning to see porno merging more with the mainstream, note that Traci was the first to morph herself into the crossover. If one wades through her films as I did, one will find a many-sided actress. In these B-movies one comes away with a feeling that Traci always gave her best regardless of the project. Bettie Page made

only a small modelling fee while someone else was making a big profit from her image. Traci, however, was quickly making top dollar even for her early porno flicks. Today she is the savvy owner of her own company: TLC, Traci Lords Company.

So who's the winner here? Both women are extraordinary, but for an image of true female empowerment, Traci Lords clearly comes out on top. The past certainly belongs to Bettie Page, thanks to the artist-who-didn't-know-he-was-an-artist, Irving Klaw, and immortality through the multi-million-dollar business that's been created around her image. The future, on the other hand may very well belong to Traci Lords. Here in San Francisco, at the Yerba Buena Center for the Arts, they're presenting 'Adults Only' nights featuring early porno flicks, now that they're seen as 'historically significant'. Bettie Page's career ended with nude modelling. Traci Lords began with it. Will Traci Lords star in a new PONY GIRLS written by Quentin Tarantino, directed by David Lynch? At age 34 Bettie Page left the modelling world never to return. At age 34 Traci Lords will be three years into the 21st Century.

The Headpress
Guide to
M⬤DERN
EXCITING!
Culture

AZRAEL PROJECT NEWSLETTER
Vol 6, No 1 Fall/Winter 98/9
40pp; Westgate Press, 5219 Magazine St.,
New Orleans, LA 70115, USA

The purpose of the New Orleans-based Azrael Project is "to put forth the word of the Angel of Death and thereby conquer fear through understanding", "to view the world through neither side of eternity, but rather from the threshold between the dimensions of space and time", and "to reconcile Life with Death, rekindle precarnate memory, and replace fear with love". To this end, under management of Leilah Wendell, Azrael put out a small, quarterly 40-page booklet full of all things necromantic, including overwritten Gothic poetry, Anne Rice-style ramblings, necrophile erotica, true-life accounts of near-death experiences, personal encounters with the Angel of Death, and the 'Necronet' — a listing page to match-up like-minded goths and ghouls. If you're not put off by the overly adjectival short stories about entropy and stagnation, and

It's old and it smells. An (unaccredited) photograph which accompanied Vol 6, No 1 of the AZRAEL PROJECT NEWSLETTER.

you're heavily into vampires, dark erotica and the 'left hand path', this is something nice for you to flick through after the sun goes down. [*With Vol 6 No 2, the newsletter folded. The editorial states, however, that "periodic updates and other mailings" will be forthcoming—Ed.*]
Mikita Brottman

BOOK HAPPY, No 1–4
34pp $5 US & Canada/$7 elsewhere
Donna Kossy, PO Box 86663, Portland,
OR 97286, USA

Give praise to all the powers of Heaven & Hell for the materialisation of this amazing little zine! A much-needed review of strange, out of print, off-the-beaten-path books and all things pulp. If you have an inquiring mind, and are not afraid of where it might lead you, this zine is for you. Likewise if you enjoy finding unwanted books in the trash, or find very peripheral pseudo science and theory your cup of tea, Ms Kossy (famed for her excellent zine and book, KOOKS) has served it up again in assembling this menag-

erie of writers and connoisseurs of unusual pulp. It's refreshing in these days of zine proliferation — where you can pick out any ten and read reviews of the same newest "cutting edge" books — to have a publication with hindsight and foresight enough to forego all that and go for the throat. The articles and reviews in BOOK HAPPY are a combination of precise criticism, wry and insightful humour and just plain interesting information for the basic bibliophile. Pick a review, any review — A STRANGE MANUSCRIPT FOUND IN A COPPER CYLINDER (1888), for example, in issue No 2, an early social commentary disguised as a fantasy novel. We get a review, a reproduction of the cover of the original book (published anonymously and posthumously) and a sample of one of the engravings from the original edition. Also a synopsis of the book and its publishing history, with a few notes on its Canadian author, James De Mille (d.1880), and his other works. The coverboy for issue No 3 is one Casimir Zwerko, a son of Polish immigrants who seems to have been a bachelor recluse of some sort, whose legacy is an attic filled with thousands of strange books, tabloids, pamphlets, magazines and personal manuscripts of a pornographic nature. This attic treasure is discovered by a student who rents the attic room for next to nothing and discovers the pulp treasure. The student hips the author of the article, who she knows to be a lover of strange and curious books, to the incredible find in the attic. The rest of the article is about the rescuing of these things and the loss of the ones left behind. It all makes for a most Lovecraftian little adventure, minus the cosmic entities. A pulp addict's dream come true! Issue No 4 leads off with an editorial about the pitfalls of ebay — the online auction site where you can find almost anything, including strange books, some cheap, some not so. I myself have acquired this bad habit, only with magazines, not so much books — yet. The problem with my addiction is I don't stop with $5 bids. The issue is rounded out with diverse articles such as 'The Epidemic of Bad Drug Books', an article on Tom Sharpe, 'master of black humour', collecting books on UFO contactees, 'Lurid Pamphlets In Merrie Olde England' and much more. All issues are heavily illustrated with reproductions of book covers as well as diagrams and illustrations from within their covers. This zine will be well loved by anyone who loves books, and drooled upon by those who love sacred and profane esoterica. My one concern is the day all these books are brought to light and there will be no more to find; when there will be 20 people bidding on each title on ebay, because they will all have become 'highly collectable' and — GULP! — fashionable! So go quietly and send for BOOK HAPPY but don't show or tell too many people... sshhh.

Tom Brinkmann

BANAL PROBE, No 13

26pp $1.50 payable Alaina Duro; PO Box 4333, Austin, TX 78765, USA

BANAL PROBE is a family-happy fanzine edited by Alaina K. Duro, with layout by husband Steve, and lots of references to the baby. This in itself is a bit off-putting, the contents are similarly worthy but not especially interesting — non-fiction accounts of encounters on the social margins. This issue features a description of a true-life combat scene in Vietnam, some-

body's experience trying to get their stuff back from a dump in Marietta, Georgia, and somebody else's experience having sex with an older woman who was still bleeding from a recent hysterectomy. Most of the accounts, however — which range from a couple of paragraphs to a number of pages — are memoirs of parents, recently-dead friends and neighbours, and the wonder of children, rather than more interesting encounters with strangers. Many of these tales of life-changing moments are by Alaina K. herself. Uplifting accounts of daily blessings for eco-friendly alternative-types who like to 'experience'.

Mikita Brottman

ZAPBRUDER HEADSNAP
No 11 & 12

44pp $3; 537 Jones St. #2074, San Francisco, CA 94102, USA

Email: headSNAP@aol.com

The best thing going for this fanzine is its title... I suppose I was disappointed to find that this wasn't some obsessive little conspiracy mag, but rather a place for the author/editor to publish snippets of stories, rants and some not very funny satire. The occasional mention of Koresh, Waco and of course JFK/Oswald is about as far as it goes in the paranoia department. Issue 11 has a piece which suggests that the death of Sonny Bono was no accident and that he'd been taken out by the CIA because of his stand on Waco. There's little detail and the whole thing feels like it was written for the sake of it rather than for any deep-seated political reasons. No, the real focus of ZAPBRUDER HEADSNAP is Sean Beaudoin's writing, which is interesting at times, but on the whole there's nothing that I'd go out of my way for. The covers are good, in a sort of cheap colour printing/DTP/collage kind of way. It's not good. It's not bad. It just leaves me indifferent.

Pan Pantziarka

HEAD MAGAZINE, No 8
Healing

Ed. Holly Mina

136pp £4; Head magazine, BM Uplift, Lon-

don, WC1N 3XX. http://www.headmag.com

HEAD magazine is a great big thick, professionally-produced black-and-white New Age periodical from BM Uplift, crammed full with articles and information on Gaia, anarchy, social subversion, 'guerrilla mobility', class war, Shiatsu, mantric prayers, crystals, magic and alchemy. There's also a section of CD, video and small press reviews. The writing is concise and professional but not without a sense of irony, and the articles present an interesting mixture of the serious/academic and the creative/personal. High points in this issue are an essay on the truth about the pet food industry (pet food contains "the rendered remains of cats and dogs"), an interview with "medical clairvoyant" Caroline Myss entitled 'Illness as a Disorder of Power', and a transcript of Howard Marks' application for the position of Drug Czar, given at Frome One World Festival. Low points include a piece about trees in Japan that "synchronise electrical biorhythms", and some blarney about loving your periods (especially the kind of dark, clotted menstrual blood that's apparently "full of life, full of magic, full of potential"). Basically, this is a very carefully crafted New Age journal, almost encyclopaedic in its coverage, with a nicely balanced variety of articles on all aspects of alternative culture in the Nineties. **Mikita Brottman**

TWOBLUE COUPLES
Vol 3 No 2

£3.50; Galaxy Publications Ltd, PO Box 312, Witham, Essex CM8 3SZ

Little more than a 'Now That's What I Call Porn' this bi-monthly mag is made up of photosets that, to this seasoned eye, look swiped from the files of other titles like CHERI, HIGH SOCIETY and FOX. This means that most of the girls are your generic Yank porn babes but, compared to the boilers you usually find in other Galaxy titles, this is most welcome.

To be fair this particular issue is class all the way — Page Three regular Karen White appears in a lively spit-dribbling dyke session with another blonde and, in one full page shot, has her arse cheeks splayed by her bleached buddy to reveal an invitingly gaping ring. Despite her impossibly cute, pixie-like nose our Karen is well stacked and I'm suddenly looking at her in a new light. Elsewhere there's splayed labia aplenty from what looks like two brunette twins, a lively threesome in a shower stall and a girl/guy session featuring whipped cream dribbled from bell-end to chin and even a precariously placed strawberry! Only the horrific Reader's Wives and Reader's Boners' (!?!) shots bring a jarring note of reality to the proceedings and the full page cartoons are some of the worst I've ever seen outside of a Student Rag Mag.

It's nowhere near 'hardcore' and not even up to speed with CHERI (which still doesn't show penetration but has recently featured 'cumshot aftermath' shots) but is a long way from the quite tame porn mags of 10 years ago.

I flick back to page seven where cute Alex (female, for those suddenly confused) firmly grips a gleaming red erection close to her gaping mouth, looking like she's just found a new religion and I'm suddenly glad that moral standards continue to decline as we head towards the end of the millennium. By December we could have cum shots on the front of THE STAR. **Rik Rawling**

VIXXXEN, No 2

44pp £3 + £0.40 UK; payable: S.J. Midwinter; Dark Carnival, 140 Crosby Ave., Scunthorpe, South Humberside, DN15 8NT
Bang on, old boy! The return of sleaze scooter VIXXXEN, the fanzine of XXX entertainment in movies, comics and the small presses.

Some pretty erudite stuff has appeared recently, focussing on the world of porn. The more the merrier, I say. But for a humorous, frivolous and flippant overview, you can't beat VIXXXEN. It

may only be 45 A5 pages long but it packs in a lot of meat including, in this second issue: an interview with Jenna Jameson, an Eighties retrospective of Christy Canyon, a feature on 'Lost Classics', a clutch of video and film reviews, and some unmissable comics articles (with the accompaniment of some down and dirty groovy illustrations) on the likes of artist Guido Crepax and publishing houses Carnal and Eros Comix.

Lots of good irreverence done in the worst possible taste! **John Carter**

MANSPLAT, No 15

Free!; Hairball Press, 2318 2nd Avenue, Suite 591, Seattle WA98121, USA
Email: mansplat@beer.com
http://home.earthlink.net/~mansplat/
"Bathroom Litter-ature for Men... but Chicks Can Read It Too!" is the tag line and based on that alone you could be forgiven for thinking that this cheaply printed tabloid paper is nothing but a low-rent LOADED. And you would be wrong.

LOADED is shite whereas MANSPLAT — despite sharing the same obsessions with beer, tits, farts and 'trash culture' — is actually pretty funny. If I were 20-years-old I would probably think it was hilarious but a page full of listings for different types of fart or coolest cars on TV is as lazy as it gets. However, a surreal and sardonic streak of wit runs through the MANSPLAT collective and is best expressed through items like the 'Shat in The Hat' column where the worlds of William Shatner (in Capt. Kirk mode) and Dr Seuss are intertwined with amusing consequences. Elsewhere there's 'Horror Movie Chicks We Wanna Do It With', 'Nixon — What A Dick' and the intriguing 'Perfect Woman' ("Would you like to watch me go down on my girlfriend", "I'm bored, let's shave my pussy") but the winner, the page you'll most want to photocopy and post to your friends comprises

Ron Jeremy Bumper Stickers ("Ron Does It Deeper"), lovingly illustrated with images of the man who physically and spiritually most resembles the MANSPLAT mentality. As it's published infrequently the occasional dose of this nonsense is welcome but repeat readings may have you longing for some Kafka. **Rik Rawling**

INFILTRATION No 9, 11 & 12
The zine about going places you're not supposed to go

28pp $1; Back issues/future issues $2 cash or postage; PO Box 66069 Town Centre PO Pickering, ON L1V 6P7. www.infiltration.org
This zine is for the — literally — underground, possibly even the chthonic. Subversion in an exploratory vein. Who knows, in the future these small thin tomes of INFILTRATION may be requisite reading! Parisian Catacombs, The Botanic Gardens of Subterranean Glasgow, Storm Drains, Chicago Tunnel Company — these are some of the themes and articles you are likely to come across. Even if you're not one of the cave/tunnel/drain world underground, this is informative, fascinating stuff. For some reason JG Ballard comes to mind... The main article in No 12 on Toronto's Union Station is fairly typical: it reads like the instructions on how to navigate through some labyrinthine video or computer game. Encounters with tunnels of opaque air, metal staircases leading to crawlspaces, hallways leading nowhere, disassembled escalators, hot metal ladders and staircases in steam tunnels etc. But instead of some virtual bullshit, these guys are breathing the dust, sweating through the steam tunnels, smelling the stench of dead vermin, and interacting with (and avoiding) security guards and employees. In these days of high tech surveillance and terrorist paranoia (not to mention in some places, submachine-gun toting security) your curiosity quotient has to be

Bumper sticker from MANSPLAT.

EXAMINING THE PATTERSON BIGFOOT FILM

high to explore some of this territory. Looking at the Manhattan skyline I've often wondered what must be underneath it all, besides the "mole people". With all manner of tunnels below tunnels below even more tunnels, what holds up all the weight? Hollow earth theory?

The back cover of No 11 even has a glossary of 'Drainspeak' and inside an interview with one of "the most active members of the Australian draining syndicate known as the Cave Clan". Down under indeed! Each issue is heavily illustrated with photos from the explorations. There are numerous web sites for those who seek these activities also. So send in your mined and minted metal or postal equivalent to the address above and go underground, way underground. **Tom Brinkmann**

X: THE UNKNOWN, Nos 32, 38/39, 40/41
Ed. Pat O'Donnell
10/16pp $1.50; subs $15/12 issues; PO Box 14, Matawan, NJ 07747, USA

You know how it is, right? You're innocently watching the skies over Arizona one night, photographing UFOs with a night vision scope, when lo and behold, out of the San Andreas fault leaps a bunch of enraged subterranean Bigfoot creatures who throw rocks at you until you're forced to run for it. Life really *is* a bitch, innit? Of course, the Bigfoots (Bigfeet?) are trying to conceal from you their complicity in the epidemic of alien-inspired cattle mutilations that have occurred in the area — it turns out that the alien 'greys' are transfusing the Bigfoots with blood from the dead cows in order to alter their genetic make-up and make them easier to control. So it's all quite simple, really.

That, at least, is what Lyle Vann, director of the ARIZONA BIGFOOT CENTER and author of MARS NEEDS BOVINE!!! would have us believe in X: THE UNKNOWN No 32. Vann writes in a breathlessly excited style and seems to think that the more words in block capitals and exclamation points he uses, the more credible his assertions will become:

As I gazed behind the brush, my curiosity and bravery was [sic] rewarded. I can claim something that no other person on Earth can: I witnessed a cattle mutilation unfolding! I saw it all with my own two eyes!!

OK, two can play at that game. I AM NOW USING CAPITAL LETTERS! NOTE HOW MUCH MORE AUTHORITATIVE AND WISE THIS REVIEW HAS BECOME!!! Vann pops up again in X No 40/41, a 'Special Double Sized News Watch Issue' with more of his Bigfoot-watching anecdotes:

… the female Bigfoot was wearing twigs in her hair like barrettes.

And also in No 38/39 (a double sized 'Exorcism' issue):

My world became unreal and mysterious the day of October 22nd, 1994 when I viewed "the message from the ape-man."

It sounds like it's been unreal and mysterious for a lot longer than that, guy!

As you will have gathered by now, X is a FORTEAN TIMES-style zine about, well, everything. Bigfoot, Nessie, spooks (both the supernatural and

CIA-funded varieties), men in black, extraterrestrials, fairies, JFK conspiracies, military cover-ups... X: THE UNKNOWN is more chokka with all the usual suspects than THE X FILES. What irks me, though, about this broad-spectrum approach is the way you are asked to believe in absolutely any loopy proposition or be seen as a crusty hidebound sceptic. Personally speaking, I'm much more prepared to believe in US military cover-ups and political conspiracies than in underground Bigfoots, and I can't really see why belief in one should imply belief in the other. And frankly, the daily behaviour of ordinary human beings is so hilarious and strange that I don't feel the need to go out looking for *outré* things to believe in — coping with 'consensual reality' is enough of a struggle.

I did get a few laughs out of these zines, though. Apart from the ever-entertaining Lyle Vann, I particularly enjoyed this gem from 'Symptoms of Demon Possession' by JF Cogan in No 38/39, an article which appears to lay the blame for almost all the woes of humanity on demonic possession:

…what makes a person risk a prominent career for no good reason at all? The answer may well be intermittent demon possession on a time-share basis.

So that's Bill Clinton off the hook, then.

Journalistic integrity compels me to point out that the back page of No 40/41 contains a rave review of HEADPRESS 17, abruptly and bizarrely spliced onto the end of an article on the typology of necrophilia (talk about guilt by association!), so I'm sorry I can't return the compliment, but, to rephrase Dana Scully, "I don't want to believe." **Simon Collins**

HOOVER HOG, No 2
A Review of Dangerous Ideas
80pp; Richard (Chip) Smith, PO Box 7511, Cross Lanes, WV 25356-0511, USA

Here I was expecting the usual 'dangerous ideas' — deviant sexuality, serial killers, porn, the stuff that HEADPRESS readers lap up — but I was quite surprised by what this deceptively low-rent magazine contains. Race, Holocaust revisionism, paedophilia, abortion... Material that really is taboo now that sexuality has moved centre stage. And, I'll admit it, this is one magazine that has left me feeling very disturbed. The lead article looks at the thorny issue of race and IQ, surveying the current state of the (non-) debate. With the establishment consensus eschewing any semblance of discussion, and with officially sanctioned 'anti-racism' the order of the day, anyone daring to ask too many questions risks being labelled a racist. I have to admit that reading this material left me feeling extremely uncomfortable, and the conclusions it draws are not the ones that I want to be drawn. However that's clearly the intention, because debate is surely what is missing, particularly in the US (where the magazine originates). Nobody disputes racial differences in IQ, what is in dispute is the cause. It's that same old nature versus nurture argument, and in this case Chip Smith of HOOVER HOG comes down on the nature side of the fence. I would still disagree with him, but he points out enough facts to give plenty of pause for thought. In the end though, and despite the persistence of differences in IQ scores between blacks and whites, I would ask why IQ scores continue to rise. If intelligence is hereditary, why is it that scores — for black and whites — are increasing? Oh, and in case you think this magazine's full of Aryan's bragging about how smart they are, the article gleefully points out that Ashkenazy Jews are way ahead of the 'master race'. Still, the whole issue of race and anti-racism is in need of being questioned. Calling everyone who questions the current orthodoxy 'racist' is certainly only going to create more racists — including such militant anti-racists as Anti-Fascist Action in the UK. Just as disturbing to read is Jewish Holocaust revisionist David Cole. To date I've always assumed that Holocaust revisionists were right-wing apologists for National Socialism (as a good percentage of them are), however to read left-wing revisionists is distinctly unsettling. I don't have the knowledge or the expertise to comment one way or another, but the questions that David Cole asks can't be dismissed easily. Other articles include anti-abortionism from an atheist libertarian perspective and a look at male attraction to adolescent females. But to be honest the other articles are more intriguing, at least to this reader.

This really is a review of ideas, and the fact that it's caused me to question so many assumptions is testament both to the quality of writing and

research, and also to the fact that honest debate on many of these issues is clearly lacking elsewhere. The fact that many of the positions adopted here are 'right-wing' makes life more difficult for libertarians and egalitarians, but somehow labels like 'left' and 'right' don't have much meaning here. If you want an interesting and challenging read then this is highly recommended. **Pan Pantziarka**

ULTRA FLESH, Vol 1
A Connoisseurs [sic] Guide to the Halcyon Days of Pornography
94pp £10.99; 1998
Available through Headpress, see p.160

In perfect-bound magazine form, how can this homage to Seventies' smut fail? It has archival Readers' Wives snaps, reviews of seminal porn films, articles on Linda Lovelace, Gerard Damiano, FLESH GORDON, the Enema Bandit, and even a crap comic strip (based on Richard Aldrich's film MS MAGNIFICENT). The soft-core pictures (erect members have been tactfully removed) and thick, glossy paper make the entire publication look less like a porn mag and more like a theatrical programme. *But what the hey! It's*

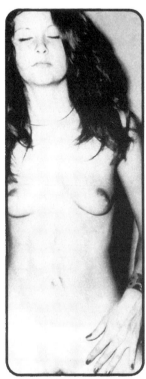

Linda Lovelace in ULTRA FLESH.

supposed to be the Seventies! There's even a John 'The Wadd' Holmes centrefold, in which the mightily donged actor is dwarfed by the majesty of his surroundings for a change (he's standing in a dramatic, arms-outstretched, Christ-like pose under a waterfall). Lightweight but fun. **Sarah Turner**

PASS THE MARMALADE
A Comprehensive Catalogue of British Horror movies
Darrell Buxton
1999; Contact the author for details:
34 Wild Street, Derby, DE1 1GN

Beneath its cheap'n'cheerful print job exterior (straightforward layout; no images; slide binder spine), PASS THE MARMALADE sets to documenting every genre related film production to have come out of Britain, which it does with a fair quota of curios and surprises. Did you know that eight versions of SCROOGE have emanated from British shores down the years, or before the end of the 1920s seven versions of FAUST had been made (one adaptation of which — dated 1898 — is promoted here as possibly the first British horror film)?

As well as full-length features and shorts (several being independents, distributed by mail-order only), a section entitled 'Problem/Borderline Films' collates those titles about which little is known, which may or may not have had British production involvement, or aren't genre films at all but do have horror references. Hence the inclusion of TV sitcom PLEASE, SIR! (because of a brief 'werewolf' gag), PREHISTORIC PEEPS (silent fantasy with a giant and an apeman), and ESKIMO NELL (because of a character supposedly based on Tigon chief Tony Tenser, and a poster for the fictitious movie 'Vampire Vomit' on a wall).

Darrell Buxton makes no apologies for this being a no-nonsense reference tool, but I can't help thinking it would have been that much better with more annotations and some consistency in the write-ups for the entries. Why, for instance, does A CLOCKWORK ORANGE get a comparatively lengthy synopsis and SHALLOW GRAVE none at all? Nevertheless, a useful source and one that stands for the moment as 'definitive'.

DEVIANT
The Shocking True Story of Ed Gein, The Original 'Psycho'
Harold Schechter
242pp £9.99; 1998, Pocket Books
ISBN 0-671-02546-5

"TOP-DRAWER TRUE CRIME"
Booklist

Deviant

The Shocking True

Story of ED GEIN,

the Original 'Psycho'

HAROLD SCHECHTER

Distributed in the UK by Turnaround

About 15 years ago, a colleague of mine was invited to a psychiatrists' party at the Mendota Mental Health Institute in Madison, Wisconsin, and at the end of the evening was surprised to learn that the small, grey-haired, docile man serving canapés was none other than Ed Gein, the Wisconsin Ghoul himself. Many 'fictionalisations' of the Gein case come over as simply absurd. I recently had the misfortune of watching a 're-construction' of the case on American television, which featured a middle-aged actor dressed in a rubbery 'woman skin' capering and gibbering ludicrously under a Hammer horror style full moon. Fortunately, Schechter's book brings us none of this malarkey. Instead, it presents a meticulously researched account, a thorough and serious recreation of the Gein case, which surely stands as the 'locus classicus' of the middle American psychopath. Schechter is especially good at evoking the heart-sickening, isolating gloom down on the farm in Plainfield, Wisconsin, the unimaginable filthiness of the old Gein place, and the crazy incongruity of the mad little old man.

DEVIANT was originally published in 1989, so it does seem a little dated in places, especially since the last 10 years have seen something of a Gein revival, whose hallmarks include Schechter's own OUTCRY, a novelisation of the Gein case, and Paul Anthony Woods' ED GEIN—PSYCHO, the handbook of the card-carrying Gein-fiend, plus a number of low-budget movies. These more recent works make Schechter's small collection of photographs look rather tame. [*The more horrible pictures which ap-*

peared in the earlier print of the book have been removed for this one, as was recently pointed out to me—Ed.] Still, DEVIANT contains some classic descriptions of this "idiot savant" of the macabre, especially Gein's mixture of childish simplicity and monstrous criminality. Schechter even seems to reveal a kind of ghoulish respect for Weird Old Eddie, appearing to relish certain details of the case. At least he doesn't attempt to diagnose him as a transvestite or avant-garde gender transgressor. Instead, Schechter believes that Gein's grave-lootings and corpse-violations were simply the instincts of a sexually normal man whose latent Oedipus complex somehow ceased to be latent. This much may be true, but there's more to be said here about the cold comforts of pioneer history and the inherent violence of the rural shotgun culture. All of America went into the making of Eddie Gein.

Mikita Brottman

DEPRAVED
The Shocking True Story of America's First Serial Killer
Harold Schechter

342pp £9.99; 1998, Pocket Books
ISBN 0-671-02544-9
Distributed in the UK by Turnaround

In 19th century Chicago, while London was chilled by tales of Jack the Ripper, Herman Mudgett (better known as H.H. Holmes), a charming, manipulative, wealthy charlatan, admitted to 27 murders. His purpose-built 'Castle of Horror' gave the fascinated locals no clue to the corpses that lay within, but incorporated stairs to nowhere, trapdoors, acid vats, torture devices and even a home-crematorium. Described as America's first serial killer, Schechter places Holmes in a detailed and convincing historical account with his usual flair for TRUE DETECTIVE-type gory details. Few reference works exist on Holmes (David Franke's THE TORTURE DOCTOR is the only other that springs to mind), which is puzzling as he was a killer of such malice, aforethought and invention that his tale is ripe for the picking.

Sarah Turner

THE OKLAHOMA CITY BOMBING AND THE POLITICS OF TERROR
David Hoffman

509pp £12.99/$18.95; 1998, Feral House; ISBN 0-922915-49-0
Distributed in the UK by Turnaround

TS Eliot once wrote that 'April is the cruellest month.' The Nineties certainly seem to be vindicating him. In April 1999, connoisseurs of atrocity could take their pick from the ongoing bloodbath in the Balkans, nail bombs in London, and the Trenchcoat Mafia shootings in Littleton, Colorado. Earlier in the decade, April 19 1993 saw the Mount Carmel compound of David Koresh and his Branch Davidian followers go up in flames in the culmination of a 51-day siege which had been catastrophically mishandled by every government agency to get involved, especially the FBI, who had taken over from the ATF (Bureau of Alcohol, Tobacco and Firearms), who had provoked the standoff in the first place with an ill-conceived attempt to raid Mount Carmel in order to search for illegal weapons. Eighty-six people died in the blaze, including 27 children. And on April 19 1995, probably not coincidentally, the Alfred P Murrah Federal Building in Oklahoma City was destroyed by a huge explosion (or explosions? See below), causing the loss of 169 lives, including 19 children, over 500 injuries, and hundreds of millions of dollars' worth of damage.

Americans, unused to acts of domestic terrorism, reacted with outrage and disbelief. Almost everyone initially assumed that Islamic fundamentalists were responsible, as they had been for the bombing of the World Trade Centre in New York in February 1993, which, until the Oklahoma City bombing, had been the worst terrorist incident seen in the United States. But within three days, the FBI had made two arrests, Timothy McVeigh and Terry Nichols, white men with military backgrounds and connections to the libertarian rightist anti-governmental 'Militia' movements. They were tried separately in Federal courts and convicted by prosecution cases based on the premise that they had together built a large (4800 pound) truck bomb out of ammonium nitrate fertiliser and fuel oil and detonated it outside the Murrah Building (a protest against the government's actions at Waco and at Ruby Ridge, Idaho, in August 1992, where federal agents had shot and killed family members of white supremacist and gun-nut Randy Weaver). In some ways, the case against the two men was strong — forensic evidence showed they had been handling explosive substances, they were both known to hold violently anti-governmental views, they had been seen setting off bombs on Nichols' farmland before, and McVeigh was placed at the scene of the crime by many witnesses. Above all, McVeigh made little attempt to argue his innocence. On closer inspection, though, the governments' case was full of holes, many of which are examined at great length in David Hoffman's fascinating book.

In some ways, the case against Tim McVeigh and Terry Nichols resembles that against Lee Harvey Oswald in the assassination of President Kennedy, the most salient difference being that McVeigh and Nichols survived to stand trial. The title of the first chapter of THE OKLAHOMA CITY BOMBING, 'The Mannlicher-Carcanno Bomb', explicitly makes this comparison. Like the Mannlicher-Carcanno Italian hunting rifle allegedly used to kill JFK, Hoffman convincingly argues that the size and type of bomb supposedly set by McVeigh simply could not have wreaked the havoc seen in Oklahoma, and he includes as an appendix an interesting bomb damage analysis report by explosives expert Benton Partin.

This is only the first in a long series of loose ends and lacunae in the Feds' case exhaustively explored by Hoffman. This is a serious and wide-ranging investigation (it took me a solid week to wade through it!), and I can only attempt to give a brief summary of the most important questions raised.

Who was 'John Doe 2', the suspect seen by many witnesses with McVeigh in the rented truck used for the bombing? An APB was initially issued for him, only to be hastily withdrawn as the authorities announced that he didn't exist after all. Suspicions remain that he was a government agent (provocateur?), who was ignored in order to protect his cover.

Why were the warnings given of the impending bombing by several different FBI informants within the Militia movement ignored? Or were they? No ATF agents were injured in the blast — they had been told not to turn up for work that morning.

What of the connections Terry Nichols had to various shady Middle Eastern people? He met some very dodgy characters on several mysterious trips to the Philippines.

A white supremacist named Wayne Snell was executed in Arkansas on the very day of the Oklahoma bombing.

Snell, convicted of two racially motivated killings, had been a member of a far-right Christian paramilitary group called the Covenant, Sword and the Arm of the Lord, which, remarkably, had plotted in 1983 to destroy the Murrah Building with a truck bomb. Why was this extraordinary coincidence never investigated?

Why did McVeigh behave so stupidly in the aftermath of the bombing? Stopped for speeding, he made no attempt to evade capture, despite having firearms in the car with him. Again, like Lee Harvey Oswald, his movements and behaviour in the weeks and months preceding the bombing seem erratic, to say the least. Admittedly, he could have been a 'lone nut', but that hardly explains how he existed with no visible means of support, apparently as an itinerant arms dealer living in the back of his car, having turned his back on a promising military career. In yet another Oswald parallel, McVeigh's time with the Marines seems to have brought him into contact with some very shadowy military intelligence operations. Was he released into civilian life only to act as an undercover agent in the Militia movement?

Ultimately, one is left not so much with a feeling that McVeigh and Nichols were innocent — they are clearly both deeply unpleasant and dangerous men — but that a much larger picture was wilfully ignored by the investigating agencies, who seemed to have an undue fervour and haste to insist that McVeigh and Nichols were the only conspirators, despite large amounts of evidence to the contrary. McVeigh in particular looks like a classic patsy.

THE OKLAHOMA CITY BOMBING suffers from the usual fault of conspiracy tomes of offering too many alternative suspects and explanations — at times, it seems there was hardly anyone in Oklahoma that fateful morning who *wasn't* trying to bomb the Murrah Building! And Hoffman's writing style doesn't really make the book a pleasure to read — earnest though it is, it's also tedious and dry, and the frequent heavy-handed sarcastic asides make it all too obvious where Hoffman is coming from, politically speaking. But like the JFK case, the bombing in Oklahoma refuses to go away — Russ Kick's invaluable PSYCHOTROPEDIA lists four other books and one video on the same topic, none of them anywhere near as sub-

stantial as this — and if you want to take a serious interest in the case, it's difficult to see how you can avoid reading this.

For those who just can't get enough (and God knows, after wading through this hefty sucker, you really should give it a rest — it's just not *healthy!*), I recommend Adam Parfrey's essay 'Finding Our Way Out Of Oklahoma', collected in his CULT RAPTURE volume. And for conspiracy buffs generally, PREVAILING WINDS is a well-researched and classy magazine covering a wildly eclectic range of topics — contact them at PO Box 23511, Santa Barbara, CA 93121, USA. No 5 contains several pieces relevant to this book, including an open letter from Oklahoma State Representative Charles Key, who also contributes a foreword to Hoffman's book, and an article by Hoffman himself on a train derailment in Arizona (this material is recycled in the book), as well as an interesting speech by Oliver Stone, himself the subject of conspiracy theories (see Feral House's SECRET AND SUPPRESSED for improbable information regarding subliminal images use in Stone's film JFK).

As William Burroughs so wisely observed, "A paranoid is someone who knows what's going on."

Simon Collins

DARK MOON
Apollo and the
Whistle-Blowers

568pp £16.99 +£1p&p; 1999, Aulis Publishers, 25 Belsize Park, London, NW3 4DU
ISBN 1-898541-10-8
Tel: +44 (0)171 431 1414
Fax: +44 (0)171 431 6644

The idea of the Apollo moon landings being nothing but an elaborate hoax

— with supposed 'live' broadcasts of moonwalks actually taking place in secret locations here on earth — has been kicking around the public consciousness for some years now. It was certainly fuelled by the 1978 movie CAPRICORN ONE (the plot of which revolves around a mission to Mars being a hoax), and is insinuated as early as 1971 (not two years after the first manned landing on the moon) in another movie: DIAMONDS ARE FOREVER. In their introduction to DARK MOON, authors Bennett & Percy claim they wish to put into "question the entire validity of the official record of mankind's exploration of the Moon especially the Apollo lunar landings themselves". It's not without some relish that they set about their task, and at times some pretty preposterous ground is covered (dressing down Santilli's alien autopsy footage is one thing, but analysing the 'flaws' in the INDEPENDENCE DAY tie-in novel...?).

One of the most 'supportive' aspects of this conspiracy theory are the snaps supposedly taken by the astronauts themselves while on the Moon. Most everything else in the book can be held up as mere conjecture, but these pictures are consistently damning when presented in the context of a hoax. It starts with the innocuous point that each picture taken by Neil Armstrong is a rather beautiful composition, and then bangs in the fact that his camera had no viewfinder. (*None* of the cameras had viewfinders — they were fixed on the astronauts' chests.) A lot of the images suffer from 'unnatural' lighting, with shadows defying logic and falling in a variety of different directions; they lack consistency, too, with some shadows being long and dark while those adjacent are short and grey. With the sun clearly visible in the background, nearside images are inexplicably clearly lit when they should be in silhouette. Such anomalies seem to indicate the presence of more than the sun as a strong light source, but NASA didn't take any lighting equipment to the Moon. 'Hot spots' — or reflections — on objects also suggest the existence of secondary lighting.

Events supposedly caught simultaneously on still-camera and TV camera reveal curious anomalies — like they never happened at the same time at all. Stranger still are the markings evident on a rock and a nearby patch of the lunar surface, interpreted as an alphabetical placement guide for the 'set dresser' in the lunar hoax landscape...

Which brings us full circle: what to believe? The authors suggest the lettering mentioned above has been airbrushed out of the photograph on its publication elsewhere, while readily admitting that they themselves have enhanced the markings here "very slightly just for clarity". Well, one man's enhancement is another man's conspiracy theory. You'd need to be very gullible indeed to swallow everything DARK MOON puts forward as indicative of foul play. However, few people will come away from this book without some suspicion that NASA has something big to hide.

TRAVELS WITH DR DEATH
Ron Rosenbaum
518pp £12; Papermac
ISBN 0-333-75031-4

No, Ron Rosenbaum didn't have to share the back seat with David Owen on his way to partition yet another country or political party (how *do* you say "troubles" in Serbo-Croatian?). Nothing so horrible. *This* Dr Death is Dr James Grigson, a Texas psychiatrist who testifies as an expert witness during the penalty phase of murder trials. His judgement is always the same: the guilty party will inevitably kill again, unless the state puts him to death. Rosenbaum rode along with the Doc as he hit three separate murder trials in three towns in two days, testified against three men, and saw all three sentenced to die. Dr Death was written originally for VANITY FAIR in 1990, and as the title piece of this collection of intriguing journalism (from one of the best feature writers in America) it may be a little misleading. Although Rosenbaum has a nose for intriguing stories (his piece 'Dead Ringers', on the Marcus Brothers, was *not* the source for the movie of the same name, but his take on the identical twin gynaecologists is even sadder than the film's) and writes well about "clandestine cultures", like people in search of illegal cancer cures, or the staffers in nuclear missile silos, his most telling work is what he terms "investigations of investigations." The most entertaining, if least successful, of these is probably 'The Corpse As Big As The Ritz', an account of the murder of David Whiting, who was the business manager of actress Sarah Miles, and was found dead in her motel room during the filming of the movie THE MAN WHO LOVED CAT DANCING. Rosenbaum's account raises more questions than it answers, though the American

Would you believe they put a man on the Moon? "The reflection in the visor [which does not have a camera positioned at eye level] cannot be that of the actual photographer of the image." **DARK MOON.**

judge's reaction to Miss Miles likely set the standard for Mary Archer's fragrant performance in the British courts a decade later. In all his exegeses of questions which perplex others, he resembles nothing as much as a theologian. For Rosenbaum brings an almost religious sensibility to almost every question, as if looking for something to believe in, when the world has been made entirely relative by physics and philosophy. Journalists become sort of secular priests, or perhaps exorcists, investigating the strange beliefs of myriad cults, and reporting back on them. As he says while checking out Dealey Plaza with Penn Jones, Rosenbaum will drop down the manhole, but he won't pull the manhole cover over his head. If this sounds like ALICE IN WONDERLAND, well, if Rosenbaum isn't a theologian then he's a literary critic, and he analyses the literature of these cults like a reviewer. Still, it becomes eerie when the characters lurking behind the cultic mysteries start popping up in each other's stories. Thus, the diary of Mary Pinchot Meyer, the JFK mistress found murdered on a towpath in Georgetown, was destroyed by James Jesus Angleton, head of counter-intelligence at the CIA. And Angleton himself is the star of Rosenbaum's best piece, about Angleton's CIA mole-hunt which nearly destroyed the Agency from within. When dealing with the levels of bluff and counterbluff, the 'they knew we knew they knew' paradoxes which drove Angleton to distraction (and was Kim Philby behind the entire game?), Rosenbaum's philosophy

teacher at Yale, Josiah Thompson, himself became a leading Kennedy assassination critic. Maybe Yale prepares you for such things, because another of the best pieces in this book delves into the Yale secret society, Skull and Bones, which has produced George Bush and just about all the CIA. Having grown up in the area myself, I can testify to the strangeness of the clubhouse where the Boners gather to exchange their sexual secrets, in echo of some Heidelberg fraternity, but Rosenbaum shrugs it off with as a joke. Maybe this is his role, to act as the sceptic for the people who read VANITY FAIR or HARPERS, and to de-mythologise and thus render safer the interpretations of our world advanced by those not as content with their Yale backgrounds. That's a cruel interpretation, but you do wish that at some point he'd let on he believes in *something* besides his deadline. But actually he does. The reason this book was given a reprint in the UK was because the essay, 'Who Was Maria's Lover?' investigating the old question of whether Adolf Hitler's father was fathered illegitimately by a Jew, and appears to have been the jumping-off point for Rosenbaum's successful book, EXPLAINING HITLER, which was his effort to try to come to terms with the idea of inhuman evil in human society. Perhaps all the essays in this volume were, in a way, his apprenticeship, paving the way for the big story where he might do more than debunk. For whatever reason, getting this exceptional collection of journalism into print was worth it by itself. **Michael Carlson**

THE PROFESSIONAL PARANOID
How To Fight Back When Being Investigated, Surveilled, Stalked, Harassed or Targetted by any Agency, Organisation or Individual
H.Michael Sweeney
195pp £9.99/$12.95; 1998, Feral House
ISBN 0-922915-54-7
Distributed in the UK by Turnaround
Moving into territory usually dominated by the likes of Paladin and Loompanics, Sweeney's hugely technical book has blood-ties with publications by Alex Constantine and Rex Feral. Mind control, law enforcement, listening-in, private mail boxes, surveillance and the like are all dissected in fanatical detail. It is at times fascinating but strangely distant, certainly the fact that Sweeney's perspective is solidly American will alienate UK readers; also its 72 page appendix of technical information will mean nothing unless you are familiar with electronic communication systems. This is not a book of dirty tricks or revenge tactics — you would have to be seriously paranoid or a contentious criminal to be in a position where such information could be put into practice. Despite its initial complexity, the book's central message is very clear: when targeted/harassed by an organisation or individual, identify your enemy and choose your allies with care. When this has been achieved, study the enemy and use the information to either assist protection or put to your own advantage (I say advantage, but self-defence is the primary motivation here).

You can look at volumes like this in two ways: fictions from a paranoid mind, or gospel. The former is certainly the least frightening of the two (only one loony out there instead of an entire network of belligerent individuals/organisations peeking in at your every move). Take all this seriously and delusions of persecution could make you unbearable!
David Greenall

THE VISIONARY GARDEN
Philippe Fichot>Die Form
H/BK; 1995, Artware Editions, Taunusstra str. 63-B, 65183 Wiesbaden, Germany
This is a very lavishly produced, limited edition photo book which contains some fairly extreme imagery. Philippe Fichot's work here recalls Hans Bellmer in its explicit yet lifeless and unerotic portrayal of the fe-

© Philippe Fichot/Artware

THE VISIONARY GARDEN.

male form, Gilles Berquet in the use of squids (always handy to have marine invertebrates around on a fetish photoshoot) and Joel-Peter Witkin in its unremitting morbidity. Almost all the women portrayed here — there are very few men — are portrayed as corpses, some looking like images from DEATH SCENES and others trapped under cars or being fed through mangles. Yet the heavy treatment of the images — black and white and universally mottled, looking in terms of style like nothing so much as a 4AD album cover design — lessens the sense of menace and danger which these images might otherwise hold, as well as losing any sense of depth perspective. More than any other fetish-related photo book I've seen, these pictures are clearly to be seen as 'art' photography rather than being in any way a titillating product, and on those terms the collection works well. The heavy treatment throughout lends a sense of sameness to the images, though, especially in terms of black/white contrast, and few of the individual images stand out as being exceptional. A mixture of some religious iconography — eroticised nuns, surprise, surprise — and some portraits add some welcome texture to the collection. All in all, though, this is an excellent collection which is unlikely to be treated kindly by customs officials. **James Marriott**

THE DRAG KING BOOK

Del Lagrace Volcano and
Judith 'Jack' Halberstam
154pp £15.00; 1999, Serpent's Tail
ISBN 1-85242-607-1

Everything you always wanted to know about drag kings but were too afraid to ask. A beautiful and intelligent book written by Judith 'Jack' Halberstam and photographed by Del Lagrace Volcano, who also did photography for the book LOVE BITES.
The trip commences with personal accounts and recollections from the macho muff divers, including their first encounter in 1995 when Jack was judge and Del a contestant at London's first ever drag king contest. We then delve into the fashioning of a Drag King and the similarities/differences between them and their drag queen counterparts. Did you realise that Male drag kings also exist?
Next is a tribute to Elvis — "who is to Drag Kings what Liza Minelli is to Drag Queens" — where various Drag Kings perform as the star through the many

stages of his career, from Fifties heart throb to Seventies huge blob. This chapter also throws up what I thought must be two of the greatest Drag King appellations ever: 'Elvis Herselvis' and 'Justin Kase'.
A more in-depth introduction to the Drag King scene follows and focuses on the Nightlife of London, New York, San Francisco and the Drag King for-a-day workshop. Designed by Diane Torr, for a nominal fee women are instructed in the manly arts of taking-up space, penis-wearing and nose-picking.
There are also interviews with Drag King icons, including The Dodge Bros, a band who perform Tom Waits covers as well as owning the Red Bearded Lady Café in San Francisco. Also included are articles on class, race, masculinity, Drag King genders and the femme versus butch issue.
All beautifully illustrated with almost a hundred of Del's prints in colour and black & white, this book gives the reader a small glimpse into a subculture that just doesn't seem to get the attention it deserves. **Rick Caveney**

ROY STUART VOL II

Roy Stuart
200pp £19.99; H/BK; 1999, Taschen
ISBN 3-8228-6870-1

This second collection of work by photographer Roy Stuart continues exactly where the first left off: with cute models in some playful, little photo-vignettes. 'Emergency Stop' has a blonde caught short and taking a pee in a side-street. Her discarded knickers are picked up by a passer-by who insists on pulling at the freshly relieved babe's skirt. A good karate kick from her stops him in his tracks and she shuts him up by stuffing the undergarment in his mouth. Another vi-

Murray Hill for Mayor.
THE DRAG KING BOOK.

gnette — 'No Smoking' — originally featured in LEG SHOW magazine, where it received letters of protest on account of an anti-smoking theme not anticipated by Stuart. In it a woman taking a crafty drag of a cigarette is confronted by her boss (mother, whatever). A scuffle ensues with knickers aplenty being flashed, and the crafty smoker is left displaying a gob full of crushed and broken cigarettes. 'The Big Surprise' is a little more unusual with its homosexual connotations. A man picks up what he perceives to be a rent boy in a darkened side-street. In a hotel room, some petting takes place, the man receives a blowjob, and finally pulls down the youngster's jeans to reveal… a very female gash. (The deceptively innocent and androgynous model is shown in the photo montage at the front of the book, holding up her ID for the camera.) Other erotic adventures take on more obvious themes (ballerinas, French maids, lesbian schoolgirls, cellists…), with the photograph of an elegant elderly lady, exhibiting what appears to be an aged and stretched caesarean scar, being curiously out of place amongst them.

CULTURE GUIDE

135

CHEESECAKE!

CHEESECAKE!
The Rotenberg Collection
Mark Lee Rotenberg
768pp £16.99; 1999, Taschen
ISBN 3-8228-7194-X

Hot-blooded males in post-war America found their pleasures in new-fangled girlie magazines like TITTER and WINK [*subjects of an earlier Taschen book; see HEADPRESS 17*]. While the models in these publications didn't reveal everything or indeed much at all, readers could find more obliging subjects through the coy classified ads elsewhere in the magazines. Glossy B&W photos measuring 4"x5" were typically available in sets of 10 or 12. Known as 'strip sets' these showed some lass getting her kit off, but so as not to draw too much undue attention were promoted using carefully selected wording like 'French' and 'art photos'.

These once filthy photographs are regarded today as sweet and kitschy, cheesecake even. This book is a collection of a *lot* of them.

Although some of the models are professional, the majority are amateurs and wear uncomfortable smiles or appear mortified at the sudden realisation of what it is they're doing.

Like the models, the photographers are largely unknown. Their 'studio' might comprise a thinly disguised bedroom, bathroom, kitchen, office or cheap motel room. Into these come

whatever props are close at hand — a half-hearted attempt at 'art' and bringing to each set a theme (The Wild West, Down a Mineshaft, Voodoo Queen, Puzzled By Cooking Utensils, and so on).

The result is a delirious catalogue of women caught in peculiar and unflattering poses, like mid-leap with a skipping rope (ripples of fat rising), tits caught in mangles, telephone cords wrapped around the neck, adjusting the knobs of an electrical gadget wearing fishnets and fag in hand, strained looks on rocky seashores…

CHEESECAKE! comes with a good informative introduction and, yes, a bundle of cheap laughs — unless of course you spot your mum.

ART AT THE TURN OF THE MILLENNIUM
Eds. Burkhard Riemschneider and Uta Grosenick
576pp £19.99; 1999, Taschen
ISBN 3-8228-7393-4

The best 'modern art' can be summed-up in neat, concise sentences. That, I think, has been the criteria for including the 137 artists that go to make up this book, whose work is prefaced by an arresting quotation.

"AN OBJECT IS CAPABLE OF CREATING THE PLACE IN WHICH IT IS SHOWN."

"MY WORK DERIVES FROM THE SNAPSHOT. IT IS THE FORM OF PHOTOGRAPHY THAT MOST CLOSELY STANDS FOR LOVE."

"WE ARE SORE-EYED SCO-POPHILIAC OXYMORONS… WE ARE ARTISTS."

'They,' the artists, would appear to be pranksters with funding. Henrik Plenge Jakobsen, for instance, has a 'Laughing Gas Chamber' installation in which two people can sit and get high on laughing gas. His very colourful acrylic painting with the wording EVERYTHING IS WRONG looks great and I can see how it is art. I can see how the 'Laughing Gas Chamber' might be art, too, but that brings with it some awkward questions on education, presentation and contextualism. Would it be less artistic if Jakobsen charged people an entry fee into his Laughing Gas Chamber? Or erected it in the street. But it's a funny concept, and I like it. I also like Sharon Lockhart's photographic studies of bored-looking curators overseeing Tokyo's Museum of Contemporary Art; Joachim Koester's boarded-up window installation (which effectively makes the gallery look like it's been closed down); Jeff Wall's 'Sudden Gust of Wind (After Hokusai)' which has figures in a barren landscape sur-

ROY STUART VOL II.

rounded by an unfeasibly large quantity of airborne papers; Cosima Von Bonin's woman with extra long arms (she stands on an elevated plank and still they reach the ground)… You get the picture/installation.

THE X-RATED BIBLE
An Irreverent Survey of Sex in the Scriptures
Ben Edward Akerley
245pp £10.99/$14.95; 1998, Feral House
ISBN 0-922915-55-5
Distributed in the UK by Turnaround
Under such chapter headings as 'Incest: Single, Double and Multiple' and 'Scatology, Bestiality & Castration', THE X-RATED BIBLE offers short biblical passages followed by Akerley's sex-related interpretation. Yes, these interpretations may occasionally be irreverent, but I can't help feeling that exposing sexual malpractice in the bible is pretty obvious and pretty cheap: the only people who might give this book the time of day will probably know what to expect and not be surprised or shocked by it. An altogether better book would have resulted if Akerley had set out to catalogue the same biblical passages but included multiple interpretations, as opposed to his singular definitions (that sex was as rampant back then as it is now). THE X-RATED BIBLE could have been a useful and fascinating book of argument, but I fear it's more of a naughty Christmas present.
Sarah Turner

SATAN SPEAKS!
Anton Szandor La Vey
Foreword by Marilyn Manson
179pp £10.99/$13; Feral House, 1998
ISBN 0-922915-66-0
Distributed in the UK by Turnaround
Anton La Vey's recent books have had neither the charm nor the relevance of THE SATANIC BIBLE — a timely tome indeed, which raised the status of popular occult paperbacks from their lowly 'pot boiler' position to one of 'best-seller' credibility. La Vey followed the BIBLE with SATANIC RITUALS — a book which revealed what all those glossy Church of Satan photographs depicting pig-headed and dog-headed ritualists were all about!
Jump to the Nineties and the release of the long-awaited DEVIL'S NOTEBOOK (replete with Adam APOCALYPSE CULTURE Parfrey's Feral House seal of approval) and now the current, albeit posthumous, SATAN SPEAKS! What we have here are two books which are

pithy, archly humorous and nihilistic but which lack the 'timely' feel of their predecessors. La Vey seems to be having to work that much harder to maintain his rancorous stance, sometimes merely exposing his own boredom without successfully identifying its legitimate source. In some ways this isn't helped by the subject matter he chooses to discuss in SATAN SPEAKS! Though perhaps inanely humorous, La Vey ranting on about panty shields, fake snot and witch's shoes (yes witch's shoes) is hardly inspiring; neither is his searing anger served well by turning it against stereo-recordings as opposed to good old mono-recordings! It's difficult to envisage anything more bathetic than this impressive-looking Satanic High Priest grouching like some ordinary old fart in an old folk's rest-home about things as mind-rottingly mundane as this…
Stephen Sennitt

'Crowd Painting #1' (detail), Donald Baechler. ART AT THE TURN OF THE MILLENNIUM.

ALEISTER CROWLEY
The Beast Demystified
Roger Hutchinson
£16.99; Mainstream Publishing
ISBN 1-85158-967-8
Far from merely demystifying Aleister Crowley, this book sets out to completely debunk the myth. Stripping away the layers of occult mysticism (and grandiose titles) with which Crowley clothed himself, it paints a picture of a man driven entirely by selfish and egotistical needs. The author doesn't paint a pretty picture, and the figure of Crowley which emerges is not only unlikeable but at times actively despicable. That's not to say that Crowley isn't given his due, his skills as chess player and mountain-

eer, for example, are clearly acknowledged. However even here Crowley's egomania over-shadow his achievements. When Crowley abandons a mountaineering expedition in a sulk, leaving behind dead and injured colleagues, it's not only the end of his career as a climber it's also an example of the petulance which stayed with him all his life. The contrast between this biography and Francis King's THE MAGICAL WORLD OF ALEISTER CROWLEY is remarkable, and in the final analysis it comes down to the authors' differing attitudes to 'magick'. Roger Hutchinson claims to be an agnostic on the matter, but it's clear that he's got no time for any occult nonsense. And where others might be tempted to apologise for Crowley's extreme hedonism and egomania as a reaction against his strict Plymouth Brethren upbringing, Hutchinson clearly shows that not only was that upbringing not as strict as would at first appear, but also that the arrogance Crowley displayed was firmly rooted in uncompromising Christian fundamentalism. By the end of the book Crowley is shown to be a sad and lonely old man, a heroin addict with delusions of grandeur, a pathetic figure in every sense of the word. And yet… There is nothing here to explain Crowley's continuing appeal. Mercenary, perverse, monstrously selfish, how is it that he attracted so many acolytes? There's nothing here to explain why a pathetic old druggy could attract so many young, attractive women into his orbit and into his bed. And why is it that all these years later Crowleyana shows no signs of abating? "Do what thou wilt shall be the whole of the law" may not strike many people as a particularly deep philosophy, but it continues to resonate. So while this book makes interesting reading, there's something clearly missing from it: Crowley's undeniable charisma.
Pan Pantziarka

BACKSTAGE PASSES AND BACKSTABBING BASTARDS
Al Kooper
$18.95; Billboard Books
SOUL OF A MAN
Al Kooper Live
MusicMasters 2CD, 1995
If you're one of the people who don't assume this review is about Alice Cooper (the first thing Al points out in his introduction) you probably already know the big story about Al Kooper, how he slid into the empty bench

behind the organ at the Highway 61 sessions, and how the licks he played on 'Like A Rolling Stone' pleased Dylan so much they became the tune's signature. Of course, Al was a guitarist by trade, and had never really played the organ before ("your son will never be a good keyboard player," his piano teacher told his father).The French horn on the Rolling Stones' 'You Can't Always Get What You Want' was Al again, and believe me, he wasn't classically trained. Al's tired of telling the Dylan story, in fact, he skips it with interviewers, but it's here in this book, and lest you think that Koop's nothing more than a rock'n'roll Zelig, showing up in the background of all the best album photos, think again. I've been a huge Kooper fan ever since the Blues Project days. When that group split up, Al started Blood, Sweat and Tears, and their first album, CHILD IS FATHER TO THE MAN, is still one of my all-time favourites. That group broke up ("we divided into factions," Al said, in an interview. "There was me, and there was the rest of the band"). BS&T went on to chart-topping success, Al went on to SUPER SESSION, the original supergroup jam session begun with Mike Bloomfield and finished with Steve Stills. He began producing, including a wonderful big band record (AUTUMN) with the Don Ellis orchestra. He discovered Lynyrd Skynyrd, for whatever that's worth. And he produced a series of solo albums throughout the Seventies and early Eighties that are a beguiling mix of the sublime and the ridiculous. He got into soundtracks, producing the noise for the late, great TV series CRIME STORY. And nowadays he's even teaching, at Boston's prestigious Berklee. Al's never been a commercial hit. Part of it is his voice ("like a soulful asthmatic" was one description), and part of it is his desire to make music to his own tastes: challenging and rarely formulaic, encompassing elements as diverse as classical strings and Hawaiian guitars, and often indulgent of his favourite influences. It's not a recipe for chart success, but it's a joy to listen to. It's partly that polyglot nature which helps make this memoir so entertaining. But there are two other factors. One is: Al can write. His songs were always full of literary allusions, bad puns, in-jokes, and sometimes striking metaphors. His albums usually featured outstanding concepts: the cover of CHILD IS FATHER

MANIAC

One of the perks of working for a publisher of erotic fiction is that I come into contact with material by a great many photographers who utilise a variety of bizarre mediums. I'd seen Gilles Berquet's work a few times before, in various fetish publications, but had been dissuaded from getting in touch with him because of my associate's complaint that "There's too much tit-binding" (to the aforementioned associate's credit, it was in fact she who first introduced me to the magazine). I knew what she meant — imagine Man Ray spliced with a Japanese bondage fanatic. But after seeing MANIAC, Berquet's highly idiosyncratic magazine, I also knew I had to see more.
When I got in touch with him, partly to ask if he had any material we could use for book covers, and partly to enquire about the history of MANIAC, he very kindly sent a whole batch of material, including a book and a signed print — I was elated by the response. Since then, typically, I've seen Berquet's work everywhere. He is interviewed in a recent issue of plush photographic magazine BLACK & WHITE, in which the interviewer brings up the hoary old chestnut of the difference between erotica and pornography. (When will these fools learn?) There's also a piece on him in a recent issue of SECRET, and his work is featured in most issues of the now sadly defunct JOURNAL OF EROTICA, one of the more intelligent and interesting British ef-

forts in this area. It was while leafing through the latter, looking for something totally different, that I found the Berquet images that have most appealed to me. I now think his work is more interesting than that of any other photographer working within a 'fetish' context. The bizarre and grotesque elements make his pictures unusable to me in a work context — we publish books which are sold in WHS, after all — but I'm more and more keen to seek it all out. Man Ray is an obvious starting point — the prodigious technical skill married to surrealist concerns — but Berquet, like a number of contemporary French photographers working with fetish images (Christophe Mourthé, Robert Chouraqui), has a far harder edge. There is, of course, the aforementioned fascination with bondage, but there is also an indefinable atmosphere of menace which runs throughout his work; a sense at times that what is portrayed on the surface as playful is, underneath, far darker.
Berquet uses, both in his photography and in MANIAC, a mixture of old and new. Stylistically, many of his pictures resemble — in the use of clothing and sepia tints — erotic prints from the early part of the century, and the magazine mixes totally new techniques and themes, both photographic and literary, with archive pictures and texts. The result, far from being uneven and anachronistic, gives a sense of timelessness, a seamless mix of intelligent pervery. Berquet himself has stated that his work is descended from the tradition of deSade and Bataille, and this sense of tradition continues in MANIAC. His photography effortlessly mixes horror and arousal, the surreal and the erotic, and would make the perfect accompaniment to Bataille's masterpiece THE STORY OF THE EYE.
The following is a translation of Berquet's aims for MANIAC, as described in a letter he wrote to me:

IN THE BEGINNING, I CREATED THE MAGAZINE AS A TRIBUTE TO JOHN WILLIE [CREATOR OF

BIZARRE); I WANTED TO DO SOMETHING IN THE SAME SPRIT, TO SHOW WHAT I LIKED AND WHAT HAD INFLUENCED MY OWN WORK, AS WELL AS RARE AND IDEALLY UNCENSORED DOCUMENTS.

I THINK THAT IT IS VERY IMPORTANT FOR ME, AS IT IS FOR ANY ARTIST WORKING NOWADAYS, TO BE ABLE TO SHOW THAT MY OWN WORK IS WITHIN AN EROTIC TRADITION WHICH REFERS TO WORK OF THE PAST.

MANIAC ACTS AS A FORUM FOR THE WORK OF YOUNG WRITERS, BUT I WRITE MOST OF THE TEXT MYSELF, AS WELL AS DOING THE DESIGN AND THE GRAPHICS. TAKING A 'CLASSIC' LOOK, MANIAC DOESN'T HAVE TO BE 'FASHIONABLE' AS IT SHOULD HAVE A TIMELESS QUALITY AND NOT JUST REFLECT WHAT'S CURRENT.

THE SUCCESS OF MANIAC RESIDES IN THE FACT THAT IT IS SOLD THROUGHOUT THE WORLD DESPITE A VERY LIMITED PRINT RUN (2000 COPIES) AND A DISTRIBUTION ONLY IN BOOKSHOPS AND GALLERIES.

MANIAC stands head and shoulders above pretty much any other fetish magazine. At the glossier end of the spectrum, SKIN TWO, MARQUIS and < <0> >, among others, are principally concerned with fetish fashion — although the articles in SKIN TWO have recently got a lot more substantial. Most other magazines cater for specific fetishes and perversions, and often seem trapped in some Seventies timewarp (check out any recent issue of KANE). If it's similar to anything else on the market, it's Jurgen Boedt's SECRET, but *Secret* is very contemporary and, while it has a far wider distribution, isn't nearly so professionally put together. MANIAC's principal strength is that it avoids both of these areas — the fashionable and the highly specific. Berquet's desire to make the magazine timeless is reiterated in the editorial of the first issue, and backed up by the

use of an incredible archive of classic erotic photos, to suit the particular theme of a given issue. This isn't cheesecake stuff either: the magazine features some of the perviest, darkest pictures I've ever seen — eroticised false hangings, men wearing what look like the real heads of horses and pigs etc. It also uses a good deal of illustrated work, and usually runs features on contemporary artists.

Otherwise, the magazine is comprised of one key essay by Berquet on the theme of the given issue, a long piece by JP Bougeron looking at various aspects of fetishism from a psychoanalytical point of view, and a focus on one particular performer or notable individual from the fetish industry's murky past. The general feel is that of a fetish magazine in the hands of a surrealist — which is, in fact, precisely what it is. This can be seen as much in the irreverence and absurdist humour as it can from the images used (woman as wardrobe, woman as side of beef, man as footstool); also, the unblinking and celebratory look at the more bizarre extremes of human sexual behaviour, and the nods to Bataille and Aragon, both surrealist writers responsible for erotic literary masterpieces. The writing in the magazine is superb, particularly Berquet's own, the photos and illustrations always at the very least striking, and the design is wonderful. There's no filler, either — the only thing resembling adverts is the news of other products from éditions Astarté, the publishers. Éditions Astarté also have a shop, Les Larmes d'Eros,* carrying a lot of illustrative and photographic material, as well as archive erotic films. MANIAC is available from them for 65FF an issue — contact them for postage charges. It's not, as far as I know, available in the UK, and you can expect to have problems with customs if you order it here — it's got some pretty strong pictures in it. Happy hunting!
James Marriott

* Les Larmes d'Eros is situated at 58 rue Amelot, 75011 Paris, France.

TO THE MAN had each band member sitting with a child-sized dummy on his lap, each dummy had the player's adult face. His liner notes were a hoot. Two: Al's got a sense of humour. He just sees things as being funny, and he's never been afraid to toss humour into the mix. Having said all that, he's never been a very good self-editor! His delight in things spelled or played backwards is strange. He's had a fascination with country music ("there aren't many Jewish guys who play the mandolin") which hasn't always fit into his music. He's often been self-indulgent in extremis, but not in the overbearing way of most rock musicians, more in the way of an excited kid who wants to show you everything he can do that might be fun. This is probably why he was musical director for a band called the Rock-Bottom Remainders, put together by a bunch of best-selling writers and big-name columnists who really just want to be rock stars. Stephen King plays guitar in this band. He wrote the liner notes for the first album by Al's new band, The Rekooperators. I hope King plays guitar as well as Al writes. That's why this book is such a hoot. As a look at the early business of rock'n'roll, it's a revelation (Al was playing in bands in his early teens, and working in Tin Pan Alley while still in high school). His stories of the mid-Sixties scene in the Village are great — Bob Dylan, Eric Andersen, Judy Collins and the like — and of course, the saga of the personality clashes in the Project and BS&T, great bands both, are worth the price of admission in themselves. He's honest and amusing about his own personal life, and the weird sort of pulling and tugging rock exerts on the emotions of its stars. Plus, Al's worked with an editor this time (the book is actually a revision and update of a volume originally published in 1977, when Al was at the peak, shall we say, of self-indulgence) and it is a genuinely funny read.

You can chart the entire process of Al's career on one two-CD set. SOUL OF A MAN was recorded at New York's Bottom Line over three days of concerts celebrating Kooper's 50th birthday. It puts together the original Blues Project, and BS&T bands, as well as the Rekooperators, who feature Al playing Hammond B-3 driven instrumentals with some of New York's best session players. Throw in the sadly-neglected producer/pianist

139

John Simon, responsible for the first two Band albums as well as BS&T's first (and that is a trio of aces), and special guests like Johnny Johnson and John Sebastian. All the strengths and flaws mentioned above are present in these two discs: the performances indulge all Al's favourite peccadilloes, and the accompanying booklet is a fascinating read. But basically, it's full of the pleasures of making music. That pleasure is contagious, and it's irresistible. So is the book. Get them. **Michael Carlson**

TOO MUCH, TOO SOON
The Makeup and Breakup of
The New York Dolls
Nina Antonia
208pp $9.99; 1998, Omnibus Press
ISBN 0-7119-6777-6
A long overdue book on the infamous New York Dolls, a band who left a huge impact on a sleepwalking music industry in the post-Warhol musical underground of NYC in the early Seventies. As hard as it may be to comprehend for some, at one time there was no MTV (a place where you might get lucky and see one of your favourite bands on Don Kirschner's Rock Concert) — a time of NY Dolls, when Vietnam was still a war and Nixon was a president. As stated on the back cover, TOO MUCH TOO SOON "is the definitive story of the NY Dolls…" — which I suppose it has to be, seeing how it's the only book that's been written on them to my knowledge. For too long the Dolls and their fans have had to be content with chapters in books on other musicians or footnotes in punk history books. Now with Ms Antonia's tome this is no longer the case! Thank God for small miracles. The author gives us glimpses of the band's childhood origins without going overboard with minutiae: Johnny Thunders' passion for baseball until he discovered rock'n'roll… Sylvain and Billy Murcias' (the band's first drummer) late Sixties' fashion outlet Truth and Soul… Then of course their genesis as a band and discovery at the Mercer Arts Center. The rest, as they say, is history, and it's all here — the infamy, sex, drugs, death and decadence. Peppered throughout with interesting anecdotes about the Dolls' influence on Aerosmith, KISS and Sex Pistols et al; Jagger going to see them and then declining to sign them to the Stones' label; Jimmy Page and Johnny Thunders chit-chatting in the backroom at Max's Kansas City, and so on… There are some rare photos and all the post-Dolls info and updates, and the untimely and close deaths of J.T. and Jerry Nolan… The only problem I have with the book is the discography which seems to list every pressing of their records around the world, but is sadly lacking in info about boots and demos (the few that are mentioned have no song listings or recording info). I personally saw the Dolls twice in '74, and the Thunders/ Nolan Heartbreakers a half-dozen times or so after that, and can attest to their sound being at the heart of rock'n'roll. Their music seems a lot more innocent in the face of what has come since, but not any less tame. It still holds its own and comes out on top in most cases. Ms Antonia has also written IN COLD BLOOD, the authorised biography of Johnny Thunders which has been revised and is being reprinted. **Tom Brinkmann**

TEIGNMOUTH ELECTRON
Tacita Dean
£19.95; Bookworks, 19 Holywell Row, London, EC2A 4JB. Tel: 0171 247 2536 Also avail from Nat Maritime museum & good art bookshops; ISBN 1-870699-36-X
This is a remarkable book. Tacita Dean was shortlisted for the Turner prize last year for an exhibition of large-scale drawings and video installations dealing with Donald Crowhurst and the issues raised by his journey — how man copes with isolation, obsession with time, and the theme of being lost at sea. I went to the exhibition and have to admit I was less than impressed — I've never been a fan of video installation art, and I wasn't aware of the broader context of Dean's work. It looked a little dull, especially when seen alongside Cathy de Monchaux' eroticised metal mandalas. But this book makes me want to see it again.
The story of Donald Crowhurst has been well documented in at least one non-fiction book, two films and a novel — Robert Stone's OUTERBRIDGE REACH. It has a resonance which continues to attract attention (a CD given away at part of Labradford's second Festival of Drifting was illustrated with one of the photos from this book). The Crowhurst saga is also cited as being the starting point for Chris Mikul's obsession in the new Critical Vision book BIZARRISM, so I won't recap the story itself here. TEIGNMOUTH ELEC-TRON is, in Dean's words, "the culmi- nation of a personal research and involvement with the voyage of Donald Crowhurst which has been part of my life now for over four years". It is a slim hardback volume which is profusely illustrated, principally with photos taken by Dean of Crowhurst's boat, derelict, stripped and bleached by sun and surrounded by lush foliage in Cayman Brac. The photos are haunting and unusual especially when juxtaposed with the other images in the book: film stills from Crowhurst's journey itself, stills from the films made about Crowhurst, and a postcard commemorating Crowhurst's departure. This last item points to a staggering tale of petty-minded England. It is widely believed that Crowhurst realised that his boat would not survive the journey, but that he felt under so much pressure from his local community — the Council of which was using the voyage to promote tourism in Teignmouth — that he didn't feel he could back out. One of the Councillors is reported to have said, after Crowhurst's boat was found abandoned, that "the voyage has brought us more publicity than this Committee has managed in 50 years. We have had this extremely cheaply, and I hope the town appreciates it." Dean's comments regarding this are worth quoting in full:

IT IS ASTOUNDING WITH WHAT EASE THEY COULD PITCH A MAN'S LIFE AGAINST THE REVENUE BROUGHT INTO THEIR SEASIDE RESORT BY TOURISM. THE LANGUAGE THEY WERE SPEAKING WAS WILDLY DISPROPORTIONATE TO THE HUGENESS OF CROWHURST'S ORDEAL AND HUMAN FAILING. YOU IMAGINE THAT IF YOU MET CROWHURST IN THE TEIGNMOUTH YACHTING CLUB, YOU MIGHT FIND HIM A BIT ARROGANT, BUT AS A HUMAN BEING, ALONE IN AN UNREMITTING SEASCAPE TRYING TO COME TO TERMS WITH HIS DETERIORATING PSYCHOLOGICAL STATE AND HIS MONUMENTAL DECEPTION, HIS STORY IS GENUINELY TRAGIC AND EXISTENTIAL, AND LEAVES THE ASPIRATIONS OF TEIGNMOUTH COUNCIL AND LITTLE ENGLAND WAY, WAY BEHIND.

Dean's angle on the Crowhurst tale, as portrayed here, reminded me of Alan Moore's epilogue to his superb psychogeographical Jack the Ripper work, FROM HELL. The epilogue deals with the peripheral issues surrounding the case — it's a document about the documentation rather than the events themselves, and comes across as being all the more interesting for it. Dean's book, similarly, constructs a tangential framework around the journey itself, with short pieces on the current owner of the boat, time-madness and the works of Ballard, Antoine de Saint-Exupéry and the two films, along with very personal recollections of her own journey to Teignmouth to discover more about Crowhurst. It's a beautifully written and lavishly constructed work, with each short piece providing a novel yet relevant context for the rest. It's an art book, so doesn't come cheap, but it's highly recommended nonetheless. **James Marriott**

BIZARRISM
Strange Lives, Cults, Celebrated Lunacy
Chris Mikul

160pp £11.95; 1999, Critical Vision
ISBN 1-900486-06-7
Available through Headpress, see p.160

Afraid that you may leave this world without having made your mark? Feeling the sands of time slipping through your fingers? Fret not — BIZARRISM is here to save you. This collection of (mainly) short articles promises 'Strange Lives, Cults, Celebrated Lunacy' and man, does it deliver. Give thanks to author Chris Mikul's lengthy obsession with such things, otherwise it's unlikely you'd ever encounter individuals such as Donald Crowhurst, the amateur sailor for whom the phrase 'plan ahead' meant nothing, or celebrity-witch Rosaleen Norton ("If she was the face of evil, she was a remarkably nice face of evil"); or even William Chidley, tunic-wearing visionary who pinpointed the male erection as the source of life's problems…

Although many of the people here roam in the two wacky pastures of the absurd — pulp sci-fi and religious cults — Mikul doesn't take the piss out of his subjects (well, okay he does when they deserve it, hence his debunkings of Sigmund Freud and the Mormons), and utilises a clear, informative writing style peppered with personal anecdotes and flashes of sly humour. As I'm a sucker for nutty musicians and turn-of-the-century crackpots, my favourites in this book were the British DIY pop producer Joe Meek (a guy who makes Phil Spector seem

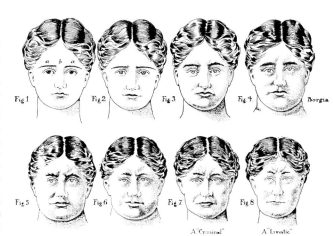

A drawing by William Chidley showing convergence of the eyebrows due to 'unnatural coition'. BIZARRISM.

well-balanced), rich-kid Harry Crosby, who pissed on rock star bullshit by actually living fast and dying young, and god-like poet-boxer Arthur Cravan who, when asked his reason for writing, replied "to infuriate!" There are many more driven individuals in BIZARRISM: mad, bad, and dangerous to know. This planet would be a much duller place without them.
Martin Jones

BIZARRISM
(Details above)

This is a bit of a departure for Critical Vision. BIZARRISM is an Australian zine covering mainly items of Forteana — it's one of the few zines stocked by Mark Pawson, which is something of a recommendation. This book is a collection of highlights from the zine; short articles, most no more than three pages long, about material like scientology, hollow earthers, lobster boy and mormons — all the usual suspects. I'm not really big on Fortean stuff, and the problem with a lot of the material on display here is that it's been mined to death already — there aren't very many surprises. Mikul was inspired to start the zine — the subject matter of which is described by him as "beacons of shining if erratic brilliance in a world of sensible conformity" — after reading about Donald Crowhurst, and the collection opens with a piece about him. It's jokey and a little dismissive and really rubbed me up the wrong way, especially as I had read sensitive treatments of his life in Tacita Dean's book TEIGNMOUTH ELECTRON [see above] and others. In a way this epitomises the whole Forteana take on its material: the reduction of complex personal

lives and struggles into throwaway freakshow fodder.

It's not a bad book, though. On the plus side, Mikul's writing is extremely readable and concise, and held my interest throughout — although most of the material is familiar, it is still fascinating, and Mikul does succeed in unearthing some truly weird nuggets. As it's an Australian zine there are a fair few pieces on Australian strangeness, and it's these pieces which are the highlight of the book for me, as they offer something truly new. I also really liked the postscript, a piece entitled 'Why I Love Cults', which offers a refreshing antidote to all the cult hysteria around at the moment. While I don't think it's one of the best Critical Vision books, it's a fun read and cheap to boot. **James Marriott**

HOLLYWOOD RAT RACE
Ed Wood, Jr.

138pp £10.99; 1998, Four Walls Eight Windows; ISBN 1-56858-119-X
Distributed in the UK by Turnaround

"YOU MUST ACT! YOU MUST! YOU MUST! YOU MUST! BUT HOW?"

Ed Wood spent most of the 1960s working on this (previously unreleased) book in answer to the most potent of all questions posed by young, Hollywood hopefuls: "How can I make it in showbiz?" It's an odd concept — Wood advising starlets on how to learn their craft and perfect their art — and remarkably conservative advice from a man whose own career appeared to rely more on charm and cheek than thoroughness and perfection. Wood's reputation as the worst director of all time simply can't be discarded when reading HOLLYWOOD RAT RACE, to the extent that it's impossible to read as the self-help manual Wood had intended. However, as a glimpse into the character of this fascinatingly and obliviously confident man, this book is great. The prose could have been written by a 17-year-old, and at times is compellingly banal. He contradicts, illuminates, amuses, and repeats the same advice over and over (don't pay for your own screen test, do get an agent, do get professional photographs printed, don't pay for your screen test…). Not surprisingly, there are frequent references to angora sweaters. Sadly they are mainly worn by starlets. Utterly priceless. **Sarah Turner**

CAMDEN PARASITES
Daniel Lux
1999, Unpopular Books
ISBN 1-871593-21-2

This apparently autobiographical book charts the rise and fall of the author, a small-time thief and junkie, from humble origins through a flirting with pop stardom to a brief stint in a mental hospital and beyond. There's no fictional framework placed around the events, and nor is there much comment made about them — just endless ups and downs, various addictions and brushes with the law. Danny's an interesting character, though, and a fairly complex picture of him is built up throughout the book, albeit more by what he leaves out than anything else. He constantly ridicules his richer peers for lacking in street smarts, and attempts to justify his stealing from them through badly digested Class War ideas — there's a quotation from a Stewart Home review on the back which refers to the book as "A savage indictment of bourgeois society". Trouble is, he rips off everyone he knows — all of his friends, who unsurprisingly eventually reject him, his long-suffering girlfriends, his parents — and the only relationship he can have with people seems to be one of exploitation. When Danny's on form he's also almost intolerably arrogant and full of himself, spraying his ego over all and sundry, and for this reason I was more taken with him when things weren't going so well — when he's institutionalised, friendless and bloated he seems somehow more human (not sure what that says about me!). In a

postscript it is revealed that the author died of a heroin overdose when the final proofs were being prepared. While saddening, it's not entirely surprising, considering the full-throttle self-destruction Danny embarks upon whenever he has any cash. The book is very readable — despite the absence of 'plot' — and makes for a far more compelling and convincing picture of this kind of London life than most novels I've come across. [*A note from Danny's flatmate and buddy that accompanied the review copy of this book suggested that Danny was also responsible for smashing the Blue Peter garden in the Seventies, see Phil Tonge's Cak-Watch in HEADPRESS 18 for details—Ed.*] **James Marriott**

A GOOD CUNTBOY IS HARD TO FIND
Doug Rice
74pp; 1998, Cyber-Psychos AOD
http://cyberpsychos.netonecom.netlcpbooks
Distributed in the UK by BBR; £5+20% p&p
Europe; payable: Chris Reed
ISBN 1-886988-08-0

Doug Rice is an English professor at Kent State University-Salem, and the author of the autobiographical fragment, 'Blood of Mugwump.' This is a collection of his short stories — tales of sexual excess and degradation, virtually non-stop sex scenes detailed in high postmodernist fashion. This means that most of the stories are virtually unreadable, full of nonsense like this, from 'The Fire Sermon':

SHE AND HER DEMONIC FLESH GONE DYSLEXIC ON ME. ALL OVER MY BODY. SHE RUDELY FORCED HER BODY BEFORE MY EYES. PERCEIVED MY DESIRES. HER BELLY WRECKED BY THE

SLAVE OF PASSION

ILLUSTRATED

XANTIA

THE PLANET THOR

WHERE WOMEN ARE SLAVES AND MEN ARE MASTERS

SOUND OF OUR PARENTS SCREAMING. FROZEN SYLLABLES FROM THE DARK LANGUAGES OF OUR ANCESTRAL PAST. WORDS LOITERING IN THE DULL CORRIDORS OF MY HOLLOW, STERILE CUT. THROBBING FOR TONGUE.

If this isn't bad enough, Rice also likes to play games with footnotes, gender, typography and identity, so we have stories about the desire of a boy to be raped by a girl, a boy-girl "suffering at the surface of mouth, cunt, word and skin", an offal girl living in a male body, characters with "mutable or nomadic gender", "pornology", sado-masochism and transsexuality. Influences — or so the introduction claims — are Artaud, The Marquis deSade, Jean Genet, Giles [*sic*] Deleuze, George [*sic*] Bataille, William Faulker, William Burroughs, and, rather less impressively, Kathy Acker and Courtney Love. Basically, this is the kind of thing that Peter Sotos does far better, and without all the bullshit.

In her introduction, the brown-nosed Lidia Yuknavitch claims that "small bands of nomads will read the book, eat the book, fuck the book". Others, less easily excited, will simply toss it away. **Mikita Brottman**

SLAVE OF DESIRE
Xantia
154pp £9.99; 1997, Blue Sky Books
PO Box 79, Blackburn, Lancs, BB1 9GF
Tel/Fax: 01254 247905
http://atyourservice.co.uk/blueskybooks/
ISBN 1-901838-00-5

Dungeons and dragons porn has never been my thing, I have to admit, but that doesn't stop me from recognising good and bad examples of this weird conjunction of genres. This one, I have to say is definitely at the bad end of the scale. The illustrations in the book are clearly a bad attempt to imitate Eric Stanton and are likely to be of interest only to the true obsessive with few critical faculties to play with. The writing isn't up to much either, but then what can you say about an author who includes a quote from Princess Di and dedicates the book to "Tweety, Mum, Dad, Amber (my dog)…". Come on now, that's hardly the mark of a hardcore pornographer, is it? Finally the story is too silly for words. Not recommended I'm afraid.

Pan Pantziarka

SLAVE OF PASSION

Xantia

156pp, £9.99, Blue Sky Books

(Order details as above)

"I AM XANTIA – RECORDER OF THE WRITTEN WORD."

There are photos of 'Xantia' at the back of this book—she's a middle-aged fetishist with the writing style of a filthy-minded adolescent who spends too long playing Dungeons and Dragons. And uses phrases like 'sex milk' and 'fuck cavern'. Anyway. this is the second book in her Thorean Master series, which is set on the planet Thor 'where women are slaves and men are masters'. The men have square dicks that, during coitus, grow a sort of sucker that attaches onto the woman's clit. Some Thorean nobles like Baal (eldest son of Titan) can deposit sex-dew inside a womb, which leads to powerful orgasms. There's also a race of yeti-type things called the Umar — they're the baddies. See what I mean about Dungeons and Dragons? It's a little puerile to ridicule this nonsense, as its author states that she writes to verbalise her sexual fantasies which are extremely masochistic by all appearances — so good luck to her, I suppose. Her first book sold 2,000 copies, a fair amount for this sort of thing, so she's doing something right. I wish she wouldn't use bold print for SM audio effects — *Wack! Wack!* (not much use for the letter H on Thor) — and get shut of her artist, who cannot draw for toffee. Her 2,000 fans will he pleased to learn that she will be writing another book under her real name, Zephyr Beau-Bradley. Yeah, I'm so fuckin' sure.

Women are slaves and men are masters, eh? I know a planet a bit like that. **Anton Black**

ABC BOOK
A Drug Primer

Steven Cerio

64pp £8.99; H/BK; Gates of Heck

ISBN 1-889539-07-4

Distributed in UK by Turnaround

The frightening thing about this ABC BOOK of drugs is the realisation that I've done damn near every one of them, and lived to tell the tale. The few exceptions I can think of are Ketamine, which is some kind of intramuscular Mickey Finn for Great Danes, and Bufotenine, which you can get by licking toads down in Texas. Somehow I always managed to lick something else before I hit Toad on

my list of things to lick in Texas, but I'm not against trying just to be able to talk loudly about it during an interval at the Royal Opera House.

Steven Cerio belongs to what I call the Hanna-Barbera Hot Rod Stoner School Of Art that also includes Coop, Frank Kozik, and several other hipsters who have cultivated facial hair at one point or another during their career. While less derivative than the two previously mentioned, Cerio is still firmly planted in the 2-D comic zone. I've always thought this kind of thing works better on skateboards or trading cards, but the kiddie format and droll little rhymes make it work. His illustrations have a Rorschach-like symmetry to them which hints at something beyond the obviousness of the subject matter. They're darned cute too. Who wouldn't want to cuddle up to the patchwork angel dust elephant? There's even a special place in the front to write your name so that when you find it over at your coke-sniffing girlfriend's place, you can pop open the cover and proclaim "This is mine, you thieving wench!"

The whole book gives a sense of what happens when toys tune in, turn on and drop out. In a way it's a shame it has a druggy theme, because I know kids would love it too. **Mark Deutrom**

THE VIDEO NASTIES!
From Absurd to Zombie Flesh-Eaters—A Collector's Guide to the Most Horrifying Films Ever Banned!

Allan Bryce

£16.99 incls p&p; 1998, Stray Cat Publishing Ltd, PO Box 36, Liskeard, Cornwall, PL14 4YT; ISBN 0-9533261-0-1

Many years ago Allan Bryce used to write for a video trade magazine and his column was entitled 'The Bryce is Right'. The title was quite often erroneous. From there Bryce went on to edit THE DARK SIDE, a fan-boyish publication that is still in print. From that same stable come this awful little work. The only point of merit the book scores is in the colour reproduction of the video sleeves, though a series of glossy pictures does not make a worthy book alone. Bryce's 'reviews' read like they've been written by a 13-year-old horror film fan trying to impress his school mates. The same amount of space is designated for each review, so when Bryce can't think of much to say about a film, the size of the typeface is increased in order to fill the allocated area. This sloppy and

F is for FenPhen.
ABC BOOK: A DRUG PRIMER.

unprofessional technique was also used in John Martin's equally bad and error-riddled SEDUCTION OF THE GULLIBLE. Martin's book is described as "excellent" in Bryce's introduction and has obviously been used as a source of flagrant plagiarism.

There are four articles which follow the introduction and all are reprints of Bryce's earlier work — the most recent having been written in 1994 — with no attempt made to update the essays. So a claim that "Certain movies, like RESERVOIR DOGS and THE EXORCIST will probably not be released on video, but then what else is new?" is utterly redundant and exemplifies the absolute laziness with which the book has been put together.

In the micro-reviews Bryce is very often wrong. In his reviews of THE BEYOND, CANNIBAL HOLOCAUST, FACES OF DEATH and ZOMBIE CREEPING FLESH he describes scenes that are not even in the video release he is supposedly reviewing. He describes I SPIT ON YOUR GRAVE as having four rapists — a well-known misnomer that is printed on the movie poster and video sleeve. In DON'T GO NEAR THE PARK he claims Linnea Quigley plays the role of "a supernatural brat named Bondy..." when the character (Bondi) is played by Tamara Taylor.

To the accusation of plagiarism: in SEDUCTION OF THE GULLIBLE John Martin writes of WEREWOLF AND THE YETI:

... NASCHY'S EIGHTH OUTING AS DANINSKY... STOCK FOOTAGE OF WESTMINSTER BRIDGE, ACCOMPANIED ON THE SOUNDTRACK BY BAGPIPES DRONING 'SCOTLAND THE

143

BRAVE'!... [NASCHY] WANDERS OFF TO COLLAPSE IN THE WILDERNESS AND IS RESCUED BY TWO SCANTILLY-CLAD [SIC] CAVE-DWELLING BIMBOS... [NASCHY IS] OBLIGED TO REDUCE THEM TO SMOKING SKELETONS WITH A HANDY-DANDY WOODEN STAKE...

Naschy is also described as a 'novelty shop werewolf'. Bryce writes of the same film,

PAUL NASCHY'S EIGHTH OUTING AS THE JOKE SHOP WOLFMAN OPENS TO STOCK FOOTAGE OF WESTMINSTER BRIDGE WITH, FOR SOME INEXPLICABLE REASON, 'SCOTLAND THE BRAVE' PLAYING ON THE SOUNDTRACK! ...NASCHY WANDERS OFF INTO THE SNOW IN SEARCH OF THE SCRIPTWRITERS AND IS RESCUED BY TWO SCANTILLY-CLAD CAVE-DWELLING BIMBOS... HE IS OBLIGED TO WHIP OUT HIS STAKE AND CONVERT THEM TO SMOKING SKELETONS...

In NIGHT OF THE BLOODY APES Martin says the doctor pronounces 'leukaemia' as "loose-seam-ia". Bryce mimics with, "what the scientist refers to as 'loose-seam-ia.'"

Indeed, there is very little in VIDEO NASTIES that can't be found almost verbatim in SEDUCTION, even the same errors are carried across. One wonders whether Bryce has even bothered to watch any of the films.

The layout of the book is as bad as its written content. Instead of having the text facing the reproduced video sleeve it refers to, you have to turn the page and find it on the back. The alphabetical ordering of the titles collapses after MADHOUSE which is followed by REVENGE OF THE BOGEY MAN, and TOOLBOX MURDERS is proceeded by MARDI GRAS MASSACRE. The publish-

Blender terror in Lamberto Bava's 'You'll Die at Midnight' aka 'Midnight Horror'. BLOOD & BLACK LACE.

ers can't event get the contents' page right even though there are only *seven* entries. But there are no page numbers in the book so the contents listing is redundant any way! A definite contender for one of the worst film books of all time, is this. **Janet Gould**

BLOOD & BLACK LACE
The Definitive Guide To Italian Sex and Horror Movies
Adrian Luther-Smith

148pp £19.99 incls p&p; 1999, Stray Cat Publishing, PO Box 36, Liskeard, Cornwall, PL14 4YT; ISBN 0-9533261-1-X

The second book in the 'Dark Side Presents' series, which fortunately stands head and shoulders above the preceding VIDEO NASTIES! volume [*above*]. This because it actually contains information to go with its pictures, penned with some authority by Adrian Luther-Smith (in the tradition of his own guide to Italian exploitation, DELIRIUM). The subject here is *giallo* — the Italian mystery genre — but it encompasses just about any film with a murder in it.

The title recognised as kicking off cinematic *giallo* is Mario Bava's 1962 production, THE EVIL EYE. Several years later — after DEEP RED, Argento's masterly redefining of the genre — the popularity of these films took an unprecedented downward turn. They came back with the US stalk and slash boom of the Eighties.

As well as cast and credit details, each entry comes with a synopsis, informed critique and cache of factoids. Hear how the US distribu-

tor of Sergio Martino's TORSO not only excised much of the film's gore, but was also responsible for the jarring guitar theme (that turns up again in Doris Wishman's DEADLY WEAPONS and Leon Klimovsky's NIGHT OF THE WALKING DEAD); or how two versions of the rape scene in Pasquale Festa Campanile's underrated HITCH-HIKE were shot for different markets.

A section entitled 'Hidden Treasures' compiles *giallo* material that remains elusive (or turned up too late for inclusion in the main text). Of these titles, THE POLICE GROPE AROUND IN THE DARK — from the aptly named Helia Colombo — sounds pretty fantastic, with a plot that includes murdered models and an invention that can photograph thoughts.

BLOOD & BLACK LACE is full-colour throughout and contains many rare images, but is a little steep at £20.

CINEMA CONTRA CINEMA
Jack Sargeant

192pp £12.99/$17.95; 1999, Fringecore, PO Box 165, 2600 Berchem 1, Belgium
Email: info@fringecore.com
www.fringecore.com
ISBN 90-76207-50-X

Jack Sargeant writes about the true independents of cinema, for whom budget generally extends no further than the price of raw film stock or videotape. For many of these filmmakers ideas are the impetus, not ticket sales. Collected together in CINEMA CONTRA CINEMA are some of Jack's most recent articles and interviews concerning the key figures in Underground's latest wave (which could be

regarded as an extension of his own DEATHTRIPPING book — the history of the Cinema of Transgression). Here you have Eric Brummer talking about set-design ("You can take any space and make Hell out of it by sprinkling body parts all over the place and writing 'Hell' on the wall") [*his DEBBIE DOES DAMNATION is reviewed on page 149*]; Charles Pinion on the necessity to feed your cast and crew; Peter Strickland on getting Nick Zedd and Holly Woodland to star in BUBBLEGUM; a discussion of mondo atrocity, TRUE GORE; and a host of others. This book is not without its flaws — what is the point of the 'Ten Brief Notes and Observations' piece? — but then I can think of no other writer who's championing underground filmmakers with the dedication and enthusiasm of Jack Sargeant.

HOLLYWOOD HEX
Mikita Brottman
201pp £14.95; 1999, Creation Books
ISBN 1-871592-85-2
The ratio for fatalities within the film and TV industry is proportionally greater than that of, say, the police and highway construction industries. The rise in explosive, action-orientated movies in the mid-1980s saw 10 fatalities on film sets with complaints of unsafe filming conditions more than doubling. In the midst of all this was TWILIGHT ZONE: THE MOVIE, an arid cash-in on Rod Serling's influential TV show of the Fifties, which has gained notoriety in recent years thanks to the circulation of out-take footage depicting the death of veteran actor Vic Morrow and two young extras. Comprising vignettes by Hollywood's young talent, it was John Landis' tale 'Bill' that met with disaster. Fleeing enemy soldiers and under simulated artillery

fire, the story required Morrow's character to rescue two Vietnamese children as around him a village exploded and above a helicopter whirred. The crew was tired from three straight weeks of filming and Landis was under pressure to call it a wrap. With multiple cameras rolling, Morrow started out across a shallow river, plucking the children from the water. The detonation of the first of the explosives created an unexpected dirt-cloud, and the heat was enough to force the nearby camera team backwards, leaving their equipment. The subsequent barrage of explosions occurred directly under the helicopter and knocked it out of the sky.

Shocked and confused, Landis couldn't understand why the helicopter was suddenly in his shot. Seconds later it became clear that Morrow and the children were dead. The footage was confiscated for investigation and used as evidence in a trial that ultimately cleared the director.

The story is a chilling one, and author Mikita Brottman uses it to help construct HOLLYWOOD HEX, a fascinating account of murder and misadventure in Tinseltown. On this literary death trip are the supposed 'cursed' movies THE EXORCIST and the POLTERGEIST series, around which cast and crew members dropped dead with rumour-inspiring regularity. Also included are the mystical connotations of Brandon Lee's THE CROW, and the less familiar John Schlesinger film THE BELIEVERS, which has been adopted by the Mexican Matamoros cult as a 'training model' for initiates (who are required to view the film 14 times).

Regular readers of HEADPRESS and those familiar with Creation's back catalogue will recognise some of the material included in HOLLYWOOD HEX. Don't be put off, as much fresh ground is covered in what is an unashamedly esoteric film book with a very entertaining premise.

BABYLON BLUE
An Illustrated History of
Adult Cinema
David Flint
188pp £16.95; 1999, Creation Books
ISBN 1-84068-002-4
One of the strange things about the "mini-flurry" (as Flint puts it) of books on the adult film industry is that they're actually all quite different — PORNOCOPIA is a fairly academic if readable tome dealing with a lot of the moral and legal concepts sur-

rounding porn; THE X-FACTORY is an enthusiastic fan's book for fans (and you can almost imagine Petkovich drooling as he meets the stars of his fantasies, who he describes in unbridled gonzo terms), and this one's an overview and history of the industry, right up to the present-day fascination with Ninn-style glossy fetish fashion, with a tone pitched somewhere between the two. Flint's clearly a fan, but he avoids dealing with the rights and wrongs (possibly feeling firstly that the ground's been covered before, and secondly that he'd be preaching to the converted) and expresses his enthusiasm in a more restrained way than Petkovich, although occasionally passages such as the following slip through:

... THE MOST ASTONISHING CLOSE-UPS AND CAMERA ANGLES THAT YOU WILL EVER SEE IN ANY HARDCORE MOVIE. *W*HEN THE MAN FUCKS GABRIELLA DOGGIE-STYLE, WE GET TWO REMARKABLE SHOTS — ONE FROM ABOVE, AND THE BETTER OF THE TWO FROM BELOW, OFFERING AN ULTRA-TIGHT CLOSE-UP OF HIS MEMBER SLAMMING INTO HER, AND A CRYSTAL-CLEAR SHOT OF HER ASSHOLE. *A* FEW MOMENTS LATER, THIS IS BETTERED BY A SHOT OF HIM SHOVING HIS FINGER UP HER ANUS, WHICH FILLS THE WHOLE SCREEN.

Whoa there! Another strange thing about these books, along with a couple of others, is that they're all British. Considering the situation — distribution of hardcore is still illegal in this country — it seems bizarre that there's so much interest here. It's similar to the situation regarding violent films — the fanzine attention paid to 'video nasties' and other restricted films often seems far out of proportion to the actual merit of most of the films themselves — the main point of interest being that these films are banned, but I digress.

Readers of this fine magazine should be familiar with David Flint — he was involved at its birth, and has since written for all sorts of publications, from Harvey Fenton's superb FLESH & BLOOD to his own DIVINITY and short-lived SEXADELIC. He's an excellent and highly readable writer, mixing incisive comment with an attention to detail which is comprehensive without quite being obsessive, and an understated humour which is the perfect foil for some of the more ludicrous areas highlighted — such as ITTY BITTY GANG BANG, a group-sex movie featuring exclusively (you guessed it) dwarves. As far as I'm aware this book was meant to come out a couple of years ago, but publication was postponed due to a police read on Flint's home, in which his video collection and computer were confiscated — the text of BABYLON BLUE being on the hard drive. The police couldn't charge him and after six months everything was returned.

The focus of the book is well-balanced, concentrating on what must be the two key areas of interest in porn history: the Seventies' golden age and the 'new porn generation' (Andrew Blake, Michael Ninn, Antonio Passolini etc). The interviews featured are with industry heavyweights, concentrating on directors/producers rather than on starlets and 'woodsmen' — namely Passolini, Lindsay Honey (aka Steve Perry aka Ben Dover), Jane Hamilton and David Friedman, all of whom come across as remarkably articulate and interesting individuals, especially Passolini, who turns out to be a big Throbbing Gristle fan. It's telling, too, that Passolini and Ninn were heavily influenced by British fetish fashion in putting together SEX and LATEX, and Passolini regards British kinkiness as the classiest in the world. Hurrah! The chapter on 'Fortress Britain' is one of the best pieces I've read on the lame homegrown industry (our classy kinkiness doesn't seem to translate to our movies), and there are a lot of stills and an excellent colour section, albeit no note of the films the colour stills are taken from. In short, the book's superb, and is a must-have item for anyone interested in this kind of material. One minor gripe — the price, which is surely a bit steep.

James Marriott

BABYLON BLUE
(Details above)

BABYLON BLUE has been a long time coming, due in part to a much-publicised police raid on the home of its author, David Flint. Beneath a somewhat uninspired front cover, Flint tackles a subject close to his heart: celluloid pornography, from stag films at the turn of the century through to the gonzo filmmakers of the Nineties. It's an entertaining and occasionally fascinating read, but — like most view-

HITMAN HART
Wrestling with Shadows
dir: Paul Jay
1998; High Road Productions/National Film Board of Canada co-production

Paul Jay set out to make a documentary about Bret 'the Hitman' Hart, the most successful of the wrestling Hart family from Calgary. Jay was interested in the conflict between fantasy and reality in the wrestling business, the difference between Bret Hart the man and his 'Hitman' wrestling character, and, by extension, the differences these implied between Canada and the USA. Although he couldn't have imagined the additional drama provided by WWF owner Vince McMahon's 'double-cross' of Hart, it's no wonder than the film was the hit of the Sheffield Documentary Film Festival in October 1998. Like many successful pro wrestlers, Bret Hart's original 'push' came because his father Stu owned the territory where he wrestled: Stampede Wrestling, a successful regional promotion based out of Calgary. Yet Stu Hart was hardly your typical wrestling promoter. A wrestler himself, he specialised in submission holds he'd learned as an orphan in a children's home, and subjected his sons (all of whom went into the business) and his other wrestling students to what could only be described as torture, in a specially fitted basement known as 'The Dungeon'. Hart eventually sold his territory to Vince McMahon, who was buying up regional promotions in order to turn his father's WWF into a coast-to-coast business with national TV, and thus compete with what is now WCW on

Ted Turner's national cable stations. Although McMahon reneged on annuity payments to Stu Hart, Hart remained the WWF's promoter in Calgary, and Bret Hart struggled up the WWF ladder, eventually becoming WWF champion as a babyface (good guy). Jay skips over Hart's earlier role as a heel (bad guy) tag team champion, because it would confuse the focus of Bret's character development. As champion, Hart became one of the few hot stars in WWF, and McMahon signed him to a massive 20 year contract. Using that contract as leverage, McMahon eventually persuaded Hart to turn heel, though because of Hart's reluctance they created a 'subtle' heel role which played the Canadian Hart against the American fans, and thus allowed him to remain a hero in Canada. This, for wrestling, was subtlety of rare proportion. Ted Turner's WCW had been quicker than McMahon to recognise a shift in wrestling audiences. They saw the creative success of a small promotion called Extreme Championship Wrestling, where good guys were disappearing: everyone broke the rules, no one showed any respect. As McMahon — feeling the pressure of slipping out of the market lead for the first time in nearly 20 years — searched for his own version of this formula, Bret Hart became redundant. So much so that McMahon tried to cancel Hart's 20 year deal, and encouraged him to defect to WCW.

Jay's film concentrates on the concept of loyalty which Hart feels: in a business like wrestling which is predicated on fraud, this seems a luxury at best, a delusion at worst. Hart remains concerned over his own wrestling character, a particularly Canadian ideal which he maintains in the face of the ruthless American business machine. As the promotion caters more and more to bad taste, sexism, rebellion, and all the things which make adolescent boys feel empowered, Hart's true-blue Canadian character becomes more and more out of place. So when the time comes that Hart finally

146

© Mark Manny

gives in and decides to go to WCW, Jay records the difficulty between Hart and McMahon over how Hart will lose his title belt. Hart does not want to be beaten in Canada at the Survivor Series in Montreal. McMahon does not want Hart showing up on WCW still holding the WWF belt and providing the opposition with a major coup. But Hart's contract allows him creative control of his character: he doesn't have to do a 'job' if he doesn't want to. Although Hart offers other scenarios, the tension comes from the expectation of trust: does McMahon trust his loyal employee to do what he says he will do, and not deliver a gratuitous hurt on his way out? Does Hart trust McMahon (and his fellow wrestlers) to allow him to go out on his own terms? Jay's cameras are there when Hart is double-crossed, when he loses the match unexpectedly and against the script. If anything, there is not enough build-up to the double-cross. The mechanics are never explained, and the reactions of people afterwards (referee Earl Hebner had sworn to Hart "on his children" that he wouldn't let any cross take place) are left up in the air. Sadly, Hart wasn't wearing a wire when he later cold-cocked McMahon in a disagreement in a closed dressing room.

Because Jay started out with the idea of contrasting Canadian ideals against US ruthlessness, he misses some of the irony implicit in portraying *anyone* in the wrestling business as an idealist. Is there really something intrinsically noble in Bret Hart's rise to the top of a business that still maintains the ethics of the carny world, and sees its fans (and most journalists and filmmakers) as 'marks'? We might legitimately wonder if it really is so tragic when Hart's script is erased by McMahon's? It is to Jay's credit that, in the end, it actually is. Bret may be naïve to take the fantasy business seriously, but he also appears to believe in a set of values which may be Canadian but do not actually seem that far removed from what people used to call

the 'American Dream'. Ironically, in the time since the film was shot, Hart has seen the WCW go down the same road as WWF, and his character has been buried far more efficiently (if not necessarily deliberately) by the battling egos and chaotic storylines of WCW than Vince McMahon could ever have done in his wildest dreams. Around the same time, his marriage, which had been pressured by untrue wrestling-business gossip documented in the film, broke up. Brian Pillman, one of the 'Hart Foundation' team in WWF, has since died of heart problems which were probably exacerbated by abuse of steroids and possibly other drugs. Davey 'Boy' Smith, 'The British Bulldog,' suffered a near-fatal back injury in a match, but is already making plans for his son — Stu Hart's grandson — to enter the business. Sean Michaels, who beat Hart in the Montreal match, has also suffered severe back injuries, and is no longer wrestling. And Bret's brother Owen, the most talented wrestler in the family, who honoured his WWF contract despite the treatment his brother received, was killed on May 23rd when he fell from a harness lowering him from the roof of the Kemper Arena in Kansas City, where he was about to wrestle under a mask as The Blue Blazer. If anything, the shadows around Bret Hart are deepening, and the events portrayed in this excellent film may well turn out to be some sort of turning point, rather than an end in themselves. **Michael Carlson**

HITMAN HART is available on video in the UK and is scheduled for broadcast by the BBC.

ers of pornography, I suspect — is over and done with rather too quickly. In the chapter 'Fortress Britain', for instance, the author rightly condemns the government's paranoia concerning matters of sex, yet he still manages to bang the entire turbulent 30 year history of British porn into a measly 13 pages! In these pages he bestows only one film (VIEWERS WIVES VOL 6) with anything more than a passing remark. For a book purporting to be one of the few devoted to the much-maligned/plain-ignored Adult genre, this is a most lackadaisical approach indeed. What about the intriguing-sounding DEATH SHOCK? Its director Lindsay Honey is interviewed in a subsequent chapter and is said to represent "the success story of the Nineties", yet DEATH SHOCK is typically awarded no plot details by Flint (though with several lines of text it still gets more space than many of the other titles he covers).

Despite a profusion of full-page illustrations, BABYLON BLUE comes in at under 190 pages. (Maybe the cops forgot to return a couple of the chapters?!) However, the author alone shouldn't take the brunt of my disappointment — the publishers must be made accountable for their absolutely awful production job, which is made even more awful by the ridiculously high price tag of £16.95. The illustrations — none of which are adventurous and comprise mainly of video sleeve reproductions — are of a piss-poor quality (one even looks like it was *faxed* to the printers!)…

And because the author claims not to be gay — ergo is without the "capacity to fully appreciate the few gay porn movies that I've seen" — gay porn is absent from this history. I was expecting more than this. **Joe Scott Wilson**

CANNIBAL HOLOCAUST and the Savage Cinema of Ruggero Deodato
Fenton, Grainger and Castoldi
111pp £13.99; 1999, FAB Press
ISBN 0-9529260-4-0
Available through Headpress

BEYOND TERROR The Films of Lucio Fulci
Stephen Thrower
311pp; 1999, FAB Press
£29.99 H/BK ISBN 0-9529260-5-9
£19.99 P/BK ISBN 0-9529260-6-7

For those readers who require a breakneck discourse on how the 'small press' has advanced in recent years, take a look at these latest film books

CULTURE GUIDE

147

from FAB. In terms of quality, CANNI-BAL HOLOCAUST is the equal of anything being put out by the major presses, while BEYOND TERROR — an oversized hardback with dust-jacket and impeccable photo reproduction — puts most quality presses to shame. Of course, no major publishing house would devote so much time and care to subjects like Ruggero Deodato and Lucio Fulci, both of whom would be considered 'non-starters' on the scale of moveable units. But that's the leverage the small press has into the marketplace: originality. Perhaps integrity. Now quality. As to the books themselves: both Deodato and Lucio are legends amongst horror film fans — the former primarily for the eponymous CANNIBAL HOLOCAUST, and the latter notably for his living dead trilogy of which ZOMBIE FLESH-EATERS is the most famous. The books are profusely illustrated with many rare illustrations (almost full-colour throughout, it's incredible that FAB managed to pull CANNIBAL HOLOCAUST in for less than £14), with incisive commentary on each directors' work. Naturally, given the page count and the fact it's been several years in the making, BEYOND TERROR has the edge, with break-downs on not only the films themselves but even the key characters

who appear in them! Author Stephen Thrower dissects every aspect of Fulci's work, resulting in a satisfyingly intelligent, eminently readable book that is complemented by some truly great illustrations and a great look.

JUICE
Electricity for
Pleasure and Pain
'Uncle Abdul'
170pp £9.99; 1998, Greenery Press
ISBN 1-890159-06-9
Distributed in the UK by Turnaround
You don't get much more bizarre than this! Instructions on how to assemble (at home) sundry torture devices for use in the bedroom — or kitchen for that matter: The Violent Wand, "a high voltage toy that uses a Tesla Coil… when the bulbs are in close proximity to the bottom's skin, a spark can jump"; The Shocking Animal Collar, a "small electronic low-voltage shocking device is placed in a pet collar"; The Electric Fly Swatter, "may not be effective on flies, but it's very effective on body parts…". JUICE claims to be the first and only book (and I believe it, I really do!) about how to use electricity safely in S&M relationships. It is as exhaustive and in-depth as you would wish a book like this to be. For all his technical expertise and know-how, the author, 'Uncle Abdul',

has created a brisk and fun-filled book which leaves your reviewer feeling bothered and bewildered — will folks actually buy this book and use it as the manual it's meant to be? Is the world really full of little would-be 'Uncle Abduls'? **Stephen Sennitt**

SPECIAL
Peter Sotos
258pp $20; Rude Shape Books
ISBN 1-890528-01-3
In Peter Sotos' two books, SPECIAL and INDEX — and the collection of magazine pieces, TOTAL ABUSE — he has demarcated an uniquely personal, extreme genre of literature. There are no pretensions, he has stated that his work is pornography. Brutal, unending, violent, unadulterated. On some levels his writing belongs to the tradition of deSade's 120 DAYS OF SODOM, and it also echoes aspects of Delaney's HOGG, and even Cooper's FRISK. But Sotos is in a league of his own, his work contains an obsession with detail, and, perhaps more importantly, information that can make the reader's flesh crawl — see for example the description of the victim of a gay torture session, throughout which Sotos drip-feeds facts to his reader, or the brutally casual description of a gang-bang sliding into a gang-rape. Flesh as degraded meat

S8 XXX SHOW
KinoFilm Festival of American
Underground Cinema, Day 7
Green Room, Manchester, Sunday 21st February 1999
KinoFilm tel: 0161 288 2494
Email: kino.info@good.co.uk

The closing evening of a week-long Super-8/shot-on-video extravaganza, which had featured some of the latest works from the American underground together with a few choice favourites from way back (including Curt McDowell's THUNDERCRACK). The theme for tonight's screenings is 'S8 XXX Show', a confrontational line-up that has numerous audience members exiting the Green Room theatre way before the flicker of the final frames.

Things get off to an innocuous enough start with Todd Lincoln's THE HONEY POT (1998), the life cycle of a disposible honey receptacle shot in the manner of an 'info-taining' SESAME STREET film clip for kiddies. Naturally, being a humorous underground short, the honey pot finds itself on a porno set and ultimately ends up being used as a bong. Anie Stanley's PARADICE [sic] (1996) and OUR US WE BONE ONE SO NAKED KNOW (1994) are next, both narrative-light exercises which feature just enough hardcore footage to keep the audience focused. PARADICE appears to be about a whore who goes on holiday and turns a trick, while the latter is a 'homage' to girl gang movies with a bunch of pistol-packing mamas rub-

bing their breasts on a car windshield. (Some of the players are from the all-girl band Fresh Fish.)
The next selection of films comprises several works by Michelle Handelman and the notorious Monte Cazzaza. SAFER SEXUAL TECHNIQUES IN THE AGE OF MECHANICAL REPRODUCTION (1988) has various sex acts represented by a solo female performer, who flicks her tongue and flaps her arms repeatedly at ambiguous ghostly superimpositions on the film ('subliminal messages' according to the programme notes). Variations on this act are repeated several times over, for the full interminable duration of a 100-foot roll of film.
The first visceral shock of the evening comes with Cazzaza's SXXX-80 (1980), a film that incorporates a giant millipede seated on a vagina, numerous gynocological insertions, and a man picking at an absess on his dick until it weeps blood and puss. Unlike the Mondo documentary TRUE GORE, on which Cazzaza worked and which incorporated censored excerpts from this, the film here runs in its unexpurgated, queasy entirety.
PIERCE (1984) is a close-up film showing Cazzaza getting an ampallang piercing. It seems much longer than its designated three-minute running time, and the auditorium fills with groans and a mass crossing of legs as first an anaesthetic is administered into the head of the penis, then the organ is wrenched this way and that before the operation is complete

has never been articulated with a greater clarity. Moreover Sotos has an uncanny skill to adopt numerous voices, and perspectives, and SPECIAL juxtaposes a mixture of interrogative Q&A with other accounts and descriptions relating to manifestations of (predominantly) sexual violence. As a writer Sotos is thoroughly engaged with his interests, as likely to reference anti-pornography feminists Catharine MacKinnon as he is to quote from Ian Brady, and as such his work defies simple analysis because he has already heard it, understood it, reworked it, and incorporated it into the writing itself. Few writers are this powerful. SPECIAL demands to be read. **Jack Sargeant**

THE YEAR'S BEST FANTASY AND HORROR
Eleventh Annual Collection
Eds. Terri Windling and
Ellen Datlow
504pp $17.95; 1998, St Martin's Griffin
ISBN 0-312-19034-4
Distributed in the UK by Turnaround
This massive annual anthology contains, in addition to 37 short stories and nine poems by writers as famous as Ray Bradbury, Joyce Carol Oates, A. Alvarez and Charles de Lint, over 100 pages of editorial material! Windling and Datlow respectively pro-

vide lengthy summations of the year's (1997, in this case) major events and publications in the fields of fantasy and horror fiction. Both of them seem to have read more books than is humanly possible in one year — not only novels, but also children's stories, collections, anthologies, poetry chapbooks, genre magazines, art books etc — and they offer passionate personal recommendations, as well as recording the winners of various awards (making this a sort of WISDEN for genre fiction fans). Other writers offer a round-up of the year's news for comics, television, films and even music, though some of the inclusions seem to stretch the definitions of 'fantasy' and 'horror' more than a little: under what criteria are the films BOOGIE NIGHTS and CHASING AMY, and the TV shows THE SIMPSONS and SOUTH PARK included here? There is also an obituary section, which includes William Burroughs, Kathy Acker, Roy Lichtenstein and Willem de Kooning (again, what have these last two to do with fantasy or horror?). All this information, as well as the extensive small press and magazine listings, should, I imagine make this an essential yearly reference book for anyone writing either fiction or criticism in these fields, and a boon to genre

fans, though it has to be said that the focus is largely on events and organisations in the USA — Britain gets a bit of a look-in, but the rest of the world is given pretty short shrift. What of the stories and poems themselves? They are all reprints from books and magazines published in

US retitle for Fulci's
'A Lizard in a Woman's Skin'.
BEYOND TERROR.

and the decorative bar is in place. CATSCAN (1989) is a collaboration between Cazzaza and Hendelman, and what appears to be a regular fuck loop is in actual fact a shot of bestiality. Following a bout of heterosexual coupling, fresh milk is poured over a woman's genetalia and a cat is encouraged to lap it up, while a guy takes to licking the bewildered feline's own privates. (The image that pops into my mind at this very moment is that of KinoFilm's more prestigious sponsers making an impromtu visit to the theatre).
Anything after CATSCAN has got to be an anti-climax, and so it is with Handelman's HOMOPHOBIA IS KNOWN TO CAUSE NIGHTMARES (1991), a cut-up monologue spoken by a woman accompanying images of male homosexuality.
Delfina Marello's ENJOY (1997) is possibly the most technically proficient film of the evening, even if it is only a one-minute stop-motion affair starring three dolls (of the Barbie and Ken variety). Against an imaginative musical soundtrack (imaginitive in that Underground cinema generally tends to suffer from a lazy overuse of schmaltzy classics of yesteryear), the three dolls fuck.

The main feature (at 80 minutes, longer than all the above put together) is DEBBIE DOES DAMNATION (1998/9). Director Eric Brummer is on hand to introduce the film, which we are assured more than once is a "work in progress". The story is set in Hell and concerns a porn star who is sent on a quest by the Devil — or what's left of him — to retrieve his horns, which have been stolen by two mercenary minions (one of whom is exploitation veteran William Smith). The porn star has committed suicide and, despite assistance from her Guardian Angel, is literally dragged towards Hell by the weight of her own sins. Following many — way too many — fight sequences in which opposing armies are represented only by a handful of extras, the porn star locates the horns, returns them to Beelzebub and is promptly killed for her troubles (moral being: never trust the Devil). The film wears its influences on its sleeve, but does come up with some impressive shoe-string ideas of its own and genuinely spooky stop-motion moments. Top marks for initiative!
These screenings are the only opportunity many people will get to see such a diverse line-up of no-budgeters. Look out for the next such KinoFilm offering.

1997, including such mainstream sources as PLAYBOY and THE NEW YORKER, and divide fairly evenly between fantasy and horror — though, as might be expected from the editorial remits discussed above, the definitions of these terms are fairly loose. Fantasy, in particular, embraces magical realism, adult fairy tales, Arthurian and classical mythology, Native American myth etc., and so not much of what is on offer here is fantasy of the old-school Tolkien-derived swords-and-sorcery type. As well as famous names, there are many pieces by authors unfamiliar, though I must admit that I haven't read much of this sort of fiction for some years.

Of the pieces that I managed to read (about a third of them), I particularly enjoyed 'The Skull of Charlotte Corday' by Leslie Dick, a post-modern look at criminal anthropology and psychoanalysis that is only debatably fictional, though it's undeniably horrible; 'Mbo' by Nicholas Royle, a modern vampire tale set in Zanzibar with, originally, a mosquito- rather than bat-based mythos, and a terrific climax; 'Safe' by Gary A. Braunbeck, a grim tale of two incidents of mass murder, one of which bears some resemblance to recent events in Colorado (this story comes with a reader advisory warning attached, and, it has to be said, really pushes the boat out in terms of violent and disturbing content); and 'Bucket of Blood' by Norman Partridge, a snappy, anecdotal piece about gunfighting and gambling in the modern mid-West.

As is probably apparent by now, I responded much more favourably to the horror half of the book than the fantasy half, though of the fantasy stories I read, the most memorable was

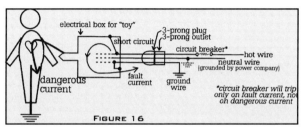

Frying tonight! JUICE.

'Wild Horses' by Charles de Lint, part of his celebrated cycle about the fictional town of Newford, and a wistful, poignant meditation on AIDS, addiction and the afterlife, with Tarot reading and shamanism thrown in.

If I have one general criticism of this anthology, it would be the repetitiousness of the settings of both the fantasy and the horror stories — of the ones I read (and maybe I was just unfortunate in my choices), over half were set in the kind of rural American small town that most of us are familiar with through the works of Stephen King and Ray Bradbury — nothing wrong with this in itself, but a bit more variety would have been nice. To some extent, this lack of variety is a result of the American bias I noted earlier. Other than that, the insufferably fey cover art — featuring a mermaid, a castle (enchanted, no doubt), a flying fish wearing a saddle and some goblins under a giant toadstool (no, really!) — put me off opening the book until the HEADPRESS deadline made it inevitable. Which is a pity, because once I started reading it I quite enjoyed it. **Simon Collins**

THE IMAGE
Jean de Berg

Nexus Classics; £5.99 + £1 p&p UK/£2 overseas; Available from Cash Sales Dept., TBS, c/o Virgin Publishing, Thames Wharf Studios, Rainville Road, London, W10 5AH
ISBN 0352333502

It's fitting that Nexus should chose to launch their new 'Nexus Classics' imprint with what is very clearly a modern erotic classic. Unlike many of the other books in the series — such as Maria del Rey's THE INSTITUTE and Aran Ashe's CHOOSING LOVERS FOR JUSTINE — THE IMAGE, by Jean de Berg, is not a home-grown Nexus classic at all. Like that other classic of modern SM fiction THE STORY OF O, it was first published by Olympia Press in Paris in the Sixties. The pseudonymous author has never been officially recognised, though most critics agree

that it was probably penned by Catherine Robbe-Grillet, though whether Dominique Aury (who penned THE STORY OF O as Pauline Reage) actually wrote the introduction to THE IMAGE (included in Nexus edition as well) is open to dispute. While THE IMAGE is less well known than 'O', the two books stand side by side in terms of literary and artistic merit. It's no surprise that Susan Sontag picked both as rare examples of porn novels which are also 'literature'. And, quite clearly, THE IMAGE is a work of pornography — the language, the focus, the intensity all mark it out as porn first and art later. The story revolves around the relationship between the male 'author'/narrator Jean and two women — the distant and enigmatic Claire and her younger, submissive partner Anne. Jean is drawn into the relationship between the women, first as an observer and then as an active participant in Claire's domination of Anne. However all is not as it appears and the end of the story manages to be at once surprising and yet obvious as the logical conclusion of the three-way relationship. This book is an auspicious start to the new Nexus series, which looks like it's going to be required reading for literate perverts everywhere.
Pan Pantziarka

THE SUBMISSION GALLERY
Lindsay Gordon
BAD PENNY
Penny Birch

£5.99 each; Nexus (Order details as above)
Ouch! Every decent S&M tale requires a Sadean baddie, and in THE SUBMISSION GALLERY it's Eliot Rilke (the literary references don't end there: another character is called Countess Nin), a sub-zero-habitat dweller and collector of film-star garments, with designs on making the book's heroine his final purchase. In futuristic (i.e. depressing) Darkling Town, artist Poppy Stanton finds her inspiration in sub/dom delights, utilising each en-

counter for her next sculpture-creation, unaware that Rilke is the man behind her success. THE SUBMISSION GALLERY's action is swift and merciless: dirty fuckers get torrid in every chapter; but the story framing the sex is well-paced enough to drag you to the end of the book, with enough imaginative set-ups to make the terrible sculptures that Poppy creates bearable. Bitter life experience as art, or just a pretentious excuse for putting it about? Whichever, Tracy Emin would give her last can of Special Brew for these kind of experiences.

Whereas Poppy Stanton takes it all ways in pursuit of her 'art', Penny Birch is much more straightforward: she's a posh slut who likes a bit of submissive tendering. The 18 stories in BAD PENNY chart her various humiliations, from having her face pushed down a toilet at a wedding to being forced to suck cock in a public lav. Lighter in tone than THE SUBMISSION GALLERY, Penny's adventures are short and sweet, much like the girl herself. In this world of upper-crust tarts and lower-class pieces of rough, every sex act is daringly 'dirty', and mostly centres on Penny's 'bottom'. Indeed, many pints of white seed are emptied across her posh peaches. Women get a look in as well (obviously), as do a set of gang-bangers, a dirty hippie, and a six-breasted creature(?). But the fact that Penny thinks her experiences are 'rude' highlights the remainder of her life to be a pretty square deal — this girl was definitely Miss straight 'A' at school. I'm all for hidden depths, but after the sex, where's the drugs and rock'n'roll in these tales? Authors, let the bitches freak-out once in a while!

Note: a dubious editorial source informs me that the Cleo Rocos lookalike on the cover of THE SUBMISSION GALLERY is currently 'co-hosting' THE BIG BREAKFAST. How far can too far go? **Martin Jones**

THE ABYSS
AND OTHER DARK PLACES
Lovecraftian Tales by
Robert A.W. Lowndes
Ed. Stephen Sennitt

60pp; 1998, Logos Press; John Beal, 170 Doncaster Rd, Mexborough, S. Yorks, S64 0JW

Another pamphlet from Logos Press, and this time it's a collection of classic weird fiction from the pen of Mr Lowndes. I have no idea if this writer existed or not — he, and the stories,

may well be creations of Mr Sennitt himself — but he is reputed to have written for a number of genre magazines in the Thirties and Forties. The stories themselves are excellent, if you like Lovecraftian fiction. They're not set strictly within the Cthulhu mythos, and indeed Lowndes invents a book which fulfils the role of Lovecraft's 'Necronomicon', entitled 'The Song of Ytse'. The writing is also in many ways tighter than that of Lovecraft — it's not as dense and multi-adjectival — and succeeds in conveying the sense of unease and otherworldliness that writers of weird fiction aimed for and only occasionally achieved. The pamphlet has a ropy cover image, and there's something inescapably tacky and formulaic about this kind of fiction — but within the genre's parameters this is good stuff, and on the basis of this and the NOX pamphlet [below], I look forward to seeing more from Logos Press. **James Marriott**

NOX, THE BLACK BOOK Vol 1
Infernal Texts
Ed. Stephen Sennitt

59pp; 1998, Logos Press (Details above)

This is "the first in a series of three volumes transgressing the definitions of modern occultism", and it makes for fairly entertaining reading. It's a cheaply produced pamphlet that appears to contain instructions for rituals such as a Satanic mass, a ritual of destruction and the "rite of nine angles", supposedly the "central mystery of alchemy". I haven't tried any of them out so can't vouch for how well they work — in any case some of them are 'bare bones' rituals and you'll have to go elsewhere for the incantations to make them complete. Other pieces in this grab-bag collection include rants about Lovecraft and Atlantis and an intriguing exploration of the demons of one's own psyche. While some of the information here strikes me as being fairly sound in its own way — rituals of deprogramming and derangement of the senses for personal 'development' — when it comes to a textual analysis of Lovecraft taking his fictions as factual accounts, or numerological analyses of the geometry of pyramids, I can't take it at all seriously. At least this is still fun, though, especially considered as fiction. Less entertaining is the undercurrent of fascism running through a lot of this, as it does through a good deal of occult/new age material:

RADIO WEREWOLF IS OPPOSED TO THE GENERAL DECADENCE OF CONTEMPORARY YOUTH-CULTURE; A SEWER OF MIND-NUMBING DRUGS, PRIMITIVE AFRICAN RHYTHMS, THE UNBALANCED ENCOURAGEMENT OF ANDROGYNY AND HOMO-SEXUALITY, THE BLURRING AND MUDDYING OF RACIAL AND CULTURAL BOUNDARIES. RADIO WEREWOLF STANDS AS THE STANDARD-BEARER OF A NEW KIND OF YOUTH — ORDERLY, DISCIPLINED, DRUG-FREE, PROUD AND RE-AWAKENED TO THEIR PAGAN HERITAGE; THE CADRES OF THE RADIO WEREWOLF YOUTH PARTY.

I've always thought mind-numbing drugs and primitive African rhythms go pretty well together. Not a good candidate for the Radio Werewolf Youth Party, then … **James Marriott**

THE CHUCKLING WHATSIT
Richard Sala

202pp £11.99/$16.95; 1997, Fantagraphics Books; ISBN 1-56097-281-5

Distributed in the UK by Turnaround

A recent offering from the consistently excellent Fantagraphics stable, THE CHUCKLING WHATSIT is Richard Sala's fifth book, though it's the first work by him that I've seen.

A fresh-faced, naïve young reporter named Broom is unwittingly drawn into the investigation of a spate of murders of astrologers, which seem to be connected to the crimes committed some 15 years earlier by the 'Gull Street Ghoul'. Along the way to the truth, he crosses paths with a bewildering array of supporting characters, all of whom have their own vested interests in the stuff he's digging up. The eponymous Whatsit is an evil-looking fetish doll with a noose around its neck. As the plot gathers momentum, fresh revelations are thrust upon Broom willy-nilly, but the last snooper to fish in these murky waters — another reporter named Cyril Root — wound up stabbed by the Gull Street Ghoul Mark II, along with all the stargazing buddies in whom he'd confided.

Critical plaudits for Sala — quoted on the back cover of THE CHUCKLING WHATSIT — mention the film noir ambience, but I discern rather earlier visual influences at work, especially German Expressionist cinema. The book's climatic denouement takes

151

place in a burning windmill, like that of James Whale's 1931 classic FRANKENSTEIN (itself heavily influenced by Expressionism); the wraith-like Celeste resembles Carol Borland in Tod Browning's MARK OF THE VAMPIRE; and the catsuit-wearing, mask-toting, roof-hopping Phoebe Duprey is a dead ringer for Irma Vep, heroine of the 1915 French serial LES VAMPIRES. Broom himself is an insufficiently embittered and world-weary protagonist to be truly 'noir' — more Tintin than Philip Marlowe!

The sinuous, hatched pen and ink work, with heavy areas of black, looks like woodcuts in general, and in particular like the Belgian artist Frans Masereel's famous 'novel without words' PASSIONATE JOURNEY, with its lonely, distorted figures scurrying through stormy landscapes.

None of this, however, is to denigrate Sala's work — it simply shows that he's seen and enjoyed a lot of the same films, books and comics as me. THE CHUCKLING WHATSIT is quirky, funny, spooky and groovy. I liked it a lot, and it made me want to see more of Sala's work. **Simon Collins**

HORRORGASMO
Psychotic Art for New Mutants

72pp L23.000; 1999, Mondo Bizarro Press, Piazza San Martino 3/d, 40126 Bologna, Italy; ISBN 88-87581-00-2

VISIONARY, PROFANE, DISTURBING, DEPRAVED. Now while I enthusiastically welcome any kind of book that promotes the work of unknown artists who specialise in 'unusual' art I can't help feeling that warnings of OPEN AT YOUR OWN RISK! went out with TALES FROM THE CRYPT.

Or maybe I'm just jaded. After years of drawing my own similarly 'difficult' material and exposing myself to the work of many, many others I am now totally desensitised to what must be for some *genuinely* shocking images. Having said that, this *is* a limited edition release (of 999 copies) that you'll never see in Waterstone's and will only be sought out by those punters who groove on pictures of crucified mutant foetuses, angels pissing on a vomiting clown or a dildo-wielding nun menaced by a Lovecraftian sex god in a cell full of bleeding walls, so I think such 'We're so bad' warnings are redundant.

Reservations on the packaging aside, this is a *good* collection featuring artists from the Italian 'underground' comics scene who all owe a debt to Charles Burns.

Stefano Zattera has the most humorous approach and blends Bettie Page and Bob Dobbs in with his own creation 'Cowgirl' — a Fresian spotted fuckbunny who shoots satanic sheriffs and lasso's mustang penises.

Gianmaria Liani is the man working closest to my own tastes. With a crisp, confident line he details the adventures of stacked horror momma Betty Sue — an ageing, sperm-slurping, fur-slippered murderess — and her mad family. His style is like Jamie Hewlett raised in a dark cellar on a diet of The Cramps and phallic hot dogs wrapped in pages torn from lingerie catalogues. Stockings, porno heels, fuck-off bulldogs and ripped flesh aplenty, his images bristle with potential *lustmord* and black as arseholes humour.

'Spiderjack' has a more idiosyncratic style that echoes early Ted McKeever, Peter Kuper, Mike Diana and, in particular, Chester Brown. Except those guys, even at the zenith of their weirdness, never drew vaginal third-eyes, crucified batwing punks with syringe pierced boners in Take That T-shirts or detachable ray gun cocks that blast holes in the cheeks of famine-victim fellatists. The *only* response is a bemused admiration for someone's willingness to open up *that* far.

But, just when you think it's peaked, in comes 'Dast' to take the doors off completely.

I don't even know where to *start* with this guy. His favoured subject matter is S&M nuclear families and religious iconography, played out by encephalic dominatrixes and skeletal junkies sporting anaconda cocks that spurt seminal napalm. Whilst possibly the least competent artist in the collection, the intensity and sheer fucking *strangeness* of his vision stays with you longer than the rest. The other three guys are 'only' artists but Dast really does seem like the asylum-bound nut that most decent people would dismiss the contributors as being.

Ultimately I think this book is long overdue. Art like this has been too long buried in obscure, small print-run magazines and deserves a much wider audience. For every vacuous

© G. Liani

HORRORGASMO.

Dave McKean book cover there should be a Dast two-headed mutant cocksucker special alongside to provide that all important yin/yang balance that keeps the universe ticking. HORRORGASMO does the job it was designed for. More of the same, please. **Rik Rawling**

JUSTICE LEAGUE OF AMERICA
Strength in Numbers
Morrison, Waid, Priest, Porter, Jorgensen, Paquette, *et al*
223pp £8.99; 1998, Titan Books
ISBN 1-840-23022-3

Superhero teams. Why take one superhero into the shower when you can take *dozens*?

The idea is to rope in dedicated readers of individual hero books by having their faves team-up with a host of others to fight heroes too big for a single hero.

And the JLA is probably the worst example of this mentality. Superman, Batman, Green Lantern, Flash, Wonder Woman and a fleet of Vauxhall League freaks are thrust together bringing all the baggage of their long and incomprehensibly intertwined histories with them. The result is a sickeningly overspiced ghoulash of absurdity that only the True Believer can stomach. The fact that STRENGTH IN NUMBERS required *three* writers and *10* artists should give you some indication of the quality of the product. As usual, because of the foreknowledge required to understand each characters' relationship with the other, the book is totally unreadable to someone like me who doesn't understand and *doesn't care*. Even the presence of Grant Morrison attempting a Lovecraftian pastiche fails to bring any much needed twat value to the proceedings.

Batman skulks in the dark, Plasticman is written with Jim Carrey in mind should this toss ever go to film, and Wonder Woman's new mini skirt is wasted as an opportunity for bruised cheeks and cheap gusset flashes. Shite, basically. **Rik Rawling**

JUSTICE LEAGUE OF AMERICA
The Nail
Alan Davis and Mark Farmer
160pp £8.99; 1998, Titan Books
ISBN 1-84023-064-9

Even more JLA! A man has his limits y'know! Fortunately, this is pretty good. An artist working from his own script usually makes for a better comic as it comes closer to a singular vision

than a clusterfuck like STRENGTH IN NUMBERS. Alan Davis first started in 2000AD and went on to work with Alan Moore on DR & QUINCH which still stands today as the Dog's Bollocks. He's now well-entrenched in the US comics scene, working exclusively in superhero comics but I have no problem with this because (*a*) he's a really good artist and (*b*) he *loves* superheroes. This makes for good old fashioned rip-roarin' entertainment as the reader regresses to eight-years-old and cheers on the ass kickin' good guys and gals.

The premise of the story is very simple — what if there was no Superman? Jonathan & Martha Kent's truck gets a nail in the tyre so they never drive on further down the road and never come across the fallen meteor with little Kal-El inside. Consequently there is no Clark Kent and superhero history is altered forever. Lex Luthor is mayor of Metropolis, Jimmy Olsen is Deputy and it gets crazier from then on as Davis throws in virtually every DC character and *almost* manages to make it work. Half of the spandex wrapped geeks I didn't recognise but it didn't matter — the whole thing moves at breakneck speed and brims with confidence and Davis displays a keen understanding of the dynamics required and an almost religious respect for the DC Universe.

Of course it all works out well in the end and along the way you get some storming fight scenes, unintentionally hilarious dialogue (Green Lantern: "My ring responds to my willpower") and cameos by long-lost crazy ass characters like Ragman, Deadman and a Superfly-afro'd Black Lightning. Verve and nostalgia delivered with a truly exemplary art job. Smooth expressive layouts, multiple POV's and impressive detail — all made to look like a piece of piss.

So there you go — the best and *worst* of what superhero comics can be. One is a waste of good tree pulp and one is well worth buying for your kid brother and sneaking a read for yourself. **Rik Rawling**

DC vs MARVEL
Marz, David, Jurgens, Castellini, Rubinstein, Neary, *et al*
200pp £10.99; 1996, Titan Books
ISBN 1-85286-750-7

"The epic mini-series they said would never happen"! I'm going to assume 'they' are not the desperate parasites at Marvel and DC who saw a perfectly

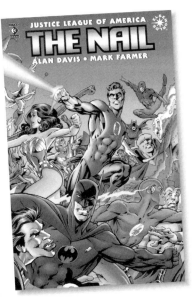

good opportunity to rake in some cash quick. The comics industry is in steady decline and the fuckers involved are so clueless as to what to do about it that they respond with this kind of speedball logic.

Maybe I'm just too old to get it? Maybe if I was younger I would have shit blood to get my hands on this? Maybe. But just flicking through the pages I'm overwhelmed by the chloroformic stench of cynicism that this venture reeks of. It's the equivalent of taking not one but two cars full of crack into a New Orleans welfare project. I know how easy it is to pick on superhero comics but this is total and utter bollocks — with obligatory workmanlike artjob throughout, big 'star' fightscenes every two pages and a breathless fear of having the target audiences attention span distracted for a split second. Lots of rippling chest muscles, gritted teeth, furrowed brows and not one fucking idea what to do with the mess they've created, as Superman kicks the Hulk's ass and Shazam leathers a faggoty looking Thor. I could have gone into high gear when Elektra faced up to Catwoman but apart from some coy 'up' shots of Catwoman's taut purple ass it fails to live up to its potential.

I cannot report on any aspect of the script because it is *impossible* to read. It comes laden with the baggage of 50 years' worth of character detail and not one shred of humour, making it nothing more than EASTENDERS on steroids.

To add insult to injury there are Writer & Artist profiles at the back, where a brain-numbing clumsiness with self-deprecating humour and 'zany' wit is evinced. They are not writing SEINFELD. They are not even writing OH, DR BEECHING! They are writing comics. Superhero comics. It's probably better than sucking cocks in the Subway Toilets to make enough change for a Big Mac meal but not by much. **Rik Rawling**

THE WATCHER IN THE ATTIC
(Yaneura No Sanpo Sha)
dir: Noboru Tanaka
Japan 1976; Pagan, Cert 18
HELLISH LOVE
(Seidan: Botandoro)
dir: Chusei Sone
Japan 1972; Pagan, Cert 18
A WOMAN CALLED ABÉ SADA
(Jitsuroku: Abé Sada)
dir: Noboru Tanaka
Japan 1975; Pagan, Cert 18
Pagan Films Ltd., PO Box 28504, London
N15 6WJ. www.paganfilms.com

Japanese Pink Cinema seems to be all the rage at the moment, these three titles arriving hot on the heels of Jack Hunter's book EROS IN HELL and Thomas and Yuko Mihara Weisser's JAPANESE CINEMA ENCYCLOPEDIA: THE SEX FILMS. Thankfully, it's a rewarding tripartite. First up is THE WATCHER IN THE ATTIC, based on a story by Edogawa Rampo, Japan's most popular thriller writer, yet filmed in arty Roman Porno style. Indeed the cinematography is excellent, but the subject matter — a landlord who spies on his sexually active residents from a dark attic — requires many very dark sequences, in some cases only a fraction of the screen escapes total blackout. The characters are however bizarre enough to make the squinting

worth while, especially the prostitute who encases men in a chair on which she sits, wears animal costume while fondling her naked breasts with hooves, eventually going so far as to suffocate a punter with her vagina. All the time she is aware, excited even, by the watchful gaze from above. As her sadism escalates, so does that of her admirer Goda who in turn kills a resident by dripping poison into the sleeping man's mouth. The result is a partnership made in Hell, a bond formed from "dreams of committing crimes". The body count rises until an earthquake reduces the guest-house to rubble — the climactic sequence of the prostitute pumping water from the bowels of her home, becoming more excited as the gushing fluid turns to blood is stunning. Throughout, WATCHER IN THE ATTIC is a film of unsettling images and sado-masochistic sex. It finds beauty in cruelty, salvation in crime. Not surprisingly, it was remade in 1994 by Akio Jissoji, this time with much full frontal nudity and stronger sex scenes.

With a similar obsession at heart, Tanaka's earlier SADA ABÉ STORY lost out to Nagisa Oshima's 1976 sexually explicit IN THE REALM OF THE SENSES. Both based on the same story, Tanaka's film has remained unseen outside Japan for years, yet is just as successful as Oshima's film. A Nikkatsu Production (the studio logo bears an uncanny resemblance to that of Toho Studios), it follows Sada, a woman sleeping with one man for financial support and another for fanatical lust for his penis. Sada and Kichi shut themselves away to indulge in a mammoth sex extravaganza lasting over two weeks, but when Kichi

must return home, Sada kills him, slicing off his penis and writing "Sada and Kichi alone" in blood on his body and surrounding sheets. She wraps up her memento with care and keeps it down the front of her underwear until the strong arm of the law finally apprehends her, the press branding her a witch. A sad end for a woman escaping a harsh past of domineering parents, abuse and rape. Despite her crimes, Sada remains a sympathetic character throughout.

Another Nikkatsu Corporation film, HELLISH LOVE is a much less harrowing affair, and somewhat disappointing. Chusei Sone, director of such oddities as DELINQUENT GIRL ALLEYCAT IN HEAT and ANGEL GUTS HIGH SCHOOL COED, here keeps his feet firmly within the realm of fantasy. A traditional ghost story, adapted from the 'Bride From Hell' tale in which the spirit of a murdered girl returns to take possession of her lover's soul. Romantic rather than fantastic (even the sex scenes are blurred or obscured by objects), it lacks the passion of the Tanaka films but is too short to induce boredom.

All these releases are simply packaged and presented not only with English sub-titles but also in widescreen. The prints are crisp and uncut. Hurrah to Pagan Films! **David Greenall**

LOVE RITES
(Ceremonie D'Amour)
dir: Walerian Borowczyk
1973; Pagan Films, Cert 18
French dialogue, English sub-titles
(Contact details as above)

Borowczyk is a master of erotic cinema, and although this simple tale cannot come close to the genius of

Courtesy Pagan Films

L–R HELLISH LOVE, THE WATCHER IN THE ATTIC, A WOMAN CALLED ABÉ SADA.

BLANCHE, LA BÊTE [*see page 37*] or DR JEKYLL ET LES FEMMES, LOVE RITES provides us with evidence that at 56 this director can still bore, stimulate and shock his audience. It begins in predictable fashion with a journey through erotic Paris, to a chance meeting on the subway of Miriam Gwen and Hugo Arnold. Prostitute and poet. There is much discourse, almost 45 minutes to be exact. This philosophical banter becomes tedious, and is far from erotic. But now I understand why Borowczyk is carefully seducing us into a false sense of security — when we eventually reach the bedroom, he constructs a ravishingly erotic love sequence. A sequence of glorious cinematography and explicit narration. Hugo's penis swells (an "arrogant mushroom" he calls it) as he watches butterflies feast on Miriam's vagina ("juicy snatch" she calls it), the oral sex and penetration that follows is as realistic as it is erotic. A successful fusion of romanticism and pornography.

Then the phone interrupts the seclusion of the lovers, Miriam answers only "yes" repeatedly. We never find out with whom she speaks, but all fingers point to a sadistic, deformed mute who terrorises her — whoever it is, the call is a short fuse, once extinguished, passive femininity becomes raging hate. Miriam, now brandishing knife-like nail extensions begins to repeatedly slash her partner's naked body. Now she is hard and he is flaccid. Here is the paradox between love and sex: tender and hard, penetration as an act of love and of violence. At last we find ourselves deep within Borowczyk territory, a territory that takes no prisoners.

Believe it or not, things get even stranger… A truly erotic film that is in turn boring, stimulating and terrifying. Essential. Fucking essential!
David Greenall

MURDER IN A BLUE WORLD
(Una Gota de sangre para morir amando)
dir: Eloy de la Iglesias
1973; Pagan Films, Cert 18
(Contact details as above)
Its title taken from a series of TV advertisements for a product called 'Blue Drink', MURDER IN A BLUE WORLD is set in an unidentified future city where a series of brutal murders have occured. Into the equation comes a gang of tearaway adolescents who drive around in a beach buggy, dress

all in leather and wield whips. For kicks they break into an apartment and terrorise and sexually abuse the couple who live there. If this scenario sounds uncannily like it belongs in another movie of the early Seventies, MURDER IN A BLUE WORLD saves you from burning out too many brain cells trying to figure out which: moments before the droogs break into the house, a TV presenter announces the screening of Stanley Kubrick's film A CLOCKWORK ORANGE, as a picture of the bearded director himself is flashed onto the screen. Maybe this is a cinematic first: I personally can think of no other movie that effectively stops to pay homage to the source of its inspiration. (Not slow to pick up on this link, the original distributors released the film onto video in Britain as CLOCK-WORK TERROR.)

But director de la Iglesias (whose name is misspelled in the opening credits) doesn't stop there: he has his own Korova Milk Bar, Strauss as opposed to Beethoven, his own Ludovico treatment (which ultimately backfires and instead of pacifying criminals, makes them more violent), and so on. Mixed into the CLOCKWORK ORANGE-isms is a curiously wonky sub-plot concerning "the unknown killer of young people", as one TV news reporter puts it.

MURDER IN A BLUE WORLD appears to be trimmed, though you'd be hard-pressed to notice. It's strange, nervy, and sexual, but lacking in the bite (no pun intended) of de la Iglesias' earlier THE CANNIBAL MAN.

THE COMING OF SIN
(La visita del vicio)
dir: José Ramon Larraz
1978; Pagan Films, Cert 18 TBC
(Contact details as above)
This film, which was originally released in the UK as VIOLATION OF THE BITCH (with the tag-line: "She asked for it") has the distinction of having one of the most un-PC video covers and titles in Salvation's superb book THE ART OF THE NASTY. Any sleazehound renting it on the strength of its cover would have been disappointed, though, especially as that earlier release was cut by 15 minutes. With Pagan's new release, it's hard to see what was cut previously as it's a pretty tame film. There's some mild bondage and a brief attempted rape along with some nudity — shocking stuff. It plays like a low-rent, poorly dubbed version of EXPOSÉ, having a

An incapacitated Chris Mitchum
in MURDER IN A BLUE WORLD.

similar atmosphere of sexual tension and a similar set-up, involving two women and one man in an isolated house surrounded by fields. The plot, which doesn't make a great deal of sense, involves a gypsy maid, Triana, staying temporarily at the house of Sally, a painter she soon seduces. The pair are visited by a naked man on a horse who, we eventually learn, knows Triana, although it's never entirely clear what their relationship is. Finally they all have sex (of sorts), and Triana kills Sally with a shotgun. Why? Fuck knows. Along the way we are treated to lengthy scenes of Sally and Triana wandering around art galleries and plenty of soft-focus canoodling between the pair. There is one standout dream sequence in which we see Triana curled up in the rear of a golden horse, presumably awaiting penetration by the other horse circling her. It's a truly startling image, and it's a shame that Larraz couldn't apply this kind of imaginative flair to the rest of the film. Larraz' VAMPYRES is a great film. This is not. It gets a good review in IMMORAL TALES, though, so what do I know? **James Marriott**

THE WASHING MACHINE
dir: Ruggero Deodato
1993; Visual Film, Cert 18
A cop is called in to investigate the disappearance of a well-known pimp, but ends up on a slippery slope when he gets involved with the three sisters who were last to see the missing man. The pimp's mangled body, one sister claims, was in the washing machine — now it's gone. But each sister has a different story and none can be corroborated. The women play the cop off against each other and ultimately against himself, teasing him with empty leads and distracting him with sex.

'From the director of CANNIBAL HOLO-CAUST,' boasts the sleeve. But don't approach this expecting to encounter anything vaguely approximating that earlier film of Deodato's. With THE WASHING MACHINE he ventures into *giallo* territory, but as the informality of the title suggests — which parodies the traditional 'animated' giallo titles, such as BLACK BELLY OF THE TARANTULA and CAT O'NINE TAILS — this isn't an altogether serious take. While it does contain the requisite sexy women, mystery assailants, radical plot twists, and some gore, it manages to have some fun and throws in plenty of humping and kinky sex (including a lesbian encounter with a blind girl). Naturally the whole thing is turned on its head in an ending that doesn't detract from the film's air of hormonal overdrive.

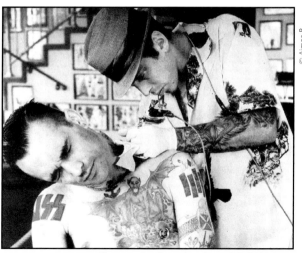

Tattoo artists Peter Loggins and Jeff Thielman in Larry Wessel's TATTOO DELUXE.

THE DRILLER KILLER

dir: Abel Ferrara

1979; Visual Film, Cert 18

Also available on DVD

How times change. THE DRILLER KILLER is one of the most notorious films ever released in Britain thanks to the 'video nasties' campaign of almost two decades ago. Now with a certificate and readily available again, it is being lauded as something of a classic. A message film. Punk. Art.

The story concerns Reno, a down-at-heel artist who is suffering a personal crisis. Heightened by outside influences, most notably the Punk Rock band that has chosen to rehearse in an adjoining apartment, Reno ultimately takes his aggression out on the street trash he previously used as subject material in his sketches, killing them at random with a portable drill. THE DRILLER KILLER naturally lacks the polish and direction of Ferrara's later works. However, plenty of his obsessions are already in evidence and the film stands up much better than when first released in the video milieu all those years ago. It's relatively blood-free for much of its running time, allowing Reno's psychosis time to slowly germinate. (It's even more blood-free in Visual's cut, which is missing some close-up flesh-rending, but plays longer courtesy of extra scenes of dialogue.) In other words: Yes, it's Art. Yes, it's great. And yes, you plankton moralists, you were wrong all along.

BREEDERS

dir: Paul Matthews

Digital Entertainment, Cert 18

At first I thought this was going to he a re-release of Tim Kincaid's sloppy 1986 monsters and babes flick of the same name. I was wrong. This is a UK originated monsters and babes flick, strangely financed by the Isle of Man Film Commission. Clearly striving to look US-based, poor attention to detail betrays the illusion in what is essentially a crap facsimile of crap American exploitation movies.

The sleeve pays most attention to cast member Samantha Janus, an actress I have never heard of who has apparently been in a couple of television shows I have never heard of. The only familiar face here for me is Oliver Tobias who plays the heroic cop figure, alongside lecturer Todd Jensen and spunky college girl Janus. This trio battle against a space monster that abducts females in which to store his eggs. This monster race is so aggressive that siblings kill each other, resulting in a desperate attempt to breed or face extinction. Following a crash landing in the grounds of a college, the monster and his hypnotised female concubine (who sports large breasts and a neat fetish outfit) make camp below the girls' showers — girls who are forced by the powers of glowing crystals to somnambulate to the monster's lair and protect its breeding programme at all costs. Armed police enter the catacombs and the usual cat-and-mouse chase follows, culminating in the destruction of the monster and return to humanity for the concubine. Of course it doesn't end there, the final shot of showering

shooting-stars implies a possible invasion of these monsters.

With full frontal female nudity, lesbian nipple play, a latex monster and gallons of slime sandwiched between CGI credit sequences (so that's where the budget went), BREEDERS will no doubt end up on Channel 5 with minor cuts. Disturbing as it sounds, I now find myself wishing this *was* a re-release of the Kincaid film after all.

David Greenall

SEX, DEATH AND THE HOLLYWOOD MYSTIQUE

dir Larry Wessel

USA, 1999 (NTSC)

TATTOO DELUXE

dir: Larry Wessel

USA, 1998 (NTSC)

US $25/Outside US $30 postpaid. Cheque or money order to: Larry Wessel, PO Box 1611, Manhattan Beach, CA 90267-1611, USA. Send SAE/IRC for catalogue.

Larry Wessel makes curious documentary features. [See *article/interview in HEADPRESS 14*.] In SEX, DEATH AND THE HOLLYWOOD MYSTIQUE, several insiders and fringe characters provide a colourful, warts and all view of what it's like to live in the shadow of the famous Hollywood sign. These range from the exuberant Forrest J. Ackerman, editor of the original FAMOUS MONSTERS OF FILMLAND whose house is a memorabilia museum, through to Kelly Monroe, a girl who had aspirations to be a movie star but is now a call girl with a drug habit. Director Curtis Harrington (NIGHT TIDE, KILLER BEES) confides that his favourite movie is FREAKS and that he uses "little people" in his own modest productions whenever possible. Nicholas Fruktow claims to be a film extra and friend to the stars (but appears to be an old drunk the film crew have bumped into) who drops names and hums the theme to DR ZHIVAGO. The key figure, however, is actor-turned-author John Gilmore, whose stories are genuinely fascinating, glamorous and lurid. He talks initially of his friendship with James Dean, of homosexual encounters with agents and the concept of the "meat rack", in which aspiring boy actors were passed down a Hollywood hierarchy of sexual abuse and false promises. Later he discusses his literary involvement with the Manson family, Charles Schmid ("the Pied Piper of Tucson"), and the Black Dahlia murder case. On a lighter note, Forry Ackerman offers one of his famous "open house" tours, delighting in stories he undoubtedly has related countless times before. Of the amazing artefacts in his possession are Lugosi's original Dracula ring and an edition of the novel FRANKENSTEIN — under the title THE MAN-DEMON — signed by Mary Shelley herself. He also has an eye for the young ladies.

Forry's reminiscences alone would have made the film worthwhile, but there is more, much more. Much, *much* more! Larry is reluctant to let anything go and it seems that everything he shoots finds its way onto the released video. Hence, we are treated to several long minutes of Kelly having her toenails painted (women's feet being one of Larry's passions), hanging around outside Forry's gate, idly waiting to be let in, and lengthy extracts from Gilmore's books, read by the author himself in a manner so deadpan none but the most ardent of fans will stay awake.

Despite several interminable sequences of its own, TATTOO DELUXE — Wessel's other new feature — is tighter and generally more engaging. It focuses on a San Pedro tattoo parlour and its clientele, who range from a shoeshine man killing time to a seasoned sea dog. The guys who run the place know their craft and some of the designs are elaborate to say the least (one customer gets a portrait of his infant son etched onto his arm). I was kinda hoping one tattoo would go horribly wrong, but it didn't happen. The surprising thing is the high number of women getting tattoos —

not with the 'cool' monochrome tribal markings that became fashionable a few years back, but honest-to-goodness traditional designs with plenty of colour (an image of Felix The Cat on a leg was particularly heart-warming). Girls tend to go for tattoos on the butt or belly (and Larry doesn't hesitate to catch their every flinch as the needle goes its merry way), while guys go for the arms or the back. Maintaining an air of *felt nowt* detachment, the guys also have more interesting things to say — like the time they visited a Donkey Sex show or got into a fight.

DEAD MAN'S CURVE
dir: Dan Rosen
1997; High Fliers, Cert 15
When it looks like he might flunk the chance of getting into Harvard, Tim decides to exploit a little known college charter that guarantees a student straight A's should a roommate commit suicide.

That's the basic premise of DEAD MAN'S CURVE, a film which draws comparisons with SCREAM (because Matthew Lillard is in both) but in reality owes more of a debt to the greatly superior HEATHERS. The plot twists are painfully stiff, while the characters are needlessly unlikeable, scheming and arrogant. The potentially funny premise doesn't make it out of the opening credits without getting a stitch. Or, maybe that's what constitutes 'black comedy' nowadays?

THE LEGEND OF THE GOD OF GAMBLERS
(God of Gamblers 3: The Early Stage)
dir: Wong Jing
1996; Hong Kong Classics, Cert 18
Two minutes into the film and we see an unscrupulous Fagan-like character about to hack the arms off the little Ko Chun whom he has just kidnapped — that way the infant might make better money as a beggar on the street. Fortunately the boy is saved by Mr Kent, a gangster and master gambler who isn't quite as benevolent as first appears. Under Kent's tutelage, Ko Chun is destined for the coveted God of Gamblers title, but discovers too late that he is a mere pawn in a much bigger game.

To give much more away would spoil things because much pleasure is derived in several completely unexpected twists. The humour for a change is funny as opposed to goofy, the fight scenes are used sparingly and to good

effect (broken vinyl records become makeshift weapons against swords; a thumbs-up is given when an opponent stops short of kicking a pregnant bystander in the belly), and it isn't necessary to know anything about card games to appreciate the gambling scenarios and the double-dealing that is taking place.

Available in two versions — both packaged as THE LEGEND OF THE GOD OF GAMBLERS — prospective viewers are advised to opt for the subtitled edition. As well as being in widescreen, it runs considerably longer than the dubbed version.

VARIOUS
Faster, Pussy...
Attack! Tora! Tora! Tora!
HELLCHILD
Circulating Contradiction
YELLOW MACHINEGUN
Spot Remover
CD albums; Howling Bull America, PO Box 40129, SF CA 94140-0129, USA
Tel: (415) 282 7755; Fax: (415) 282 7711
http://www.howlingbull.com/
This is all metal, and as far as metal goes I'm afraid it's pretty nondescript. The bands are Japanese and the label American. Unlike some instances in which the Japanese have taken Western rock music and regurgitated it in distilled and hyperkinetic form — bands like High Rise spring to mind with their take on Blue Cheer-style psych rock — this doesn't really offer much in the way of new kicks. There's none of the Keiji Haino-style intensity commonly associated with Japanese rock here either — it's all pretty standard stuff, and would be difficult to place geographically if the lyric notes weren't in such strange English:

I'M NOT YOU, YOU'RE NOT /
LIVE IN SOMEWHERE
DIE IN ANYWHERE
Yellow Machinegun, 'I Know'

Occasionally a spazzy lead guitar breaks ranks for extra value but for the rest of the time the bands just chug along with predictable metal riffs. Any distinguishing characteristics? The FASTER, PUSSY CD is a compilation with one or two good tunes on it, Yellow Machinegun is an all-girl band whose appearance defies all rock convention (they look like the Japanese chapter of Natalie Imbruglia's fan club) and Hellchild have a slightly more morbid edge than the other bands. That's it. Oh, and the Yellow Machinegun CD is covered with pretty

157

nifty Panter-style skulls — but it's still not enough to make you love it.
James Marriott

CONTAGIOUS ORGASM
Loop Contamination/
Earache Floor
7" single; Speeding Across My Hemisphere, 58285 Gevelsberg, Germany
Fax: 0049 2332 81613

This group or band or whatever the hell three monkeys in a room call themselves these days, gets a blue ribbon for having the gumption to enlist someone called Marvel. He plays percussion, but so does another guy — so, unfortunately for me and the rest of music history, what Marvel did on this single will have to remain a mystery, not unlike Aztec astronauts. I'll just have to live with that, along with the possibility that I listened to this at the wrong speed. At any rate, it sounded OK.

One side is called Loop Contamination, the other side is called Earache Floor. I think this comes from Japan, and evidently something has been lost in the translation of these titles because I'm drawing a blank. I've taken into account the admirable deviousness of the Oriental mind. I've taken into account the groovy poster and fetching plastic bag. I've taken into account that it was composed *and* — wait for it — performed, by said ensemble, but there just isn't much performance or composition going on. I can't figure out what they must have been doing in the studio for the three months it took to do this. Either the engineer had an excellent collection of filthy video tapes, or they had to rebuild the studio before they could start, just like Fleetwood Mac did once or twice.

Still, I can't damn this indigestible smattering of loopy avant-gloop as I think it has virtue in the evocation of certain imagery involving heavily rusted car spares and a legion of nymphomaniac amputees. It's been a long

day and I'm tired. Just buy it and hump that stump. **Mark Deutrom**

FIFI AND THE MACH III
New Race/Too Fast To Live, Too Young To Die *et al*
4-track 7" EP; Wrench Records, BCM Box 4049, London, WC1N 3XX

Fifi and The Mach III are from Tokyo. They get points for that. I just read a book about the guy that designed the Mitsubishi Zero in WWII so I'm all hot for the Japs right now. I also love sushi, and own a widescreen edition of TORA! TORA! TORA! There's a chick in this band called Fifi, and I think she might be pretty good-looking, but I can't really tell from the photo so I'll have to tap into some of the more exotic URL's and indulge in a little substitution therapy. She's got a damn firm grip on that mic stand and that's certainly obvious.

At first I had the gramophone set on 45rpm and Fifi sounded just like Geddy Lee from Rush. At any moment I expected her to scream "Of Salesmen!!" No joy... Slowed the sucker down to 33, and came up with a Blondie/L7 thing that wasn't half bad. Nice thick out-of-tune guitars with a Japanese Geddy Lee girl over the top. The clean recording deballed the overall effect, but hey, this is a CHICK band so deballing is not only called for, but insisted upon. Definition of chick band: any band with a chick in it. At least there is minimal or no digital

tomfoolery, and the band sounds like it is actually playing, which is always refreshing these days.

Just like Trad Jazz, there is a whole school of Trad Punk which conforms strictly to a given set of parameters. Fifi and the boys are right in there, obeying every rule and playing it as safe as cake. There's something comforting in knowing exactly what you're getting. Personally, I haven't discovered what that something is yet, but I'm sure the kids will love it, and possibly some 30-year-olds with spiky hair.

I wholeheartedly recommend these four songs to anyone who likes Rush, Blondie, L7, The Mitsubishi Zero, Trad Jazz, or cake. **Mark Deutrom**

LIL BUNNIES
Bunnie Hole/
Be Kind To The Animals
7" single; Wrench Records (Details above)

Well... Ummmm... This is almost funny. Wait, no, it's not at all funny. As we all know, there's nothing worse than something that is not funny. Apparently, this is some kind of inside joke that has gone on far too long, and has now found its way onto vinyl. I know this band is from Sacramento (nuff said) and are allegedly punk rock and wear rabbit ears onstage, but I have an alternative theory to explain away this horseshit. I think a really big band did this to try to be cool and punk and counter culture and vaguely controversial. I heard a tasty guitar riff for a nanosecond. I heard an American accent. I heard competent musicians pretending they couldn't play. Before I reveal who this is, I feel duty bound to say that this is horrible. It's really bad, and not how Michael means bad. Worst of all, it's not funny and that's the biggest crime of all. The bastard in me couldn't even laugh at how bad it was. 'Get Out Of My Bunnie Hole' gave me violent thoughts, so I suppose it was successful in a sense. The other side was just distorto-crap rehearsal-room nonsense and a waste of perfectly good vinyl.

I really wish Metallica would stop trying to be cool and get back to the good ol' days of 'Creeping Death' and 'Trapped Under Ice'. For now, at least their fans will have another obscure 7" to chase after until the BLACK SYMPHONY, or whatever they're going to call it comes out... I think this is a limited edition, so better get hopping.
Mark Deutrom

SEND REVIEW MATERIALS TO

Headpress, 40 Rossall Avenue, Radcliffe, Manchester, M26 1JD, Great Britain. Be sure to include the following details on a separate sheet of paper (preferably not a tiny scrap):

(i) Title, (ii) ISBN if applicable, (iii) Price, (iv) Postage, including overseas p&p, (v) Contact address. The following details are optional: Telephone/Fax number, Email and URL.

We endeavour to review everything that comes our way sooner or later, but cannot guarantee the fact.

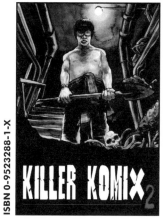